LEADERSHIP THROUGH EXCELLENCE

LEADERSHIP THROUGH EXCELLENCE

*Professional Growth
for School Leaders*

Raymond L. Calabrese

The University of Texas at San Antonio

Allyn and Bacon

Boston • London • Toronto • Sydney • Tokyo • Singapore

Series editor: Arnis E. Burvikovs
Series editorial assistant: Karin Huang
Manufacturing buyer: Suzanne Lareau

Between the time Website information is gathered and then published, it is not unusual for some sites to have closed. Also, the transcription of URLs can result in unintended typographical errors. The publisher would appreciate notification where these occur so that they may be corrected in subsequent editions. Thank you.

Library of Congress Cataloging-in-Publication Data

Calabrese, Raymond L. (date)
    Leadership through excellence : professional growth for school leaders /
Raymond L. Calabrese.
        p.   cm.
    Includes bibliographical references and index.
    ISBN 0-205-30613-6
    1. School administrators—In-service training—United States.   2. Educational
leadership—United States.   I. Title.
LB1738.5.C285 2000
371.2'011'0973 21—dc21   99-046206

Printed in the United States of America
10 9 8 7 6 5 4 3 2 1   03 02 01 00 99

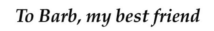

To Barb, my best friend

Contents

Preface

"Nothing stops an organization faster than people who believe that the way they worked yesterday is the best way to work tomorrow. To succeed, not only do your people have to change the way they act, they have got to change the way they think about the past."[1]

Change surrounds us. It always has been a part of the human situation. The difference between today and fifty years ago is that change has accelerated to the point where we can often no longer anticipate change, but must adapt to it as part of the natural flow of life. Those who adapt to change will survive and thrive in the future. Those who resist change will be left behind. The future is bleak for any species that refuses to master its environment. However, for leaders willing to embrace change, acquire new knowledge, and learn to apply new skills, the future is full of promise. These people will be our leaders in the twenty-first century. These people will transform society. These people will facilitate the discovery of solutions to perplexing problems. These leaders will be found in all races, among men and women, at every age, and in every profession. Their competence will build bridges across society's chasms of fear and hopelessness. These are the excellent leaders.

Leadership through excellence is the central theme of this book. *Excellence* refers to a superior state of performance. Leadership through excellence means that top-quality leaders transcend the conditions of their context to extend their roles through the superior value of their performance. Top-quality leaders excel because they operate at high levels of competence and seek to attain even higher levels to enhance their performance further. Their high levels of competence are expressed in many ways—for example, through their integrity and their ability to work with people, solve problems, communicate vision, and build a sense of community. The gestalt of high levels of competence in an array of areas results in leadership through excellence.

There is no single route to improving leadership through increased excellence in performance. Each of us has a different starting point, environment, demands, training, experiences, and mentoring. In essence, our leadership journey toward excellence is intertwined with the paths of those affected by our performance. They will judge our leadership by their assessment of our performance. We can control the outcome of their assessment by achieving excellence in performance. If leadership is to be acquired through excellence, then the starting place is in determining one's level of leadership competence.

This book allows educational leaders to assess their current level of leadership competence. This process provides more than twenty different assessments including a comprehensive 360° Administrator Feedback format. Among the array of self-scoring instruments are a personality profile to determine your specific ways of relating to people or situations, a profile of decision-making style, an analysis of leadership and management styles, and an assessment of the differences between high performers and those who have potential yet derail their careers. These differences are explained and followed by a self-analysis and prescription for growth. The educational leader can use these self-scoring instruments to complete the professional growth plan provided in the final chapter. This chapter gives leaders an example of a completed professional growth plan as well as a plan for the leader to complete. The educational leader can use this plan for individual and professional leadership development. The plan can be used in conjunction with the growing national trend to require professional growth plans for educational leaders. The development of a professional growth plan is essential to achieving excellence through leadership.

Leadership through excellence occurs in a public forum. The more competently leaders perform, the more they excel in their role, thereby adding value to the community. Consequently, excellent leaders make their competence known by securing positions in which they can make the greatest contribution. This book shows educational leaders how to accelerate their professional advancement. Educational leaders will discover the secrets of creating a winning resume, preparing an outstanding application package, eliminating the three myths that retard professional advancement, and developing a career action plan.

In the end, each of us must take personal responsibility for developing and maintaining our leadership ability. Leadership through excellence is a path to a fulfilled professional life. "Make professional development your first loyalty. To that end, keep dreaming, keep planning, and keep enhancing your skills in ways that will help ensure your employability in and outside of your organization. Make your second loyalty your profession; it is likely to be a longer-term springboard to career opportunities than your job. And make your third loyalty your company; in the short to medium term, it will most likely provide a venue for interesting and challenging work assignments that can polish your professional pedigree. Do these things and you'll stave off professional obsolescence and position yourself for continued career success."[2]

Are you ready to realize leadership through excellence? Chapter One is waiting for you. I have used many examples to illustrate points related to essential leadership skills. The names and places are all fictional, but each story can be found in many organizational settings.

I also used the personal pronouns *he* and *she* to avoid awkwardness in reading.

It is impossible to write a book like this without a great deal of assistance. I would like to acknowledge the help of many individuals and organizations. I have had support and encouragement from The University of Texas at San Antonio, my family, and my colleagues Bambi Cardenas, David Hinojosa, Alan Shoho, and Quintin Vargas. Of special note, I want to thank my wife Barb, whose faith in my ideas and in me never wavers. Special friends along my journey who have given me many ideas, examples, and learning experiences include Bob Anderson, Christopher Borman, Leonard Chaffee, Richard Clifford, Janis Fine, Tom Koerner, Clem Seldin, and Sally Zepeda. Anthony Robbins's work in human performance provided me with a source of ideas and inspiration.

Many people at Allyn and Bacon have helped the writing process and encouraged my efforts. I thank Ray Short for exploring and supporting the idea of linking the concepts of leadership, excellence, and competence, as well as Karin Huang, editorial assistant, whose patience with my many questions and requests for information was never ending, and Rowena Dores, whose timely feedback came at a critical moment. Also, thanks to Judy Ashkenaz, the project manager, who facilitated my book through its final publication stages, and to Laura MacKay for an outstanding job as copyeditor. A special thank you to Arnis Burvikovs, acquisitions editor and Ray Short's successor, whose accessibility and advice on many items has been constructive and supportive. Finally, I wish to thank the reviewers, William C. Hine of Eastern Illinois University and Dennis McNaughten of Tarleton State University, who provided valuable feedback in the development of this book.

NOTES

[1]Blanchard, K., & T. Waghorn, (1997). *Mission Possible.* New York: McGraw-Hill, (p. 25), quoting J. Madonna, Chairman, KPMG International.
[2]Koonce, R. (1998). How to prevent professional obsolescence. *Training & Development.* 52(2): 17.

Why Competence?

Richard Koonce, elaborating on the "4 Ms of career success," stated: "Ever say to yourself: 'I should do more with my career. I'm not developing as much as I should or being used to full potential in the job I have right now.'"[1] Career success is important to each of us. Each of us has a different and personal standard for career success. Regardless of the standard used for measuring career success, our working careers shape and influence our lives and the lives of those who surround us. Career success is a venue in which we can use our skills to contribute to society. It enhances our self-esteem. It provides psychological and material rewards. It gives meaning to our lives. In addition, it contributes to a personal sense of career fulfillment. We will spend the majority of our lives at work. Therefore, it is critical to make our careers "work" for us.

In the current global economic and political climate, there is more pressure than ever for career success–minded people to continually adapt to changing environments. No longer can a person go to college, earn a degree, and fit into a lifelong career. A career such as school principal retains the same title, but the role of school principal today bears little resemblance to the role of school principal twenty years ago. Rapid societal change impacts careers; jobs appear and disappear, driven by economic and political forces. Raelin tells us: "Employees can become expendable before their time. Thus, the need to be in control of one's career is more critical than ever. Security is available, but it comes in a new form. It's not derived from mere seniority, but rather from the continuous accumulation of human capital from the growth in skills that can prepare one for the next assignment. Jobs are less fixed in the information age, so workers need to be flexible and mobile to keep up with new knowledge requirements."[2]

If we are to make our careers "work," we must systematically update our professional skill level to conform to contemporary demands. This systematic update occurs through the creation of a professional growth plan. The professional growth plan has the sole purpose of increasing our level of competence. Ken Blanchard contends: "To stay competitive today, you not only have to pay attention to what you are doing now in order to perform better, but to what you have to do tomorrow to stay competitive in the future. In other words, you have to simultaneously manage the present and plan the future."[3] To the extent that we systemically use a professional growth plan to "manage the present and plan the future," we ensure our career success.

An effective professional growth plan is a map that leads its maker to greater levels of professional competence. This chapter explores what it means to be competent, and the subsequent chapters provide the means for you to assess your current competency levels. These competence assessments will provide the data for you to create your professional growth plan in Chapter Eight. Everyone wants to be competent and believes they are competent at what they do. Yet, if you take a cursory survey of any profession, you will find that many "competent" people do not reach their full potential. You will find people who believe their performance is competent. Yet, if experts judged their performance, they would have significant shortfalls.

Competence is the cornerstone of a professional growth plan. It is the cornerstone because it is "both the possession of knowledge and the behavioral capacity to act appropriately. To develop competencies you must be both introduced to knowledge and have the opportunity to practice your skills."[4] The demand for increasing levels of competence will drive future professional career success. Competence is a mental model needed by school administrators in the twenty-first century. It is a tough-minded formula for making one's career thrive while adding value to the community and organization.

What is your attitude regarding competence? The *Competence Attitude Assessment* at the top of page 3 will ascertain your use of competence thinking. Each YES response indicates a personal desire to become more competent and a recognition that competence is an essential core value.

Competence creates trust. We trust those who respond competently and mistrust those whose competence we question. The more we experience competence around us, the more confident we are of potential outcomes. Consequently, competence prevents anxiety! It allows us to function effectively in the present and prepares us for the future. Competence is rapidly becoming the ultimate key to job security in the twenty-first century. Koonce says:

> If the less aggressive learner gains new knowledge and skills at a rate of 4 percent a year, by the time he's in his 50s, his 100 units of talent will have increased to 256 units, and he'll be able to cope effectively with tasks at least twice as hard as the ones he could handle at age 25. Let's say the aggressive learner increases her knowledge and skills by 9 percent a year. By the time she's in her 50s she will have multiplied her 100 units of talent to 862, and she'll be able to handle tasks eight times as difficult as those she could handle at 25. Clearly, she'll be in a league apart from the person who was once her peer.[5]

Competent people will be sought after and rewarded for their competence. You can be one of these sought-after individuals. You can move

COMPETENCE ATTITUDE ASSESSMENT

The following statements ascertain your use of competence thinking. Answer each statement with a YES or NO response. When you finish, total the number of YES responses and the number of NO responses.

1. My future is important to me.	YES	NO
2. I want to contribute to my community.	YES	NO
3. People really need me.	YES	NO
4. Technology is moving faster than I am.	YES	NO
5. The demands on school administrators are rapidly changing.	YES	NO
6. I want to acquire greater skills, but the demands of my job limit my time.	YES	NO
7. Sometimes I feel overwhelmed with all that is demanded of me.	YES	NO
8. I wish I had a year off to catch up with everything I have to know.	YES	NO
9. The university did not prepare me for my present position.	YES	NO
10. If I could have tailor-made my preparation, I would have done it differently.	YES	NO

ahead and stay ahead of your competition. You can use your competence to change your environment. This chapter walks you through the essential components of competence. Are you ready for the challenge? If you are, you are an adventurer, a risk-taker, and a natural leader.

COMPETENCY-BASED DEVELOPMENT—THREE CHALLENGES

Challenge 1: Understanding Competence as a Public and Relational Activity

Competence is a multidimensional construct. On one hand, people are competent when they perform a designated task to specific standards. To the degree that they repeatedly perform this task, they demonstrate competence. On the other hand, life is not static. It constantly changes and places an evolving set of demands on people. For example, farmers who milked cows in the nineteenth century performed this action by hand. That action demanded competence on the part of the farmer. If a farmer in the twenty-first century were to milk cows by hand, regardless of how efficient the performance, few people would consider the farmer competent. In simple terms, competence is being good at what you do and is relevant to the needs of the community.

Competence goes deeper than performing a series of technically sound tasks. For example, a great basketball player does more than shoot a ball through the basket. The great basketball player has a synergistic impact on team members, fans, and opposing players. The great basketball player's presence on the court is often sufficient for victory whether or not the player scores points. People look to this person for leadership, attitude, and skill. In essence, the basketball player's competence is multidimensional and is directly related to his impact on other people. The basketball player would not be considered competent if baskets were made in the solitary confines of the playground, without teammates or opponents.

Competence is a complex phenomenon comprising four specific actions. These four actions are part of any human behavior that is judged competent.

1. **The action is relevant.**
2. **The action meets the standards set by a social group.**
3. **The action expresses itself publicly.**
4. **The action is expressed through work-related relationships.**

The action is relevant

The actions of a person performing any given task have to be *relevant* if they are to be competent. Relevant actions address the demands of the present context. If they are not relevant, they do not meet the *standards* that are implicitly or explicitly stated by the members of the organization where the actions are performed. For example, a school administrator who is arbitrary and authoritarian may make excellent decisions; yet, this school administrator may be viewed by the faculty as incompetent if the organization demands participation in the decision-making process. Authoritarian leadership may be competent in one organization and inappropriate in another organization. Relevance as it is related to competence meets three criteria.

Criterion 1: The action addresses a problem identified by the organization. Everyone has heard of people who are ahead of their time. They are called visionaries. Without them, society seldom advances. Yet, although visionaries who are unable to communicate to their contemporaries may be proved correct by history, they seldom advance the needs of their society. The competent person understands and addresses the problems faced by his organization. He educates the members of the work environment in terms of existing problems and potential solutions. The person who addresses the right problem at the right time is well on his way to being judged as competent. In the eyes of his constituents, he is able to understand the problem, propose an acceptable solution, and see that the problem is solved.

Criterion 2: The action in addressing a relevant problem is consistent with the values and beliefs of the organization within which the action occurs. The values and beliefs of a group drive its understanding of competence. The success-driven person who focuses solely on achievement will be seen as competent in those organizations that esteem success. However, the same person will be seen as incompetent in organizations that value relationship building. For school administrators, this is especially true in communities that include large numbers of immigrants from cultures that place a high priority on relationships. The school administrator in this situation would do well to focus on building relationships as a way of collaborating with parents and students in moving toward greater achievement. Actions that indicate a lack of understanding and respect for the values of the organization are irrelevant and incompetent.

Criterion 3: The actions in addressing a relevant problem are efficient and effective. Problems that affect the organization are also public problems. Public issues are meteoric in nature and hold the focus of attention. The intensity of attention relates to the American culture's focus on efficiency and effectiveness. When a person is unable to resolve the relevant problem efficiently, this person is viewed as less than fully competent. In the same manner, the person who resolves the problem efficiently but does not address the source of the problem is, in the end, not seen as effective. The competent person is one who is both efficient and effective. For example, a school administrator may face the challenge of student gangs in school. The school administrator may rapidly organize the teachers and community to address the problem and implement a solution within weeks. The community responds favorably to the school administrator's actions. In this case, a need was identified and action was taken. But imagine that within a month graffiti are seen on school walls, gang activity is taking place on campus, and rumors of gang control of lavatories are rampant. Now, the school administrator no longer is seen as competent. Effectiveness was missing from solving a problem relevant to the organization and community. Efficiency and effectiveness are linked.

The action meets the standards set by a social group

Each social group has a set of explicit or implicit standards to judge actions. These standards may be passed down from one generation to another, formed by an evolving context, based on economic factors, or developed by consensual designation. More often, they are implicit rather than explicit. In this sense, the school administrator has to identify the standards inherent within the organization. For example, one school administrator has a highly dogmatic and structured approach to discipline. The community has strong conservative values and believes that strong-handed discipline is important. Therefore, this community views this school administrator as highly competent. On the other hand, a neighboring community is very liberal. Students in this community have a much greater voice in decision making. The school administrator in the conservative community would be viewed as incompetent if she used the same strategies and tactics in the liberal community as she uses in the conservative community.

These community-driven standards may conflict with the school administrator's personal standards. When the school administrator meets the standards of the organization while simultaneously ignoring her standards, she experiences cognitive dissonance. If she attempts to impose her beliefs, she will be at odds with the community. Competence is more easily achieved when the school administrator's personal standards are aligned with those of the organization. Achieving competence depends not so much on an understanding between the school administrator and the organization as it does on the school administrator's understanding of community expectations. When she understands these expectations, she focuses her energy to address specific community needs.

The action expresses itself publicly

The competent person practices his craft in a public domain. That is, his work is publicly visible, subject to public scrutiny and public judgment. As Parker Palmer says: "No significant vision can find full expression within the confines of private life. Sooner or later, if it is to be fulfilled, it must find an outlet in the public realm."[6] The school administrator's work is a public activity. It affects a wide audience. The school administrator's actions directly influence the members of the community. All members form judgments of the school administrator's actions. Their judgments are linked directly to the impact they feel the school administrator has on their lives. If we return to the sports metaphor, the competent basketball player has little, if any, influence on someone who has no interest in basketball. There is little concern for how well he plies his craft. On the other hand, a rabid basketball fan with an emotional interest in the team is deeply concerned with how well this basketball player performs. To the degree that this basketball player successfully shoots, rebounds, and assists other team members, he will be judged as competent. To the degree that his performance is detrimental to the team's overall mission (winning games) he is judged as less-than-competent. It is public perception that is the final arbiter of competence. In the end, performance cannot be submerged in team play or in cooperatively working with others. The final judgment on competence is always solitary in nature. One who seeks to be seen as competent must seek a public venue.

The action is expressed through work-related relationships

A competent act affects other people. Consequently, it is openly expressed. Mozart would never have been judged as competent if his music had not been heard. When the action is hidden, competence is missing. When the action is open, it affects other people. In this sense, it is relational because of the interaction created by the performer's action. A rock cannot be tossed into a pool of water without creating ripples.

When it is tossed into the water, a series of ripples follow the action of the rock. Each ripple pushes the preceding ripples farther away from the place where the rock entered the water. In the same way, any action by the school administrator causes a series of ripples affecting people beyond his office. The relational aspect of competence is manifested through a series of characteristics present in the competent person's actions.

- **Competence is expressed through communication.**
- **Competence is expressed through empowering others.**
- **Competence is expressed through meeting the needs of others.**
- **Competence is expressed through integrity.**

Competence is expressed through communication

A competent relationship exists through communication in which the parties in the relationship each take responsibility for communicating. The competent school administrator realizes that "the beginning of all successful communication is desire—the desire to communicate. This desire cannot be vague and negotiable. It has to be a flint-hard posture of the will, an inner resolution, a firm promise made to ourselves and to others with whom we are trying to relate."[7] Through this desire, the competent school administrator initiates efforts to make sure that communication takes place by exchanging information in several ways, such as talking, writing, and gesturing. It is the school administrator's system for sending and receiving messages. Therefore, actions are explained, opinions sought, dialogue invited in order to enhance the relational nature of competence. Often, highly skilled people are viewed as incompetent because they are unable to communicate effectively. Their competence is undermined by futile attempts to communicate in a one-dimensional, linear fashion without effort to facilitate communication in a multidimensional, complex fashion. Communication is an integral part of leadership competence because it forms and reconciles political and social relationships.

Competence is expressed through empowering others

The competent school administrator empowers the members of the school community. Empowerment is at the heart of leadership efforts in a democratic society. If the school administrator fails to empower, she acts as a demagogue at worst and, at best, a benevolent dictator, with the actions of her employees based either on fear of retribution or on the desire to be rewarded. This is not relational, nor is it competent. Her actions fail to be competent because she creates situations in which she stifles the growth of the members of her organization. Empowerment is a centerpiece of competence because it creates a synergistic/relational environment in which each member understands the importance of the gestalt of each person's actions. Members recognize that the whole organization is much greater than the sum of its parts. The school administrator who embraces empowerment gains the respect of the organization because she first respects the inherent strength and goodness within the organization's membership.

Competence is expressed through meeting the needs of others

Maslow spoke of one of the basic conflicts that confront many people as that of the struggle between autonomy and homonomy.[8] This is the struggle between the desires of the ego and the need to include and involve others in one's life. The competent person balances both needs. The person has a need to succeed, achieve, and have personal ambition. Yet, this need is channeled toward building a better society for other people. For the competent person, the world exists to be served, to add value to, and to meet the needs of others. To quote Spears (1994):

> There is a revolution underway. In corporate boardrooms, university classes, community leadership groups, not-for-profit organizations and elsewhere, change is occurring around the ways in which we, as a society, approach the subject of work and leadership. Many people are seeking new and better ways of integrating work with their own personal and spiritual growth. They are seeking to combine the best elements of leadership based upon service to others, as part of an exciting concept called "servant-leadership." It has been, to be sure, a slow-growing revolution—but one which is now sending deep roots throughout society.[9]

For example, consider the high school administrator who desires to become superintendent of schools. If she uses her technical ability to promote herself without considering the needs of her organization, she will be viewed as self-serving. Any demonstration of competence will be viewed as one-dimensional and not focused on meeting the needs of her community. However, if she maintains a dual focus, and also reaches out to meet the needs of her organization, she will discover that her career-driven desires will be met. There is a synergistic relationship between autonomy and homonomy. In effect, autonomy follows homonomy.

Competence is expressed through integrity

The foundation of the relational aspects of competence resides in integrity. Stephen Carter, author of *Integrity*, states: "Integrity is the crucial element of good citizenship. It's more important to know if someone has integrity than to know whether I agree or disagree with him. If you lack integrity, nothing else you say you believe matters."[10] Integrity is the alignment of the school administrator's internal positive value system with his external actions. The competent school administrator is fully cognizant of his duty, the breadth and depth of its scope, and the consequences of any failure on his part to fulfill his duty. Extending beyond fulfilling his duties, the school administrator has a deep sense of responsibility. That is, he does not need someone to follow him and direct his activities. He acts on what needs to be done and is willing to be held accountable for his actions. In the eyes of the competent school administrator, the buck stops with him. He is ready to assume full responsibility for any action without attributing blame to others. This sense of duty and responsibility leads to deepening trust by the members of his organization. In his organization, the members recognize that he serves their best interests. They recognize that the school administrator's actions are designed to help, heal, and foster a healthy community. Ironically, this deep sense of trust can be destroyed by a single act that lacks integrity. The competent school administrator who, in a moment of weakness, allows himself to play favorites and unjustly rewards a supporter to the detriment of a nonsupporter, loses the respect of the members of his organization. The motivation for each future action will be questioned; these actions will be seen as self-serving. The actions of the school administrator are devoid of innocence once integrity is missing. Integrity, once lost, is seldom regained.

Challenge 2: Identifying the Seven Essential Competence Characteristics

Psychologically healthy people desire to be competent. Psychologically healthy people have to sharpen their competence to increase their contribution to society. Increasing one's competence provides greater benefits to society as well as to oneself. Becoming competent is akin to Maslow's concept of the "self-actualizing" human being. When people are competent, they achieve their human potential. In this sense, becoming competent is a highly personal endeavor. Each person's competence is like his or her DNA. It is individual. It is matched to the unique set of experiences, abilities, and beliefs that each brings to his or her environment. Interaction with one's environment is expressed in a competence domain.

Living demands a competent response. It is our primal way of survival. The competence response is inherent in surviving members of any species. The tiger cub that does not learn to hunt does not survive. Predators soon devour the cardinal that cannot fly. The human being who does not learn to form relationships becomes isolated. Each situation demands a competent response. There are serious consequences to incompetent actions. These negative consequences are felt directly in the animal world, where survival is threatened each time an incompetent action is taken. As human beings, we are often able to recover from incompetent actions. However, they have a cumulative effect on us. There are startling differences between people who live competently and those who live incompetently.

In effect, competence is essential in our professional and personal roles. We must move from a narrowly constrained view of competence as related solely to work to an expansive view of competence as related to everything that we do. Understanding that all aspects of our lives are integrated makes us more fully human and provides a greater degree of security. Moreover, it makes us more competent because it moves us closer to Maslow's concept of self-actualization. The closer we are to self-actualization, the closer we are to manifesting the seven essential characteristics of competence. These characteristics drive competence in every human endeavor.

The seven essential competence characteristics
- Competence is *value driven.*
- Competence provides *positive benefits.*
- Competence is *adaptive.*
- Competence is *time centered.*
- Competence is *correctly focused.*
- Competence is *problem generated.*
- Competence is *results oriented.*

Competence is value driven

The competent school administrator is driven by a set of values that defines the school administrator's contribution. This set of values influences each action of the school administrator. When the school administrator internally integrates these values, they are expressed in her actions. Each of us has a set of values that we express in each of our actions. The competent person identifies these values and determines if they are to be reinforced or set aside and replaced by a set of values that contributes to becoming more fully competent. Recently, a large urban newspaper reported the investigation of a school superintendent regarding the misuse of school funds. The superintendent was charged with using school funds to purchase expensive home furniture. Technically, this superintendent was competent. Yet, this superintendent had a set of values that allowed the use of taxpayers' dollars for personal gain. This superintendent was removed, tried, and convicted. The superintendent never examined a core set of values. On the surface, the superintendent never would have admitted to possessing a poorly derived set of values. Yet, competence-limiting values were driving this superintendent's actions.

THE VALUES TEST

Take the *Values Test* to discover if your competence is *value driven.* Identify any deficiencies before they harm your professional success.

Each of the following statements elicits the motivation for your values. As you read each statement, you may feel that it does not apply to you or that the statement does not perfectly fit. Assess if the statement is more *True* or more *False* about you. You *must* choose an answer.

1. My career is more important than are people. **T** or **F**.
2. The organization is better off when I am assertively leading. **T** or **F**.

3. I have the answers to many problems, but I only share them when I am asked. **T** or **F**.

4. I have a difficult time saying no to people. **T** or **F**.

5. I prefer to control the process and outcome of a situation. **T** or **F**.

6. I prefer to let people stumble and then ask me for help. **T** or **F**.

7. If people refuse my help, I will not offer it the next time they need it. **T** or **F**.

8. I enjoy challenging authority regardless of the issue. **T** or **F**.

9. I would rather be left alone than work with other people. **T** or **F**.

10. I have never spent considerable time reflecting on the efficacy of my values. **T** or **F**.

You have completed the *Values Test*. The test is explained below. Each statement is illustrated and followed by a prescription (℞). Each prescription is designed to help you make your competence more value driven.

If you answered *True* to the statement, "My career is more important than are other people," it indicates that your values are ego driven.

℞. Competence demands that the value be balanced between self and other interests. Identify ways that you can set aside your ambitions to promote the interests of your constituents. Those who have mastered this value have discovered that the more they move away from being ambition driven to being other driven, the more their ambitions are realized.

If you answered *True* to the statement, "The organization is better off when I am assertively leading," it indicates a great sense of self-confidence, yet it also indicates a lack of confidence in other people.

℞. Competence demands confidence in other people. This is an important value of highly competent people. They realize that any success they achieve comes through the cooperative efforts of others. Those who have mastered this value have discovered that the more confidence they demonstrate in others, the more confidence others demonstrate in them. It is a synergistic activity.

If you answered *True* to the statement, "I have the answers to many problems, but I only share them when I am asked," it indicates that you value your intelligence but also hoard it and do not readily put it to the use of others.

℞. Competence demands that one's abilities, intelligence, and skills are put to public use. Highly competent people have this core value. They realize their lives' signatures are written by the way that they proactively contribute to others.

If you answered *True* to the statement, "I have a difficult time saying no to people," it indicates a lack of value placed on one's personal space and an inability to prioritize. It is also indicative of codependent behavior.

℞. Competent people value their time and space. They never do for others what others can do for themselves. They may give advice or coach someone, but they do not take responsibility by removing the duty that rightfully belongs to that person. In this way, the competent person demonstrates respect of the other. It is a sign of trust in someone else's ability to perform a given task.

If you answered *True* to the statement, "I prefer to control the process and outcome of a situation," it indicates a strong value of personal control.

℞. The competent person realizes that chaos often reigns. Exercising total control is the way of tyrants and is not consistent with the values of a democratic society. The greater the desire for total control, the greater the degree of insecurity that a person expresses. Total control over any situation is nearly impossible. The competent person knows what he can and should control, and is also aware of what he cannot and should not control. It is the understanding of this loose–tight fit that enables the competent person to guide the organization through turbulent times.

If you answered *True* to the statement, "I prefer to let people stumble and then ask me for help," it indicates a value of power.

℞. Competent people recognize that a constructive application of power is always employed at the service of others. It does not subjugate or obligate others. There is an interactive synergy between the competent leader and his followers. In this synergy, the competent leader and his followers understand how and when to respond to each other. The response of the competent person is appropriate to the need.

If you answered *True* to the statement, "If people refuse my help, I will not offer it the next time they need it," it indicates a value of oversensitivity.

℞. Competent people are not overly sensitive. They have "thick skin" and "broad shoulders." It is not easy to lead a group of people. The leader is always the focal point. As the focal point, the leader receives deserved and undeserved criticism. The competent person has personal security in knowing who she is and what she has to offer. She recognizes the inherent limitations in each person and does not let these limitations fester into barriers that prevent collaboration.

If you answered *True* to the statement, "I enjoy challenging authority regardless of the issue," it indicates a mistrust of superiors.

℞. The competent person views respect for authority as an essential value. He recognizes that a person in authority is not always right. In such cases, the competent person discerns appropriate ways of enlightening those in authority. However, the competent person recognizes that no civil organization survives without respect for authority, society's symbols, and society's inherent values.

If you answered *True* to the statement, "I would rather be left alone than work with other people," it indicates a value of privacy.

℞. The competent person values privacy but not to the extent that it inhibits duty or responsibility. She recognizes that any organization operates effectively based on how well people collaborate on common issues. It is with and through people that the competent person gets things done. This means that competence moves from privacy toward social engagement. As Einstein said, "The value of a man, however, should be seen in what he gives and not in what he is able to receive."[11]

If you answered *True* to the statement, "I have never spent considerable time reflecting on the efficacy of my values," it indicates a deep need to emphasize the reflective nature of your humanity.

℞. Competent people have a clear awareness of personal identity. New trends, political pressures, and continually changing demands do not alter their basic personal identity. They have values that resonate and that drive their actions. These are personally discovered values, not values adapted or adopted from others. It is from this reservoir of values that they find strength in times of struggle.

Competence provides positive benefits

Any competent action produces positive results. These results benefit humanity. They add value to the quality of life or the quality of work of others in the organization and community. When a result adds value to the quality of a person's life, it is a direct consequence of actions that met or exceeded the expectations of the person affected by the actions. Mozart's *Symphony Number 41 in C Major* performed competently brings delight and pleasure to the audience. The quality of life of the recipients of this action is enhanced. On the other hand, if the symphony orchestra did not practice and performed poorly, those in the audience would feel cheated because of the less-than-competent performance.

Competence provides benefits that add value to the quality of work. Work is the vehicle through which we express ourselves. It is tightly tied to our sense of self-esteem. A competent leader understands the importance of work for each member of the organization and focuses actions on enhancing the work environment so that work is meaningful. She acts to make sure that people have the skills and tools to do their work. She realizes that effective performance builds self-esteem. People feel good about themselves when they can see that their efforts are effective and recognized.

Competence provides benefits because it is other directed. Because competence is other directed, it moves away from the person performing the action toward others. Competence is practice of a craft that brings benefit to the self as well as others. Each competent action performed by the school administrator has the inherent capacity to provide benefit to others. In this sense, the work of the school administrator is a craft that must be practiced. The craftsperson does not act on rote memory, but views each act in detail with the final image in mind. The competent, other-directed school administrator responds in the same way. Consequently, competent leadership provides benefits that result in the growth of others, contributes to a psychologically and physiologically healthy environment, and resolves problems with the least degree of effort.

Competence *is* adaptive

Competence can only be sustained if it adapts to evolving contexts. What was seen as a competent act by one generation may be viewed as a marginally competent act by the succeeding generation. For example, the school administrator of the 1950s led highly traditional schools. In many parts of the United States, schools were not integrated. There was no call for large-scale achievement testing. After the launching of Sputnik in 1958, the role of the school administrator changed. Competence began to be related to student achievement. The school administrator of the 1960s focused on social issues stemming from integration and social unrest grounded in the Vietnam War. The school administrator of the 1970s focused on previously disenfranchised groups such as students with disabilities and women, and had to discover ways to integrate these populations into school programs. The school administrator of the 1980s and 1990s is challenged by external accountability. State legislatures, for example, take a more intrusive look into instructional outcomes.

The demands on school administrators continue to change. The competent school administrator adapts to new demands and anticipates paradigm shifts. School administrators who are only now preparing to be competent in a technological age have missed the paradigm shift. Joel Barker, the futurist, states: "Simply put a paradigm shift is when the basic rules are FUNDAMENTALLY CHANGED. The boundary or limits rules are changed and the operational rules for success within the boundaries are changed. Both sets of rules must change in order to have a paradigm shift."[12]

The questions asked by competent school administrators as they make a paradigm shift are: "What will be demanded of me in the next ten years?" "What new skills, evolving vision, or knowledge are essential to greet the evolving paradigm?" It is not easy to anticipate a paradigm shift. However, competence requires an adjustment for what is needed. When Joel Barker described the paradigm shift, he noted that by the time most people climb onto the paradigm shift, a new shift is already taking place. The ability to anticipate the shift, prepare for the shift, and await its arrival with a set of solutions is one of the traits of the highly competent leader. Those who are marginally competent are buffeted by the winds of change. The former fills his sails with the air of change. The latter is capsized by the turbulence.

Competence *is* time centered

Competence is connected to the past and the future while operating in the present. Competence is rooted in the past because it has a history. Its history is rooted in the following areas:

- Maintenance of high personal performance.
- Continuous personal growth.
- Personal impact on increasingly complex environments.

- Evolving and widespread recognition by the recipients of competent actions.
- Confidence in personal competence.

Maintenance of high personal performance. The competent person maintains, over time, a history of high personal performance. There is a consistency to this level of performance. Any "down time" is only temporary and is followed by resurgence. The history of a competent performer is not checkered, but a continuous stream of clearly identifiable results that exceed the performance of competitors. This is known as the Ideal Performance State (IPS). The Ideal Performance State is that area in which you reach your potential and achieve at your optimum capacity. There is a link between being able to dominate life's challenges and the mental toughness that makes it possible to attain IPS.[13] People who constantly operate in IPS are inducted into "halls of fame" or recognized by their professional organizations as having withstood the test of time.

Continuous personal growth. Competent people are never satisfied with the status quo. They desire to learn, evolve, and stretch to make the ascent to the next level of competence. This happens to people committed to continuous personal growth. They have a history of commitment to lifelong learning. Remarkable athletes, musicians, writers, and teachers make a study of their craft. They are never through learning. They are simultaneously teachers and students of their craft. A story circulated among baseball people was that the famous Boston Red Sox player Ted Williams studied every pitcher to learn about the pitcher's tendencies. Consequently, he was ready to face the pitcher when it was his turn to bat. His .406 batting average in 1941 stands as a testament of his competence.[14] There is no dichotomy between teaching and learning. They are synonymous to the competent professional.

Personal impact on increasingly complex environments. The competent person has a history of personal impact on complex environments. This person begins by resolving simple tasks and progressively moves to higher levels of complexity. It is a way of life. A child learns to crawl, walk, and then run. The competent person recognizes that gaining competence is much like climbing a ladder. At each rung of the ladder, a new set of competencies is demanded. A person must teach before becoming a school administrator. A surgeon, however brilliant as a medical student, must first become an intern, then a resident before fully practicing medicine. Competent people have a history of success at increasingly difficult levels of complexity.

Evolving and widespread recognition by the recipients of competent actions. The competent person has a history of increased recognition. The competent person does not act in a vacuum. His actions are public actions and as each action succeeds, he becomes more of a public figure. His stature elevates the members of his organization. John Gardner tells us, "Societies are renewed—if they are renewed at all—by people who believe in something, care about something, stand for something."[15] Competent people cannot help but make a recognizable difference. There is an increasing demand on their time to share their competence with a wider array of groups. Competence cannot be hidden. It is such a rare commodity that people want to know more about this person, they want to be close to this person, they want to be part of this person's life. Competence is always recognized and rewarded. The eclipsing of major league baseball's home run record in 1998 by Mark McGwire illustrates this point. People wanted to know more about McGwire, they wanted to be close to him because of his significant level of competence.

Confidence in personal competence. Competent people are confident. They are not afraid of tackling tough problems. They are confident in the outcome because they have a history of competence in similar situations. They know how to perform under pressure. They have a sense of tranquility as they move into uncharted waters, while others shy away. They identify dangers and devise strategies to overcome dangers. Their confidence engenders greater confidence in followers. It is contagious. Winston Churchill was able to demonstrate confidence to the people of England even when Germany appeared to be sure of victory. Churchill's confidence was fueled by his competence to lead even in the most difficult of times.

Competence is acted out in present tense, but the present is not static. The lessons of the past inform the actions of the present; the actions of the present are driven by a vision of the future. Competence cannot rest in the glories of the past, nor can it live in the illusions of the future. It is alive. It is action oriented. It is forced to respond to the demands of the moment. It does so, because competence is not worried about the acclaim of the critics. It allows its actions to speak to the critics and to let the future be the judge. Competent people cannot waste time fretting about how their actions will be received. Copernicus was not discouraged when he shared his views regarding the organization of the solar system. He was criticized during his lifetime, but history has proved him correct.

The future awaits the actions of the competent person. The future's destiny is determined by the present. A present moment filled with incompetent actions does not lead to a future. A future can only occur through competent leadership. Each competent act prepares for the birth of the future. Each competent act becomes a brick in the building of a new world. Each competent act in the present is the continuation of a legacy and the passing of a torch to a future generation.

Competence is correctly focused

The actions of competent people are correctly focused. Those who are highly competent recognize that they have limited energy and that the diffusion of energy has little return. They take their full attention and channel it toward the right issue. Competence when correctly focused:

- Acts on the right issue.
- Acts at the right time.

- Acts in the right place.
- Acts with the right people.
- Acts with the right response.

Acts on the right issue. School leaders are confronted with a wide array of competing issues. Yet, competent school administrators have an intuitive sense as to the issues that are the most critical to their organizations' survival. They know that these critical issues, if resolved efficiently and effectively, provide the organization with the greatest benefit. For example, in today's political culture there is a strong movement to fund alternatives to public schools. Private religious and nonreligious schools are growing. Charter schools are sanctioned in many states. Homeschooling is attracting a growing list of adherents. Public schools are in direct competition with each of these alternatives. Yet, many school administrators sit idly by and watch their brightest students move to alternative educational settings. Competent school administrators sense the highly competitive nature of this climate and proactively move to make their schools competitive. They are able to integrate the concerns of parents and communities to make their schools the competitive choice.

Acts at the right time. Competent school leaders have a sense of timing. It is neither delayed nor premature. They know when to act. An exceptional proposal prematurely presented to the school board will be ignored. The school board may not be ready for the proposal because it is not fully cognizant of the issues the proposal addresses. There is a window of opportunity in which the competent leader acts. Actions taken outside this window fall short of their full potential. In an age in which information is rapidly communicated, the window for action has shrunk. There is little margin for error. There is a demand for decisiveness. Competence is expressed in decisiveness. One example of this scheme of decisiveness is the launching of the space shuttle. When the space shuttle is launched, the astronauts have seconds to decided whether to continue or abort the mission and be separated from the rocket. They are making rapid, life-threatening decisions in split seconds. They must be competent.

Acts in the right place. The competent person focuses on the right issues at the right time in the *right place*. He knows that actions applied where they are not needed are useless. Martin Luther King Jr. provides an excellent example of acting in the right place. His march to Selma, Alabama, brought the right issues at the right time to the *right place*. If Dr. King had marched on Berkeley, California, he would not have roused the national consciousness. Instead, he chose to focus his energy and the energy of his movement on Selma, and he roused the moral indignation of a nation. School administrators, to be competent, must understand the notion of place. Place is where the impact of the action has its greatest effect. As Gallagher says in *The Power of Place*, ". . . we are apt to act in certain ways in certain places; the more clues a place provides about what we should do or not do, the more we will conform to them."[16]

Acts with the right people. Imagine leadership as a play. The play has a number of acts; each act has a series of scenes. In each scene, there are different characters. Throughout the play, the main actors and actresses sustain the play's theme. Those who participate in the play know its outcome. Those who participate in the real-life drama of leadership can only anticipate the outcome. Competent leadership understands the need to align the right issue, at the right time, in the right place, with the *right people*. The wrong players appearing in the right scene create chaos for the acting company. The play stops until order is restored. No one would be able to play his or her part. The competent school administrator recognizes this phenomenon. She identifies the *right people* who are essential to the resolution of a problem. There is no wasted energy because she understands the talents of these people and assists them in focusing their energy on the specific parts of the problem for which they have expertise.

Acts with the right response. The competent person knows how to respond. This response is used to judge him as competent. The *right response* is accurate in terms of its depth, breadth, volume, and density. Imagine a gardener applying herbicide in inordinate amounts to a garden. Weeds and wanted plants alike are destroyed. The competent gardener knows the amount and type of herbicide to apply so that weeds are destroyed and the wanted plants are protected. The competent school administrator acts like a competent gardener. She understands her people. She recognizes their strengths and limitations. She knows how to motivate each member of her staff. She recognizes the need to fine-tune her response, so she constantly monitors its application. Competent people are aware of the importance of addressing the right issue, at the right time, in the right place, with the right people, with the *right response*.

Competence *is* problem generated

Competence exists in a problem-filled, challenging, and unpredictable environment. The competent person understands that life demands that he respond competently to challenges. The ability to respond competently is a part of our genetic makeup. This is why the fragile human species has survived against countless obstacles. The human species is wired to solve problems. Each set of solutions generates a new set of problems. It is a never-ending cycle. It is why competent people are constantly in demand. Identify a problem and you discover that competent people are needed to resolve the problem.

For example, one school district had a high school that was plagued by poor discipline. The teachers in this school were constantly threatened. Students viewed class attendance as an option. Drugs were freely distributed on the campus. The school board sought an administrator to bring order to this school. It believed that the process for change would take months. The newly hired administrator caused a dramatic turnaround within a matter of days. The problem of chaotic school discipline was a deep-rooted challenge to the community. The new school administrator saw it as a personal challenge. She knew how to restore order and refocus student and faculty attention on learning. Although she was able to restore a sense of order, she discovered other problems that demanded different types of competence. She had to deal with a long history of marginal teaching, a poorly constructed curriculum, and poor SAT scores. Competence identifies and resolves problems.

If we refer again to Dr. King, we see that he created a sense of moral indignation. Segregation was no longer an option. This presented the United States with a new series of problems. Leaders and citizens had to determine how to ensure that segregation would not recur. Leaders had to determine how to redress the historical evil consequences of segregation. They had to address how to bring together peacefully people who had been purposely kept apart. Some of these issues remain to be resolved. Yet, competent people address these issues and continue to address them until they are resolved.

Competence is results oriented

Competence is attached to results. Competence is a measured phenomenon. A baseball player who makes a large number of fielding errors is not competent. One who makes few errors and many outstanding plays in the field is given the Golden Glove Award. The cellist who is acclaimed as a virtuoso and asked to perform at Carnegie Hall is judged competent by peers, critics, and her audience. Competence is seen through the results of the performance. People know when they are in the presence of competence. An awe overtakes the atmosphere. This is why standards are so important. If standards are absent, performance cannot be measured. In addition, if performance is not measured, it cannot be judged as competent. When this occurs, less-than-competent performances are accepted as competent and the general level of performance declines.

In an environment that fails to measure performance against a challenging standard, it is up to the individual to set personal standards. Competence requires us to continually drive ourselves to a greater level of performance measured against the best-known standards. A tennis player may win every match against lower-ranked opponents, yet this tennis player is not competent. The tennis player failed the competence test because the standard used was flawed. He failed to challenge himself by selecting a standard that exceeded his current level of performance.

Challenge 3: Preparing for the Adventure

Competence is "a characteristic of an individual that leads to behaviors that meet the job demands of the individual within the parameters of the organizational environment and that bring about desired results."[17] It is a multidimensional and complex activity. It is not for the weak, timid, or those who seek the easy path. It is for the strong, courageous, and those unafraid of hard work and personal challenges. The challenge of preparation for the adventure asks you to judge yourself in terms of *readiness* and of the *relative nature* of your competence.

Are you set to define your stage of readiness? *Readiness* speaks to your willingness to accept the challenge to become more competent. It challenges you to admit that you have not arrived. Readiness allows you to demonstrate that you have not withdrawn from the task of living and growing. It is a statement that you are ready to tackle a new adventure. Determine your level of readiness for this challenge. Respond to the following statements:

1. I am ready to set higher personal standards. **YES   NO**

2. I am ready to challenge my set ways of thinking, acting, and seeing others. **YES   NO**

3. I am ready to make a personal commitment to increased competence. **YES   NO**

4. I am ready to take on the challenge of the work involved in becoming competent. **YES   NO**

5. I am ready to allow my personal competence to become public competence. **YES   NO**

If you answered YES to each statement, you have a high state of readiness to take your current level of competence to higher, more complex levels. Your response indicates that you have a clear understanding of the personal investment required to achieve this desired state. It also indicates a belief in your self-worth and in the contribution that you can make to society.

Assume that you are already competent. Assume that you desire to become more competent. When desire is translated into positive action, powerful forces align themselves to bring about the desired result. The willingness to initiate is the first critical step to becoming more competent. The second step is to leap into the unknown, not knowing what you will discover. This is a gift of all risk-takers. As Joseph Campbell stated: "We must be willing to get rid of the life we've planned, so as to have the life that is waiting for us. The old skin has to be shed before the new one can come. If we fix on the old, we get stuck. When we hang onto any form, we are in danger of putrefaction."[18] If you answered NO to any question, try to discover the reasons for your response. Is there a sense of fear? Is there a sense of arrival? Identify the motivation. In the end, take a chance on yourself! You have nothing to lose and everything to gain.

READY—SET—LEAP!

Now that you have made the commitment to competence assess the *relative nature* of your current state of competence. The relative nature of your current state of competence references many of the issues addressed in this chapter. As I talk about the relative nature of competence, I want you to respond in personal terms. I am going to guide you through a process that will provide you with a baseline identification of your current competence level. You will need to be reflective. To encourage you to reflect on your current competence status, you should have a *competence journal*. Maintain your competence journal for one week.

A competence journal comprises three parts: **A**, **B**, and **C**.

A stands for actions

Record a major action that took place during the day. As you record this action, describe it as completely as possible. What caused you to act? What forces influenced the situation? Who were the players? What level of competence was demanded? Moreover, why was it important for you to act?

B stands for behaviors

What were the behaviors that you exhibited regarding this situation? What did you actually do? When did you do it? Was your behavior public? Where did you do it? Who was the recipient of your actions?

C stands for consequences

What were the consequences of your actions? Was there a previously set standard? Did you achieve this standard? What could have been done better? How would you do it again if you could start over?

The A, B, Cs are essential to follow in assessing the relative nature of competence. By reflecting on our actions, we begin the process of self-diagnosis. Self-diagnosis starts with an awareness of one's actions and their consequences. Once we become aware of what we are doing, we can then analyze that behavior. Consider the following pattern:

$$S \quad B \quad A$$

In this pattern, **S** stands for stimulus, **B** stands for behavior, and **A** stands for awareness. Most people respond to a problem situation, and only after responding are they aware of their actions. This patterned way of acting leaves room for many negative consequences. This is not the competent response. It is an automatic response rather than one that is weighed, calculated, and reasoned. When awareness replaces behavior, the behavior is no longer instinctive or reactive. The competent response pattern looks like this:

$$S \quad A \quad B$$

The competence journal, carried out over time, provides opportunity for becoming more aware of your reactions to the various stimuli to which you are subjected. As you become aware of your reaction/behavior to stimuli, you can anticipate your behavior. The more you become aware of your typical response, the freer you are to choose a behavior that is competent for the situation. For example, Jill Carson is the school administrator of Johnson Middle School. A few teachers discover they can bully Jill into agreeing to their position. They enter Jill's office and become very loud (stimulus). Jill becomes anxious and agrees to their suggestion in order to end their tirade (behavior). When the teachers leave, Jill feels guilty and wishes she had acted differently (awareness). Now that Jill is starting to maintain a competence journal, she can review these situations and her behavior. Now she can generate strategies to deal with faculty bullies.

The following is an example of a competence journal.

COMPETENCE JOURNAL

Date: April 27, 1999

Action
What caused you to take action? Sheila Timmons, parent of Sean Timmons, met with me today regarding Sean's algebra teacher. Ms. Timmons requested that I transfer Sean to a different teacher. She claimed that Sean was not learning from his present teacher.

What forces influenced the situation? Ms. Timmons's husband, Robert, is an influential member of the community. He has connections with the school board; he is a member of several well-known community organizations.

Who were the players? Obviously Ms. Timmons and her son Sean. I cannot forget that her husband, although absent, is also a player. The algebra teacher, Charlie Nastoes, is a player. The husband is connected to James Madison, the school board president.

What level of competence was demanded? A high level of interpersonal and negotiation competence was demanded in this situation.

Why was it important to act? The parent, Sheila Timmons, was right in front of me demanding action. She wanted a response. She wanted a very specific response, and I knew that she would not be happy if I did not give her the response that she expected.

Behavior
What was the behavior that I exhibited concerning the situation? I got defensive. I reacted by defending my algebra teacher and letting Ms. Timmons know that she could not demand a transfer for her son. After all, I cannot transfer the other twenty-five students out of the class!

What did you actually do? I told Ms. Timmons that a transfer was impossible. I also shared with her information that demonstrated that the students in Mr. Nastoes's class do as well on achievement tests as those with other teachers.

When did I act? I allowed Ms. Timmons to explain her position and then I responded.

Was my behavior public? No, the activities took place in my office. Ms. Timmons and I were the only participants.

Who was the recipient of your actions? Ms. Timmons was the initial recipient of my actions. However, I was trying to send a message to all other parents that they could not demand transfers for their children just because there was a conflict with the teacher.

Consequences

What were the consequences of my actions? I received a telephone call from the superintendent asking me to explain what had happened. It did not take long for Ms. Timmons to call her husband to start the political ball rolling. The superintendent told me that he did not want this to become an issue and for me to take care of the problem. Chalk one up for Ms. Timmons.

Was there a previously set standard? There was no official policy regarding this problem (boy, that sounds like part of the problem!).

Did I achieve this standard? I will think about standards next time. This will not happen again.

What could have been done better? Many things could have been done better. First, I should have gotten as much information from Ms. Timmons as possible. Second, I should have spoken to her son. Third, I should have spoken to the teacher. Fourth, I should have had the teacher, Sean, Ms. Timmons, and me at a meeting to work collaboratively toward a solution. Fifth, there should be a policy regarding student transfers from one class to another during the school year.

How would I do it again if I could start over? I would listen to Ms. Timmons. I would try to understand her motivation for coming to me; for example, what was behind her solution to change classes for her son? I would negotiate a time frame to investigate the issue and set a new meeting with her.

Maintaining a competence journal is essential if you want to understand the relative nature of your level of competence.

This chapter explained the nature of competence. It gave you a chance to assess your attitudes toward competence. The **competence journal** provided you with a critical tool on your journey to becoming more competent. Act now and begin your competence journal. Use this chapter as a foundation to move to greater levels of personal and professional competence. The choice of becoming more competent is up to you. Do not make any excuses. Your contribution to society is vitally important. Your contribution is limited until you take personal responsibility to move toward a program of continued competence growth. As you involve yourself in this journey, you will begin to explore your unlimited potential.

COMPETENCE CHECK

Do you understand:

☐ That competence is relative to the environment?

☐ That competence is a public event?

☐ That competence occurs in the relational exchange between the leader and the environment?

☐ That competence is expressed through personal integrity?

☐ That competence in a democratic environment is letting go of personal control and empowering others?

☐ The essential aspects of the seven essential competence characteristics?

☐ The positive benefits that are derived through competent action?

☐ The importance of timing in competent action?

☐ How to maintain your competence journal?

Were you able to place a ✓ in each of the boxes in the competence check? The competent person leaves no stone unturned. If you have any confusion, quickly return to that part of this chapter and review the material. The journey has begun. You are on your way to increasing your competence. You have a clear understanding of what it means to be competent and how your competence affects your environment. There will be a growing demand for you because there is always a demand for competence. You have accepted the challenge. In the next chapter, you will be guided through a series of personal assessments to establish your level of competence.

NOTES

[1] Koonce, R. (1997). The 4 Ms of career success. *Training and Development. 51* (12), (p. 15).

[2] Raelin, J. (1997). Internal career development in the age of insecurity. *Business Forum. 22*(1), (p. 22).

[3] Blanchard, K., & T. Waghorn. (1997). *Mission possible.* New York: McGraw-Hill (p. xiii).

[4] Quinn, R., S. Faerman, M. Thompson, & M. McGrath. (1996). *Becoming a master manager: A competency framework.* New York: Wiley (p. 24).

[5] Koonce, R. (1998). How to prevent professional obsolescence. *Training and Development. 52* (2), (p. 17).

[6] Palmer, P. (1981). *The company of strangers.* New York: Crossroads (p. 45).

[7] Powell, J. (1985). *Will the real me please stand up?* Allen, TX: Tabor Publishing (p. 18).

[8] Maslow, A. (1971). *The farther reaches of human nature.* New York: Viking Press.

[9] Spears, L. (1994). *Servant leadership: Quest for caring leadership.* Reprinted from *Inner Quest* (#2). *http://greenleaf.org/carelead.html.*

[10] A conversation with Stephen Carter, "Integrity: why we need a transfusion." An interview by David L. Miller, senior editor of *The Lutheran.* [Online]. Available: *http://www.thelutheran.org/9607/page6.html.*

[11] Einstein, A. (1970). *Out of my later years.* Westport, CT: Greenwood Press (p. 35).

[12] Barker, J. Paradigm shift. *TIPS: A Newsletter of Trends, Innovations, and Paradigm Shifts.* [Online]. Available: *http://www.jbtips.com/Definitions.html.* Accessed February 6, 1999.

[13] Loehr, J. (1993). *Toughness training for life.* New York: Plume Book.

[14] Thorn, J., P. Palmer, M. Gershman, & D. Pietrusza. (1997). *Total baseball: The official encyclopedia of major league baseball.* New York: Penguin.

[15] Gardner, J. (1964). *Self-renewal.* New York: Harper and Row (p. 115).

[16] Gallagher, W. (1994). *The power of place.* New York: Simon & Schuster (p. 190).

[17] Wexley, K., & R. Klimoski. (1990). Performance appraisal: an update. In G. Ferris & K. Rowland (Eds.), *Performance.* Greenwich, CT: JAI Press (p. 5).

[18] Campbell, J. (1991). *A Joseph Campbell companion: Reflections of the art of living.* Selected and edited by Diane K. Osbon. New York: HarperCollins (p. 18).

Identify Your Competence

In this chapter you will

- Understand role-based competence.
- Discover a baseline for competence.
- Identify the basic competencies essential to leadership and management.
- Identify your level of political competence.
- Identify your level of personal competence.
- Identify your level of perceptual competence.
- Understand how to balance leadership and management.
- Identify leadership standards essential for the competent school administrator.
- Develop a map to greater competence.

ROLE-BASED COMPETENCE

To increase your competence you have to identify your current competence status. Your competence status is measured by how well you perform your job against the benchmark potential for job performance. Satisfaction with current performance has little to do with competence. It has more to do with culturally acceptable standards. Competence is ongoing and evolving. It is continually sought after but never fully achieved. It is the mark of a lifelong learner and a learning organization. As Starkey states: "Learning is seen as the key to making organizations more democratic, more responsive to change, and to creating organizations in which individuals can grow and develop."[1] Competent people understand their professional roles. Your professional role has unique demands. The demands of the role determine the type of skills you need and the extent to which your array of skills is used. School administration demands the application of leadership and management skills. Leadership and management are interwoven throughout the school administrator's day. Tompkins tells us: "To sustain peak performance, we must undertake four major shifts: One, from management to leadership. Two, from individuals to teams. Three, from customer service to partnerships. And four, from traditional compensation to performance-based rewards and recognition. . . . What is required today is both good management and good leadership."[2] One critical component of competence for the school administrator is to recognize when the role demands leadership or management. The competent school administrator recognizes the difference and responds appropriately and accurately.

Leadership and Managerial Competence

Dubrin says: "Broadly speaking, leadership deals with the interpersonal aspects of a manager's job, whereas planning, organizing, and controlling deal with the administrative aspects . . . leadership deals with change, inspiration, motivation, and influence."[3] Leadership competence is different from managerial competence. If a school administrator continually responded as a leader throughout the school day, he would not be competent because his role includes a managerial function. Managerial functions, such as organizing graduation, evaluating teachers, preparing an agenda for a school board meeting, developing a budget, and preparing for the first day of school, are all essential to the proper functioning of the school. On the other hand, if a school administrator becomes overly involved in managing a school, there is a sense of drifting without vision. Without a vision, the members of the organization lack direction. In this directionless vacuum, the seeds are planted for discord, competition among special interest groups, and the politicization of the environment. Work may get done in this environment, but it lacks an over arching purpose and sense of interrelatedness.

Leaders and managers have multiple but not mutually compatible competency needs. The sense of incompatibility between leadership and management requirements seemingly forces a person to opt to be a leader or a manager. This separation of roles is unhealthy and diminishes competence. Competent school administrators must be competent leaders and managers. They recognize that they are neither full-time leaders nor full-time managers. The changing requirements of the school environment obligate the school administrator to move fluidly from leadership to management and management to leadership. Therefore, the school environment demands a constant transitional flow between leadership and management competence. At times, these competencies are distinctive. At other times, they overlap. Table 2.1 represents the differences in leadership and managerial competence.

TABLE 2.1   **Leadership and Managerial Competence**

Leadership Competence		Managerial Competence
Requires a global perspective	versus	Operates with a micro perspective
Requires strategic planning	versus	Focuses on task implementation
Operates in highly complex, sophisticated environment	versus	Operates with an uncomplicated orientation
Requires flexibility	versus	Requires control orientation
Comfortable in chaos	versus	Requires order
Tolerates ambiguity	versus	Requires clarity
Responsibility driven	versus	Duty driven
Puts people prior to task	versus	Puts tasks prior to people
Awareness of value/goal alignment	versus	Awareness of time limits
Intuitive/creative orientation	versus	Linear orientation
Long-range orientation	versus	Immediate orientation

EVALUATING BASELINE COMPETENCE

Leadership and Management Distinctions

Each of the above leadership and managerial competencies are essential for the school administrator. The competent school administrator recognizes the continuous flow between leadership and management. However, this flow can become "stuck" when the school administrator loses sight of what the environment requires. When the flow is "stuck," the school administrator becomes a full-time leader or a full-time manager. Neither extreme meets the environmental demands for competence by the organization.

The following explanation of each leadership and managerial characteristic provides an opportunity to evaluate your baseline competence. After you read each description, rate yourself as to where you place your emphasis: *leadership* or *management*.

Characteristic 1: Global perspective versus micro perspective. Leadership operates from a global perspective. The leader is required to see the larger picture and continually seek strategic advantage for the organization. In this global picture, the leader is aware of a variety of forces shaping the environment surrounding the organization. The leader knows that he may not be able to control the forces influencing his organization, but he is able to maneuver his organization through these forces while being consistently aware of the immediate and long-range consequences of any action. The leader has a sense of the interrelatedness of his actions. He realizes that actions taken within his organization impact other organizations within his environment.

The manager seldom focuses on the global perspective. He is affected by what is happening within his immediate environment. He is concerned with his organization's day-to-day operations and works to see that the specific duties and functions are satisfactorily carried out. The manager may recognize that there are external forces impacting his work, yet his concern with these external forces is minimal and only insofar as they have a direct bearing on his current task. Further, he focuses on the task and not on the impact that it may have outside of the organization.

Self-rating: Global perspective (circle your current level)

Low 0 1 2 3 4 5 6 7 8 9 10 High

Characteristic 2: Strategic planning versus task implementation. Leadership involves long- and short-term strategic planning. Strategic planning focuses on the organization's relationship with similar organizations and the organization's ability to respond assertively to existing opportunities. Steven Covey in his *Seven Habits of Highly Effective Leaders* spoke of this difference: "You can quickly grasp the important difference between the two if you envision a group of producers cutting their way through the jungle with machetes. They're the producers, the problem solvers. They're cutting through the undergrowth, clearing it out. The managers are behind them, sharpening their machetes, writing policy and procedure manuals, holding muscle developing programs, bringing in improved technologies and setting up working schedules and compensation programs for machete wielders."[4]

Management takes the plans of the leader and makes them operational. The school administrator who focuses on management sees planning as essential to her role. She plans how to carry out the assigned tasks. She organizes the tasks to focus on efficiency. To the manager, implementing the task correctly is a major concern.

The need for balance of leadership and management is seen in a number of areas. For example, the Johnson City High School principal must operate as a manager to ensure that graduation ceremonies will be effectively conducted. He realizes the community will judge him by the sense of organization that is apparent in the graduation ceremonies. The same school administrator as leader has a different focus. He sees his plans in a much more global scheme. He looks at graduation as a means of showcasing his school and creating prestige by having a well-known graduation speaker. He will be highly aware of how the graduation at his school compares to other high schools in his district or region.

Self-rating: Strategic planning (circle your current level)

Low 0 1 2 3 4 5 6 7 8 9 10 High

Characteristic 3: Highly complex versus uncomplicated orientation. Leaders have a highly complex orientation. The leader can see highly intricate patterns of themes and forces influencing his school. The leader understands how these patterns and forces impact each other. Because of his ability to see patterns and their interaction, he can shape the interchange among a wide array of diverse groups. The leader examines the gestalt. He focuses simultaneously on his school, curriculum, various departments, and academic standards necessary for student achievement, parent support, and continued evolution toward greater effectiveness.

The manager tries to make the task uncomplicated. He moves away from complication and toward simplicity. He is the efficiency expert. As manager, he focuses on a single aspect, the English curriculum, and analyzes its effectiveness.

Self-rating: High complexity (circle your current level)

Low 0   1   2   3   4   5   6   7   8   9   10   High

Characteristic 4: Flexibility versus control orientation. Leaders are highly flexible. There is a fluid nature taken to the events that swirl around their organizations. The leader finds that she has to adapt to forces and events as she guides the school toward greater effectiveness. Her sense of flexibility makes her aware of ever-changing dynamics in her school environment. As leader, she recognizes that tight control, although creating a predictable environment, also creates unnecessary tension.

As manager, she has a high discomfort with flexibility. She prefers a more tightly controlled environment. In her tightly controlled environment, events are highly predictable. She is able to anticipate what will happen. Tight control is necessary where safety and public accountability are concerned, whereas loose control is seen by the manager as an invitation to chaos.

Self-rating: Flexibility (circle your current level)

Low 0   1   2   3   4   5   6   7   8   9   10   High

Characteristic 5: Comfortableness in chaos versus demand for order. The leader understands that the context of leadership is often the crucible of chaos. In this dynamic environment, he maintains a sense of presence and calm. He is a stabilizing influence on the organization. The members of the organization look to him for confidence in the midst of chaos. Warren Bennis speaks about leaders in chaotic environments when he says: "These leaders have proved not only the necessity but the efficacy of self-confidence, vision, virtue, plain guts, and reliance on the blessed impulse. They have learned from everything, but they have learned more from experience, and even more from adversity and mistakes . . . Grace under pressure might be this group's motto."[5] Because he is comfortable with chaos, he is able to bring a sense of order to the organization. Chaos, for the leader, is a normal condition. Consequently, it is not frightening and does not cause the leader to panic.

As a manager, the school administrator demands a sense of personal and organizational order. Chaos is the antithesis of order. It is to be eliminated or avoided at all costs. In his search for order, the manager sets tight schedules, establishes firm policies, and expects the environment to respond predictably. Eliminating chaos requires the manager to operate in a left-brain, linear function.

Self-rating: Comfort level with chaos (circle your current level)

Low   0   1   2   3   4   5   6   7   8   9   10   High

Characteristic 6: Tolerates ambiguity versus requirement for clarity. The leader tolerates ambiguity. She knows that outcomes cannot be prescribed. Yet, she is willing to trust the process she sets in place. The ability to tolerate ambiguity allows her to focus on the potential of others, her organization, and herself. This tolerance of ambiguity is an expression of faith in her ability and experience. She understands that neither she, the people whom she leads, nor her organization has arrived; each is in the process of arriving.

As manager, she needs clarity. She needs to understand what is demanded of her. She needs to know what can be demanded of others. Thus, her need for clarity often results in needing to have situations, expectations, and demands clarified. She feels more comfortable when there are rules, policies, and guidelines to follow. The presence of rules, policies, and guidelines prevents her from making mistakes. She is uncomfortable with ambiguity. Ambiguity is a nebulous foundation that creates problems for her and others. It is to be avoided.

Self-rating: Toleration of ambiguity (circle your current level)

Low   0   1   2   3   4   5   6   7   8   9   10   High

Characteristic 7: Responsibility driven versus duty driven. The leader is responsibility driven. James MacGregor Burns, in his seminal work, *Leadership,* tells us: "leadership is relational, collective, and purposeful. Leadership shares with power the central function of achieving purpose. But the reach and domain of leadership are, in the short range at least, more limited than those of power. Leaders do not obliterate followers' motives. . . . They lead other creatures, not things. To control things—tools, mineral resources, money, energy—is an act of power, not leadership, for things have no motive. Power wielders may treat people as things. Leaders may not."[6]

Leadership is a responsibility toward meeting the needs of people and not the acquisition of things (money, space, and so on). Because the leader is responsibility driven, comfortable acting independently, and accepts responsibility for his actions, he understands that he is responsible for his decisions. He does not attribute blame to others nor see others as the cause for his problems. He sees himself as the primary cause for the good or bad he creates and accepts responsibility for the consequences of his actions. The leader sees the job description as a non-binding set of guidelines. He uses these guidelines to expand his sphere of influence, often acting without prior approval and always accepting responsibility for his actions.

The manager focuses on duty. He wants to know what is required, and then he carries out those requirements to the letter. As manager, he is driven by a job description. The manager sees his work as an obligation that he has to his employer and to the people in the organization. He understands the importance of fulfilling his job to the letter. For example, if a budget request is due by April 3, it will be in on or before that date. The job description becomes his identity.

Self-rating: Responsibility driven (circle your current level)
Low   0   1   2   3   4   5   6   7   8   9   10   High

Characteristic 8: People prior to task versus tasks prior to people. The leader always places people prior to her tasks. The leader recognizes that people are the basis of success for herself and the organization. In an effort to move her organization toward the fulfillment of its mission, she is willing to deviate from the assigned task if it is in the best interest of the organization. Her concern for people and their welfare generates a high degree of loyalty and respect. People will often follow her wherever she asks them to go because they trust her. They know that she will never give tasks the primary priority.

The manager makes task completion the priority. She drives the members of her organization to meet deadlines or other obligations. The manager believes her reputation and the reputation of her organization are at stake if tasks are not completed on schedule. The manager can become overzealous in her desire to complete her tasks. Her overzealousness frequently takes its toll on people, resulting in low morale and organizational chaos, the very things that she wanted to avoid.

Self-rating: People prior to task (circle your current level)
Low   0   1   2   3   4   5   6   7   8   9   10   High

Characteristic 9: Awareness of value/goal alignment versus awareness of time limits. The leader is constantly aware of the alignment of his values with the goals of his organization. He knows that this alignment demonstrates his integrity to the members of his organization. When he acts, he is acting out of a value base that others recognize as being part of his identity. Because he is value driven, he is predictable. Organizational goals are not chosen because of political appeal but because of alignment with values.

The manager is not so much concerned with value/goal alignment as he is with his awareness of time limits. As manager, he often suppresses his value system and adopts the value system of his superordinates. He is highly aware of time limits imposed by his superordinate to complete tasks. His primary value is one of task completion within specified time requirements. By following someone else's priorities, he is able to prove his worth to himself and others, especially his superordinate.

Self-rating: Value/goal alignment (circle your current level)

Low   0   1   2   3   4   5   6   7   8   9   10   High

Characteristic 10: Intuitive/creative orientation versus linear orientation. The leader is comfortable with her intuitive/creative side. She trusts her intuition when making decisions. She understands that her feelings are ways of experiencing reality. The leader believes that her intuition detects information that her consciousness seems to miss. Bennis says: "In any corporation, managers serve as the left brain and the research and development staff serves as the right brain, but the CEO must combine both, must have both administrative and imaginative gifts. One of the reasons that so few corporate executives have successfully made the leap from capable manager to successful leader is that the corporate culture, along with society as a whole, recognizes and rewards left-brain accomplishments and tends to discount right-brain accomplishments."[7]

Consequently, the leader makes decisions to head in a new direction against prevailing wisdom. In moving creatively into a new direction, she is often proved right. The members of her organization learn to trust her intuition and know that her instincts are a good indicator of what should be done. Her ability to act intuitively is not something she was taught. It is something she believes she has always had. As she grew as a leader, she realized that she had good instincts and listened carefully to her intuitive voices.

The manager does not readily trust her intuition. She is analytical. She wants facts. She wants information. She is hesitant to decide based on feelings. She looks at the figures and then decides. Decisions are made carefully after long deliberation and weighing the possible consequence of each possible course of action. Each action is based on the previous action and leads into the next series of actions. Intuition is not trusted; facts are valued.

Self-rating: Intuitive/creative orientation (circle your current level)

Low   0   1   2   3   4   5   6   7   8   9   10   High

Characteristic 11: Long-range orientation versus immediate orientation. The leader is constantly thinking of the future. He is able to see how the present connects to the future. The leader recognizes that any decision he makes today impacts tomorrow. There is a fit between today and tomorrow. The leader has a sense of the forces that will prevail in the future and orients his organization to be prepared for those forces well before they are encountered. He seldom is surprised because he is able to anticipate events. As leader, he is constantly moving people and the organization toward change. He realizes change is the lifeblood of the organization.

The manager is not concerned as much with the future as he is with today. He wants to make sure that the organization is stable. He wants to address problems as they are encountered. He is firmly entrenched. This immediate orientation provides a strong sense of stability to the organization, yet it leaves the organization as a possible victim to the changing nature of its environment. As manager, he is trying to control the pace of change to maintain a sense of stability and control.

Self-rating: Long-range orientation (circle your current level)
Low   0   1   2   3   4   5   6   7   8   9   10   High

Rating your preference for leadership or management
Add your total number of points.

- If you scored between 85 and 110, you are centered on leadership competencies.
- If you scored between 0 and 35, you are centered on managerial competence.
- If you scored between 35 and 85, you balance your leadership and managerial competence.

Make *balance* your reference point. As a school administrator, you need to be manager and leader. You need to recognize when it is time to lead and when it is time to manage. The highly competent school administrator recognizes the environmental demands for leadership and management. If you scored high as leader or high as manager, consider the areas in which you need more balance. Incorporate the necessary skills to become a better leader or more effective manager. Competency for the school administrator is a balance between leadership and management, and knowing the difference between the two.

BASELINE COMPETENCE—KNOWING HOW TO SURVIVE

The primary drive of any species is to survive. Frequently, a person, filled with idealism, takes a new position. Within weeks her idealism is shattered as the reality of the job chips away at her good intentions. The administrator's dream of creating a collaborative atmosphere becomes victim to staff bickering. She finds herself trapped between opposing forces and at times feels as if she is hanging on for dear life. She slowly becomes cynical and her idealism is lost. If she had understood and applied the baseline measure of survival competence, she would have been able to maintain her idealism in the midst of a chaotic environment.

FIGURE 2.1   **Three dimensions of survival competence**

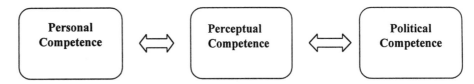

Survival Competence

Survival competence comprises three dimensions: personal competence, perceptual competence, and political competence (see Figure 2.1). Each of these competence dimensions is interrelated. If the school administrator is to survive and thrive, he needs to be competent in each of these three dimensions. These three dimensions are baseline survival competence dimensions. They drive all competency development. Without a firm grounding in these baseline dimensions, the administrator, whether acting as leader or manager, will not consistently perform at a highly competent level. Skilled, experienced, and knowledgeable school administrators will be seen as competent to the degree that they possess these dimensions.

Dimension 1: Personal competence

Personal competence is related to the school administrator's characteristics. Those who form the school administrator's cultural and environmental context judge these characteristics. These people are faculty, staff, students, parents, school board members, and other community members who interact or have a special interest in the education process. They consciously and subconsciously ask the following questions about the school administrator:

- Is the school administrator truthful?
- Is the school administrator trustworthy?
- Is the school administrator genuine?
- Is the school administrator friendly?
- Is the school administrator supportive?
- Does the school administrator have a good sense of humor?
- Is the school administrator cooperative?

Is the school administrator truthful? Baseline survival competence requires truthfulness. The members of the school organization want the truth from their administrators. They do not want to be manipulated or misled by half-truths or lies. Eventually, administrators who practice deception are caught in a web of deceit that results in their losing the trust of the members of the school and community. When they tell the truth, they gain the respect and admiration of the members of their organization. Two of America's greatest presidents, Washington and Lincoln, have long-standing myths that relate to their truthfulness. It is an admired quality.

Self-rating: Level of truthfulness (circle your current level)

Low 0 1 2 3 4 5 6 7 8 9 10 High

Is the school administrator trustworthy? There is an expectation that the school administrator will keep secrets and not betray a confidence. When the administrator refuses to participate in gossiping cliques, sharing information given to him in confidence, he builds his trustworthiness rating among the members of the school and community. The members of the school and community sense that the school administrator is a person of integrity with a sound character. They know they can count on him. They know that his word is his bond. Nilsen relates: "A few years back, our colleague David Campbell conducted a study that asked people to rate the most effective and ineffective leaders they had ever known. He provided a list of more than twenty attributes, including dynamic, empowering, productive, ambitious, and credible. Several of these differentiated between the two groups of leaders, but credibility was seen as the most significant factor. Credibility (or being credible), which was defined in this study as a person's being believable and worthy of trust, is a major outcome of integrity."[8]

Self-rating: Level of trustworthiness (circle your current level)

Low 0 1 2 3 4 5 6 7 8 9 10 High

Is the school administrator genuine? The members of the school community want to make sure that what they see is what exists. This person is authentic. There is no hiding of positive or negative characteristics. In a sense, "what you see, is what you get." When the school administrator is genuine there is no guile, false self, or masks. This person is "real," understands his limitations, and is willing to admit to his limitations. Conversely, the school community can discern when the school administrator is not genuine. They see a lack of substance. By being genuine, the school administrator relates on a personal level to each member of his community.

Self-rating: Level of genuineness (circle your current level)

Low 0 1 2 3 4 5 6 7 8 9 10 High

Is the school administrator friendly? Members of a democratic society do not want to work for a person who is not friendly. By being friendly, the school administrator moves easily into the social dynamics of the organization. He is able to be a part of and yet remain apart from these dynamics. Being friendly means that the school administrator is approachable, someone that the members of the school community can engage. He is likeable. He engages easily in conversations about the profession as well as discussions about the lives of the members of the community. Others like to be near this person. This person is not fearful of diluting power by being friendly. Rather, he recognizes that a willingness to operate relationally enhances and extends power.

Self-rating: Level of friendliness (circle your current level)

Low   0   1   2   3   4   5   6   7   8   9   10   High

Is the school administrator supportive? Members of the school community want to work for a supportive person. A supportive school administrator is one who encourages people to improve and move toward self-actualization. Senge says, "Leaders in learning organizations are responsible for building organizations where people are continually expanding their capabilities to shape their future—that is, leaders are responsible for learning."[9] The competent school administrator is capable of bringing out the best in a person because he sees the best in each person. He is supportive when he encourages the members of the school community to risk, take on a new adventure, or act on their intuition. When he is supportive, he is also compassionate. He is able to empathize with the unique situations faced by each member of the school community. Yet, he never loses sight of what is in the best interests of each person. His support is always grounded in the best interests of the person with whom he is conducting business.

Self-rating: Level of supportiveness (circle your current level)

Low   0   1   2   3   4   5   6   7   8   9   10   High

Does the school administrator have a good sense of humor? A school administrator needs a sense of humor. He is able to laugh at situations and at himself. Frequently, the effective use of humor is the best way to defuse potentially hostile situations. The effective use of humor in hostile situations releases tension and allows the parties to focus on the central issue. Humor directed at the self allows others to relate to the school administrator. The members of the school community recognize that through the administrator's use of humor he has a clear sense of his abilities and limitations. Through humor, he moves beyond defensiveness to the recognition that he is not omnipotent. His humanity shows through his humor.

Self-rating: Level of sense of humor (circle your current level)

Low   0   1   2   3   4   5   6   7   8   9   10   High

Is the school administrator cooperative? Democratic organizations work best when people work together for a common cause. Members of democratic societies do not like to be told what to do and how to do it. They want to have their voices heard. When the school administrator works with people rather than over them, he is seen as a member of the group. He has a belief in people. He has, as Saul Alinsky said: "A complete commitment to the belief that if people have the power, the opportunity to act, in the long run they will, most of the time, reach the right decisions."[10] This faith in others is expressed through the school administrator's friendliness toward others. He is seen as a person who understands and is able to integrate the experience of the members of the school community. He is also seen as a person who validates the knowledge and experiences of the members of the school community. He views the success of the school as a joint venture in which all share in a cooperative journey.

Self-rating: Level of cooperativeness (circle your current level)

Low   0   1   2   3   4   5   6   7   8   9   10   High

Rating your personal competence

How do you rate in baseline personal competence?

- If you scored a 50 or higher, you have strong personal competence.
- If you scored 50 or lower, examine those areas that need to be improved.

Remember that personal competence is one of the three essential dimensions inherent in survival competence.

Dimension 2: Perceptual competence

Perceptual competence is the school administrator's ability to recognize, analyze, and construct meaning from the events in her environment. The school administrator is judged on perceptual competence by the way that she answers the following questions:

- Do I jump to conclusions?
- Do I understand the environment?
- Do I have a sense of perspective?
- Do I overreact to a situation?
- Am I able to listen to other people?
- Am I a part of the chaos or apart from the chaos?
- Do I have fixed thoughts about the environment?

Do I jump to conclusions? The competent school administrator resists jumping to conclusions. Conclusions are based on our need to judge, classify, and place objects in neat boxes. They are part of our human need for order. However, this need for order creates havoc when the school administrator assumes that her view of reality is correct. She does not realize that her view is limited. Imagine a school administrator who walks into a classroom and perceives a high degree of chaos. The school administrator quickly makes a note to speak to the teacher about the lack of learning that is taking place in the classroom. When the school administrator confronts the teacher regarding the lack of learning, the teacher becomes defensive and explains that the disorder was actually a highly planned and well-conceived learning environment. The teacher claims that the students were actively engaged in a meaningful group experience that focused on a collaborative learning activity. The school administrator is embarrassed. The school administrator, in jumping to conclusions, did not recognize the teacher's reality. The competent school administrator reserves judgment, resists her initial impulse to jump to conclusions, and assimilates the environment.

Self-rating: Resists jumping to conclusions (circle your current level)

Low   0   1   2   3   4   5   6   7   8   9   10   High

Do I understand the environment? Perceptual competence requires an understanding of the work environment. Perceptual competence is the ability to size up the situation as it exists. This is an instinctive ability. Each person has this ability. Some people are able to use this ability more easily than others. In a way, it may be described as being "street smart." "Street smart" people are those who instinctively know how to react to an unfolding situation in an urban environment. The competent administrator needs the same kind of perceptual competence. When administrators do not understand the environment, they respond inaccurately. Their response is based on what they believe exists. For example, one new school administrator, when meeting with faculty, openly announced how he planned to increase observations and tighten the evaluation process. The school administrator was unaware of faculty anxiety; consequently, the faculty distrusted the school administrator. He failed to develop a working relationship with the faculty and left for a different position after two years.

Self-rating: Understands the environment (circle your current level)

Low   0   1   2   3   4   5   6   7   8   9   10   High

Do I have a sense of perspective? Perceptual competence demands a sense of perspective. Events are placed in context. No single event is placed out of context; it is seen as part of the evolutionary growth of the organization, person, or program. By placing events in perspective, the school administrator resists overreacting to any event or person. A sense of perspective requires the competent school administrator to have a view of history. She is able to look back into the past and see the impact of a similar event. She realizes that this event, although momentarily volatile, will soon be forgotten, and her reaction to this event will either create a deeper memory or reduce the memory of it. Competent administrators learn to embrace the saying "this too shall pass." They also understand when an event has the potential to influence the future. If this is a positive event, they are able to construct a collaborative and joint perception of its perspective. Peter Vaill said: "Perception is not a stop-action photograph that I take of a situation in order that I may determine what sort of competence is required in it. Perceiving is an act occurring continuously in parallel with my action in situations. Situations unfold before me, partly as a result of my efforts and partly as a result of other factors. But perceiving what I am doing and what is happening, and what I *am* doing and what *is* happening, are inextricably interwoven."[11]

Self-rating: Sense of perception (circle your current level)

Low   0   1   2   3   4   5   6   7   8   9   10   High

Do I overreact to a situation? Perceptual competence demands accuracy of perception. The school administrator who has accuracy of perception can see events as they exist. When the school administrator has accuracy of perception she responds appropriately to the existing situation. The school administrator who views a student flashing gang signals and has accuracy of perception sees a single student flashing gang signs. She does not overreact and assume that gang members control her school. She has an accurate perception of an event. She is able to reduce the event to specific terms. When she speaks to the faculty, she informs them of what she saw and how many people were involved. Because she has accuracy of perception, she reduces the chance that she or the members of her faculty will respond inaccurately or inappropriately.

Self-rating: Accuracy of perception (circle your current level)

Low   0   1   2   3   4   5   6   7   8   9   10   High

Am I able to listen to other people? Perceptual competence occurs, in part, through the school administrator's ability to listen to other people. When she is able to include other people's viewpoint as to what is occurring, she expands her view of reality. For example, at this moment, as you read this book, your view of reality is the printed words on this page. However, there is a much greater reality within your immediate environment. There is the reality of what is happening behind you, above you, and below you. Imagine a group of people gathered in a large circle. Each person in the circle is looking straight ahead. It takes the views of all the people to explain the environment in which the circle is located. Accuracy of perception is gained, in part, through effective listening. Paul Swets lists six steps to more effective listening: one, choose to listen; two, listen actively; three, listen for ideas and feelings; four, listen with the heart's ear; five, listen to yourself; and six, know when to keep silent.[12] The competent administrator increases her perceptual competence by listening to other people. She realizes that they, like her, have limited views. Yet, she realizes, taken collectively, those views can reduce distortions and give her a truer understanding of her environment.

Self-rating: Ability to listen to other voices (circle your current level)

Low   0   1   2   3   4   5   6   7   8   9   10   High

Am I a part of the chaos or apart from the chaos? Perceptual competence demands that the school administrator be apart from the chaos. Chaos is a part of the typical school administrator's day. The average school administrator, for example, has more than four hundred interactions in any given day.[13] The majority of these interactions last less than one minute. Even the well-organized school administrator finds it difficult to predict what will occur in any school day. He is often adrift as teachers, students, parents, and central office personnel come into his life with an unrehearsed script. He is forced to play by ear and hope that he responds accurately to instantaneous demands. The school administrator who is trapped in the chaos has lost control of the situation as well as his response. The school administrator who removes himself from the chaos and acts with a sense of detachment responds more accurately. He is able to bring a sense of calm to those caught in the chaos.

Self-rating: Detachment from the chaos (circle your current level)

Low   0   1   2   3   4   5   6   7   8   9   10   High

Do I have fixed thoughts about the environmental context? Perceptual competence demands that the school administrator have a sense of openness to have accuracy of judgment. Fixed thoughts about how an environment appears create a sense of rigidity and require the school administrator to make existing people and programs fit well-established mental models. He ignores the fluid nature of life and of organizations. Pat Gordon, for example, had been superintendent of schools in Literton for twenty-five years. Dr. Gordon had never had a request for resources turned down by the school board. He went to the school board with a request for a major bond issue. The board was reluctant. Dr. Gordon was adamant. The board gave reluctant approval. Voters defeated the bond issue causing Dr. Gordon to resign. Dr. Gordon's view was rigid. He did not realize that the community was no longer willing to allow the school district to acquire resources without strict accountability.

When the school administrator is open to the environment, he is able to discover a wide array of potential benefits. He has an accuracy of judgment regarding what exists. He does not resist acknowledging what exists in the hope that something better may exist. This accuracy of judgment is tied directly to his sense of openness. The greater the degree of flexibility the school administrator has, the greater the latitude of responses available.

Self-rating: Sense of openness to the context (circle your current level)

Low   0   1   2   3   4   5   6   7   8   9   10   High

Rating your baseline perceptual competence

How do you rate in baseline perceptual competence?

- If you scored 50 or higher, you have strong perceptual competence.
- If you scored 50 or lower, examine those areas that need to be improved.

Remember that perceptual competence is one of the three essential dimensions inherent in survival competence.

Dimension 3: Political competence

Political competence is an essential component of survival competence. The school administrator's role is a political role in that she works with and through people to develop and implement a common agenda. Her success is directly related to her level of political competence. If she is intellectually capable, yet politically naive, she will ultimately fail in her mission to lead. Political competence is judged by superordinates and subordinates on how well the school administrator is able to successfully move the school organization toward greater levels of effectiveness and maintain high levels of support. Political competence is determined, in large part, by the relationship the school administrator forms with the people in her organization and community. Thomas Jefferson spoke of this relationship more than two hundred years ago: "It behooves [a chief executive] to think and to act for [himself] and for [his] people. The great principles of right and wrong are legible to every reader; to pursue them requires not the aid of many counselors. The whole art of government consists in the art of being honest. [He need] only aim to do [his] duty, and mankind will give [him] credit where [he fails]."[14]

Political competence asks the following questions:

- Am I able to act with self-restraint?
- Am I able to recognize the rights of others?
- Am I able to yield to others?
- Am I able to empower others?
- Am I able to transcend self-interests?
- Am I able to work with others?
- Am I able to express political courage?

Am I able to act with self-restraint? The politically competent school administrator realizes that her position provides her with considerable power and leverage. The indiscriminate application of power causes great harm to members of the organization even when the ultimate aim of the use of power is for a beneficial purpose. Followers view the indiscriminate use of power negatively. They see this school administrator as a threat, one who "walks over" people to achieve her purposes. On the other hand, when the school administrator uses self-restraint in the application of power she is able to inspire others. Her followers recognize her ability to temper her approach to events or people.

Consider the school administrator who tells a teacher how to conduct class. How do you think the teacher will respond? In most cases, the teacher responds defensively; the teacher reacts to protect his fragile self-image. On the other hand, there is the school administrator who asks the teacher how the class could be conducted differently or if the teacher has ideas that could add value to what was already done. How do you think this teacher responds? In both cases, the school administrator has the same power. In the former case, the school administrator uses the power; in the latter case, the power is withheld. It exists in potential; it is applied with restraint.

Self-rating: Sense of restraint (circle your current level)

Low   0   1   2   3   4   5   6   7   8   9   10   High

Am I able to recognize the rights of others? Political competence demands that the rights of others be recognized and respected. It is as if the school administrator operates on a *quid pro quo* basis. By respecting the rights of the members of his school organization, he gets their respect. Before he can recognize the rights of others, he must be aware of their rights. Often, political incompetence occurs when the school administrator tramples on or ignores the rights of the members of his organization. One school administrator, for example, issued a work demand to a teacher. The teacher responded by filing a grievance against the school administrator. The school administrator told the teacher to either halt the grievance or face an uncertain future. The teacher filed a lawsuit against the school administrator and school district. The teacher had contract rights that this school administrator failed to recognize.

The politically competent school administrator recognizes legal and contractual rights of the members of his organization and honors those rights. He also recognizes noncontractual but inherent rights among members of a democratic society, for example, the right to voice a dissenting opinion or the right to be involved in the decision-making process.

Self-rating: Recognition of others' rights (circle your current level)

Low   0   1   2   3   4   5   6   7   8   9   10   High

Am I able to yield to others? The inability to yield to others is a sign of anxiety and insecurity. The politically competent school administrator recognizes when it is time to back off from a stated position and yield to others. This sense of political competence is not so much a wise political move as it is the recognition that she does not have all answers. It is a wise political move to include others so that they feel part of the political process. The politically competent school administrator understands and recognizes the necessary balance between yielding and asserting one's position. To achieve this balance, the school administrator has to identify a narrowly constructed set of circumstances in which assertion of political power is essential. Political power should be asserted to ensure the safety and legal rights of the members of the organization.

Self-rating: Willingness to yield to others (circle your current level)

Low   0   1   2   3   4   5   6   7   8   9   10   High

Am I able to empower others? The politically competent school administrator shares power with the members of his school organization. He realizes that the more power he "gives away" the more real power he retains. He understands that power is more an illusion than a reality, and that in a democratic society, power is provisionally lent to leaders. His understanding of the nature of power in a democratic society encourages him to empower others. He knows that when others feel empowered they are more likely to perform at higher levels, feel a greater part of the organization, and operate interdependently. Cicero stated: "A people is not just any collection of human beings brought together in any sort of way—but an assemblage of people . . . associated in an agreement with respect to justice and a partnership for the common good."[15] When the school administrator fails to empower others, he centralizes power within himself and makes others dependent on his actions. In his absence, people are unable to act. They feel powerless and have a low sense of control. Empowerment is a synergistic activity that builds thriving organizations.

Self-rating: Willingness to empower others (circle your current level)

Low   0   1   2   3   4   5   6   7   8   9   10   High

Am I able to transcend self-interests? Political competence requires that self-interests be put aside to promote the group's interests. When the school administrator places primacy on self-interests, she is viewed as selfish and self-serving. Conversely, when she places self-interests in a subordinate position to the needs of the group, she is seen as concerned about the members of her organization. Ironically, most people who become school administrators reach those positions because they have a high degree of ambition. Their ambition enabled them to succeed in college, succeed as teachers, and succeed in their pursuit of administrative positions. Political competence demands that personal ambition be transcended. That is, ambition can no longer be used for personal gain, but must be placed at the disposal of the community. In this way, the school administrator uses her skills, abilities, and strategies for the benefit of others. She moves beyond personal interests to group interests.

Self-rating: Transcends self interests (circle your current level)

Low   0   1   2   3   4   5   6   7   8   9   10   High

Am I able to work with others? Political competence demands that school administrators have the skills and the ability to work with other people. It is through other people that the school administrator is able to accomplish his political agenda. When the school administrator lacks the ability to work with others, a wide riff develops between the administrator and the members of the organization. The school administrator becomes isolated because there is little communication, trust, or desire to collaborate. As isolation increases, the school administrator loses contact with the members of his organization. He no longer hears the voices of the members of his organization. This lack of connection inevitably produces a dysfunctional organization.

Conversely, the competent school administrator has an innate ability to work with people. He likes, accepts, and builds trust with the members of his organization. The school administrator's ability to work with others finds its basis in his confidence in the inherent goodness of people. The competent school administrator has an innate belief that people work hard, desire to become increasingly competent, are trustworthy, and act with integrity.

Self-rating: Willingness to work with others (circle your current level)

Low   0   1   2   3   4   5   6   7   8   9   10   High

Am I able to express political courage? Political competence demands political courage. The school administrator expresses political courage when she supports an issue even when there is strong opposition. Political courage is always exhibited when the school administrator is in the minority. She has an internal compass that tells her that what she is doing is right regardless of the pressure she feels from the greater population. The school administrator who refuses to suspend a student because she knows that the student's actions were provoked by a teacher commits an act of political courage. The school administrator who challenges the school board's intention to ban certain books in her school library not on the literary merits of the books but because of a personal belief system is acting with political courage. Acting with political courage may be painful in the short term, but it always pays off in the long term. The school administrator is seen as a person of strength, courage, and moral integrity. This school administrator is a *transforming leader* because she: "can also shape and alter and elevate the motives and values and goals of followers through the vital teaching role of leadership. . . . The premise of this leadership is that, whatever the separate interests persons might hold, they are presently or potentially united in the pursuit of 'higher' goals, the realization of which is tested by the achievement of significant change that represents the collective or pooled interests of leaders and followers."[16] She is the kind of person others want to follow. When the school administrator tries to discover what others want and is aligned with these perceptions, she eventually is viewed by the school community as lacking political courage. She loses her loyal following.

Self-rating: Level of political courage (circle your current level)

Low   0   1   2   3   4   5   6   7   8   9   10   High

Rating your baseline political competence

How do you rate in baseline political competence?

- If you scored 50 or higher, you have strong political competence.
- If you scored 50 or lower, examine those areas that need to be improved.

Remember that political competence is one of the three essential dimensions inherent in survival competence.

Establishing Baseline Competence

You derive your baseline competence from two specific components:

1. **What level of competence do you desire?**
2. **What level of competence is called for by your position?**

Your baseline competence is determined, in part, by your internal motivation. Some people feel an internal drive for higher and higher levels of performance. We find these people in all occupations. They may be teachers, school administrators, artists, musicians, athletes, mothers, fathers, or doctors. They are not satisfied with the level of their performance. They continuously reflect on and question their past performance to improve their current and future performance. Other people plateau. They become satisfied at a performance level and are not motivated to move beyond that performance level.

Your baseline competence is also determined by your professional position. Each position demands certain skills and abilities. A computer programmer has a set of competency requirements far different from those of a teacher. A teacher has a set of competency requirements that are different from those of the school administrator. Although there is overlap in competency roles, specific requirements are demanded of each position. Each of us has to make a decision as to the level of personal competence we seek to acquire and put into practice. Are we satisfied with minimal competence? Or, are we lifelong learners regardless of the level of competence we attain? Ask yourself the following questions to discover the level of personal competence that you desire:

1. Am I frequently dissatisfied with my performance?

    Low   0   1   2   3   4   5   6   7   8   9   10   High

2. Do I often seek information to help me improve my performance?

    Low   0   1   2   3   4   5   6   7   8   9   10   High

3. Do others view me as a "go-getter"?

    Low 0 1 2 3 4 5 6 7 8 9 10 High

4. Do I engage in self-talk regarding past performance?

    Low 0 1 2 3 4 5 6 7 8 9 10 High

5. Do I constantly seek to acquire new skills and sharpen my existing abilities?

    Low 0 1 2 3 4 5 6 7 8 9 10 High

Add your scores. If you scored 40 or higher, you have a high personal standard of competence. You will not be satisfied with the status quo. It is part of your nature to seek continuous improvement. Your role does not matter; you will seek competence levels far exceeding the role's demands. If you scored between 25 and 40, you have a moderate standard for seeking to improve your competency level. There are areas of your professional life with which you are satisfied. You may find that your dissatisfaction with the status quo reaches a point at which you are forced to act. In this case, you may find yourself enrolling in college courses, reading self-help books, or seeking the advice of professionals. If you scored below 25, you are satisfied with your current status and competency level and have little motivation to increase your level of competence. Be aware that the rapid changes of society may move swiftly beyond your current position and leave you without a firm foundation for professional survival.

Bringing it together
Use the chart on the next page to record your baseline competence. Remember, baseline competence is a self-reported analysis that expresses your baseline competence status in regard to your ability to balance managerial and leadership issues. It also is an assessment of your survival competence in three domains with twenty-one subareas. Each area provides you with an opportunity to identify whether the area is a current competency. If it is a current competency, you receive positive feedback indicating your proficiency in this area. The final decision as to whether you identify an area as a current competency or as an area of growth is a personal decision and has much to do with your set of competency standards. If an area does not meet or exceed your personal and/or role-related standards for competence, then it is *an area for growth*.

Mapping the Future

You have identified your baseline competence. You may have discovered that you have specific survival competence areas to address. These are your areas of growth. You may have discovered that you have an imbalance between leadership and management or that you are

Personal Analysis of Baseline Competence

Area	A Current Competency	Area of Growth
Leadership		
Management		
Survival Competence (Overall)		
Personal Competence (Overall)		
• Truthfulness		
• Trustworthiness		
• Genuineness		
• Friendliness		
• Supportiveness		
• Sense of humor		
• Cooperativeness		
Perceptual Competence (Overall)		
• Avoid jumping to conclusions		
• Understand the environment		
• Sense of perspective		
• Avoid overreacting		
• Listen to other people		
• Apart from the chaos		
• Flexible views of current context		
Political Competence (Overall)		
• Act with self restraint		
• Recognize the rights of others		
• Yield to others when necessary		
• Empower others		
• Transcend self interests		
• Work effectively with others		
• Express political courage		

confused as to when you should lead and when you should manage. Armed with this information you can now *map your future*. Mapping connects short-term and long-term competence. Your map begins by focusing on short-term competence.

Identify three areas to be immediately addressed. These areas become your targets. They are your focus to acquire immediate competency gains. Employ this simple equation for success:

$$S = St + Sg + A + F$$

S stands for *Success*. Success in competence means that you move from your current level of competence to a higher level of competence.

St stands for *Specific targeting*. To be successful, you have to aim for a specific target, or you become confused. You act with disorientation as to what you are supposed to be doing and soon become frustrated and quit.

Sg stands for *Specific goal*. When you aim at your target, you need a specific goal that you want to produce as the result of aiming at your target. You know what you want to accomplish. This is not a general goal such as "I want to lose weight" or "I want to improve my golf game." It is specific: "I want to lose five pounds." "I want to shoot a 76 in golf." There is no question as to what you want to accomplish.

A stands for *Action*. You must act if you are to succeed. You cannot leave your target and specific goal on the planning table. All success requires action. The quality of the act does not matter as much as the direction.

F stands for *Feedback*. We need to gain appropriate feedback to adjust our action. With feedback, we have the opportunity to fine-tune our actions. Each time we fine-tune our action we align our specific goal with the desired target. Success happens.

EXAMPLE

Specific Target: Empowering my assistant principal

Specific Goal: Today I will empower my assistant principal to set up a committee to make recommendations for staff development to improve school discipline. I will support these recommendations.

Action: I spoke with my assistant principal specifically as to what I wanted her to do. I gave her the power to set up the committee and make recommendations to the entire faculty and me.

Feedback: I asked the assistant principal (a week later) how she was doing and if she needed additional support. She provided me with feedback regarding my empowerment. I can use this feedback when I empower my department chairpersons.

This school administrator uses the competence gained in this activity to continue to empower other people in his school. The more he empowers and then receives constructive feedback on his actions, the more skilled he becomes at empowerment. He is on his way to making empowerment of others a peak performance survival competency skill.

Next Steps
1. Seek feedback related to your baseline competence from colleagues and others you trust. Ask them to assess your balance between leadership and management. Ask them to assess your baseline competence.

2. Look for differences between perception of your baseline competence from the feedback you receive and your perception of your baseline competence. Oftentimes, those who are detached from the process are more objective than those who are closer to the process. If you feel defensive about any area where there is a difference, look hard at that area—your critics are probably correct. Defensiveness is a sure sign that we are trying to protect our egos.

3. Employ the *success formula* to make immediate competency gains.

4. If there is an *area of growth* in which you feel you lack the knowledge and/or ability to improve your competence, identify one person who models the behavior you need. Make contact with this person. Identify his recipe for success. Ask him to guide you through the process. The only difference between you and your model is that he has perfected the recipe. Identify the recipe, ask for coaching, and make the recipe your own. You do not have to reinvent the wheel. You have to discover what is already successful.

COMPETENCE CHECK

Do you understand:

☐ That competence in school administrators is a balance between leadership and management?

☐ The differences between leadership and managerial competence?

☐ The concept of survival competence?

☐ The characteristics associated with personal competence?

☐ The characteristics associated with perceptual competence?

☐ The characteristics associated with political competence?

☐ The success formula?

☐ The importance of immediate application of the success formula?

☐ The importance of identifying an appropriate success model?

Were you able to place a ✓ in each of the boxes in the competency check? The competent person is resolute in her task. She does not jump ahead unless she is sure she has mastered the content. She understands that each step on the road to competence builds the foundation for greater success through competence. One of the most trusted ways to ensure complete comprehension of the material is to teach the material.

Identify a person in your organization to mentor. As you gain greater competence, mentor that person. You will form a synergistic relationship that facilitates mutual growth toward greater competency.

NOTES

[1] Starkey, K. (1998). What can we learn from learning organizations? *Human Relations. 51* (4), (p. 536).

[2] Tompkins, J. (1997). Peak-to-peak performance. *Executive Excellence. 14* (5), (p. 17).

[3] Dubrin, A. (1998). *Leadership: Research findings, practice, and skills.* Boston: Houghton Mifflin Company (p. 3).

[4] Covey, S. (1990). *The 7 habits of highly effective people.* New York: Fireside (p. 101).

[5] Bennis, W. (1989). *On becoming a leader.* Reading, MA: Addison-Wesley Publishing (p. 111).

[6] Burns, J. M. (1979). *Leadership.* New York: Harper Torchbooks (p. 18).

[7] Bennis, W. (1989). *On becoming a leader.* Reading, MA: Addison-Wesley Publishing (p. 103).

[8] Nilsen, D. & G. Hernez-Broome. (1998). Integrity in leadership. *Leadership in Action, 18* (2), (p.13).

[9] Senge, P. (1994). The leader's new work. *Executive Excellence. 11* (11), (p. 8).

[10] Alinsky, S. (1969). *Reveille for radicals.* New York: Vintage Books (p. xiv).

[11] Vaill, P. (1991). *Managing as a performing art.* San Francisco: Jossey Bass Publishers (p. 38).

[12] Swets, P. (1987). *The art of talking so that people will listen.* New York: Fireside Books.

[13] Manasse, A. L. (1985). Improving conditions for principal effectiveness: Policy implications for research. *The Elementary School Journal. 85* (3), (pp. 439–462).

[14] Jefferson, T. J. Thomas Jefferson: Rights of British America, 1774. Papers, 1:134, In *Thomas Jefferson on politics and government.* Available: *etext.virginia.edu/jefferson/quotations/jeff1240.htm.*

[15] Cicero in *De Republica,* taken from J. Gardner's *On leadership* (1990) (p. 113).

[16] Burns, J. M. (1979). *Leadership.* New York: Harper Torchbooks (p. 425).

Personal Assessment

In this chapter you will

- Assess your current level of competence.
- Determine your personality type.
- Understand how your personality type affects your decision making.
- Understand how your personality type affects your leadership style.
- Determine your decision-making style.
- Understand the process of making quality decisions.
- Determine your leadership style.

This chapter guides you through an assessment process in the three critical competence areas of personality, leadership, and decision making. Assessment in these areas provides personal insights into professional performance. Insights into personality, leadership, and decision-making styles establish the competency context. By understanding this context, you can develop strategies to optimize personal competence and minimize potential derailing characteristics.

PERSONALITY STYLE

You have a unique personality style. Your personality style is much like your DNA—there is no other you! Each human being is unique. Yet, within our unique nature there are similarities. These similarities are based on physical appearance, that is, the normal human being has two legs, two arms, two eyes, two ears, and so on. They are also based on the ways that we express ourselves. The way you express yourself to the external world is your personality. Your answers to the following six questions demonstrate that you have a unique personality. Respond to the following statements to begin to get a sense of your unique personality.

1. There are certain kinds of people I don't like to be around.   **YES   NO**

2. There are certain kinds of events that cause me stress.   **YES   NO**

3. There are predictable ways that I react to stressful situations.   **YES   NO**

4. There are specific kinds of people whom I like to be around.   **YES   NO**

5. There are specific ways that I make decisions.   **YES   NO**

6. I know what I like and what I don't like.   **YES   NO**

How did you respond to the statements? Most likely, you answered YES to each of the statements. Your responses demonstrate that you have a personality. Your personality, as it developed over time, provided you with distinct likes and dislikes. It provided you with a set pattern to make decisions, respond to people, respond to events, select specific types of restaurants, identify people you like, and enjoy your profession. Healthy people enjoy their personalities and the personalities of others. Our personality is as much a part of us as is our body. There may be some aspects of our personality that we don't like (e.g., I wish I were less extroverted). However, we learn to adapt our personality to our environment. Thus, seemingly negative aspects are transformed into positive aspects by the psychologically healthy person.

The adaptive responses that are part of our personality are, most often, successful for psychologically healthy people. At other times, these responses create problems. For example, have you ever had a telephone conversation and simultaneously continued doing paperwork or working on your computer? This is a common experience among busy people. Yet, either the conversation suffers or the work suffers. Those who try to do two or three things at a time share this response as part of their personalities. It allows a person to complete tasks, but it also detracts from conversations. The impatient personality who gets edgy at stoplights, long lines, or meetings can cause harm through driving recklessly, behaving abusively toward store clerks, or trying to steer meetings toward quick conclusions. By being aware of our personality we can empower our positive traits and constrain our negative traits. Awareness of our personality is a critical component of competence for the following reasons:

- **It helps to understand personal motivation.**
- **It helps to understand the motivation of others.**
- **It helps to understand how personality affects leadership and managerial style.**
- **It helps to understand how personality affects one's worldview.**
- **It helps to understand how personality affects reactions to stress situations.**
- **It helps to understand how personality affects decision making.**
- **It helps to identify positive personality traits.**
- **It helps to identify derailing personality traits.**

Understanding personal motivation. There is a reason behind each of our actions. Conscious or subconscious motivation drives our actions. Take an ordinary activity such as getting out of bed. Why did you get out of bed? Did you get out of bed to go to work? Why did you go to work? Did you go to work to earn a living? Why did you brush your teeth? Perhaps it was the desire for healthy gums. Every action has a reason. We are aware of many of our motives. There are many motives of which we are unaware. Understanding these hidden motives can remove obstacles to successful leadership and skilled management. Understanding these hidden motives can vastly improve our decision making. Erich Fromm said: "Because the optimum of efficiency in living depends on the degree to which we know ourselves as that instrument which has to orient itself in the world and make decisions. The better known we are to ourselves, obviously the more proper are the decisions we make. The less we know ourselves, the more confused must be the decisions we make."[1]

Understanding the motivations of others. When we understand our personality profile, we gain greater understanding into the motivations of other people. It helps to understand the differences in personalities because we all have different reasons for our behavior. One school administrator, for example, calls a parent because she wants to provide close customer service to parents. This school administrator moves toward people. Another school administrator calls a parent because he is anxious that if he does not call, the parent will contact a member of the school board or his superintendent. Two different people, each performing the same action, each having different motives for their actions. When we understand the motives of other people, we can frame our interactions to provide the greatest mutual benefit.

Understanding how personality affects leadership and managerial style. We are our personalities. We take our personalities to work, play, church, and school. We cannot leave our personalities at home and transform into something different based on the environment. If we attempt to do this, it leads to *identity confusion.* As Erikson says, "A lasting sense of self cannot exist without a continuous experience of a conscious 'I,' which is the numinous center of existence."[2]

This sense of identity or our personality drives our leadership and managerial styles. Because our personalities have precise ways of responding to the environment, we have fixed ways of reacting to environmental stimuli. These fixed patterns operate on automatic pilot when we are under stress. We don't take the time to analyze how to best respond. This is one reason why situational leadership seldom occurs. Situational leadership makes common sense, yet in the heat of crisis our personality directs our actions. If our personality is one that wants a high degree of control, then in crisis situations we attempt to assert a high degree of control. If our personality is one that desires a low degree of control, then during crisis situations we may delegate responsibility, ask for a series of opinions, delay our actions until consultations are completed. When we understand the impact that our personality has on our leadership and managerial styles we can consciously select patterns of behavior we would not normally select.

Understanding how personality affects one's worldview. Your personality affects how you view the world. You have often heard the expression, "Is the cup half empty or is it half full?" The answer to this expression separates optimists from pessimists. How you answer this question also indicates a *worldview.* According to Karen Horney, there are three dominant worldviews:[3]

- The world is a friendly place and people will help me.
- The world is a hostile environment and I must be strong in order to survive.
- The world exists, but I want my private space.

Each of us can express any of these three worldviews. However, one will be more dominant than the others. Our personality drives our worldview and impacts how we adapt to our environment.

Understanding how personality affects reaction to stress situations. Our personalities are most visible during high stress situations. Have you seen people who "fall apart" during stress? Perhaps you've seen people who shut down all emotions during periods of high stress. Our reaction to stress is driven by our personality. This is enormously important to the school administrator because the school day is a stress-filled environment. Events are unpredictable; they seem to arise at any moment. If we are able to identify our personality and how we typically react in stress-filled situations, we can learn to act in more responsive, competent ways.

Understanding how personality affects decision making. The decisions we make may surprise us, but they do not surprise the outside observer who understands our personality. Our decisions are predictable because they are personality driven. We gain control over our decision-making process by understanding our personality and making it work for us rather than against us. Our personality has well-trained, finely honed paths that it follows when we make decisions. These decisions can be personal in the sense of how we buy a car, or they can be professional in the sense of how we respond to the school board president's latest comments. When we understand our personality, we can slow the decision-making process and consider alternatives other than those that automatically occur to our minds. Simon, in his seminal work *Administrative Behavior,* says: "All behavior involves conscious or unconscious selection of particular actions out of all those which are physically possible to the actor and to those persons over whom he exercises influence and authority. The term *selection* is used without any implication of a conscious or deliberate process. It refers simply to the fact that, if the individual follows one particular course of action, there are other courses of action that he forgoes. . . . Here the action is in some sense rational, yet no element of consciousness or deliberation is involved."[4]

Identifying positive personality traits. When we understand our personality, we identify positive traits associated with it. These positive traits are often taken for granted in our day-to-day activities. When we identify our positive traits, we become aware of the wide array of resources that are naturally at our command. Awareness of these resources allows us to apply them to the daily challenges that confront us. Identifying these resources also builds a high degree of confidence and raises our self-esteem. We become aware that we are capable of survival. We have natural resources to overcome challenges. We are not helpless or powerless in a hostile environment. Competent people are well aware of their resources and allow them to naturally interact with their environment. The following thirteen positive personality traits are associated with competent people. These are adapted from characteristics identified by researchers.[5] Which of these positive traits do you associate with your behavior?

1. **People view me as unselfish in sharing my time or resources.**
2. **People view me as highly empathetic—I am able to connect with their feelings.**
3. **People view me as a highly considerate person—I fully respect who they are and what they represent.**
4. **People view me as self-sacrificing—I put aside my interests to help others get their jobs done.**
5. **People view me as a strong leader—I get things done.**
6. **People view me as highly efficient—I don't waste people's time or energy; I stay focused.**
7. **People view me as one who relishes challenges—I have always been a risk-taker.**
8. **People view me as strong—I am able to stand up to confrontation and challenges.**
9. **People view me as fair-minded—I try to see both sides of the issue.**
10. **People see me as a tireless worker—It's easy to work when it is fun.**
11. **People see me as self-motivated—I am a self-starter.**
12. **People see me as a team player—I work well with others.**
13. **People see me as independent—I am willing to walk my own path.**

The more you integrate these positive traits into your personality, the more resources you have at your disposal. Accurately identify the personality traits you exhibit. Identify those that need to be more fully integrated into your personality. Develop a plan to increase these positive personality traits.

Identifying derailing personality traits. Unfortunately, we are not a composite of positive personality traits. Our personality is a double-edged sword. For every personality strength there is a corresponding weakness. When we are not aware of our weaknesses, they become *derailers.* That is, they have the potential to move us off the track to success and onto the track of failure. When we are unaware of our derailers, we blame others for our failures. The competent person recognizes that final responsibility for success or failure is internal.

The competent administrator knows that responsibility for behavior starts with the self. The competent administrator is aware of personal derailers and consciously moves to minimize their impact on himself and others. For example, the extroverted administrator can use his extroversion to meet people, make people feel comfortable, and publicly promote his school. On the other hand, if he allows his extroversion to get out of control, others will view him as loud, brash, and egotistical. His personality will be viewed as overwhelming. People will avoid him. His overwhelming extroversion may not derail him, but it contributes to the ease with which other people recognize his major derailing traits. Each of us has powerful derailing traits. However, we do not have to be held prisoner by these traits. We can identify them and minimize their power over our behavior. The following thirteen derailing personality traits are common among leaders and managers. These traits are adapted from derailing characteristics identified by a number of researchers.[6] Which traits do you believe others would associate with you?

1. **People view me as not being able to make a commitment.**
2. **People view me as resisting collaboration.**
3. **People view me as a loner.**
4. **People view me as power hungry.**
5. **People view me as a manipulator.**
6. **People view me as ambitious.**
7. **People view me as demanding.**
8. **People view me as overly compliant.**
9. **People view me as weak—too trusting of others.**
10. **People view me as not being able to decide without getting permission from a supervisor.**
11. **People view me as aloof.**
12. **People view me as selfish.**
13. **People view me as uncaring of others' needs or feelings.**

To some degree, each of us manifests all of these traits. It is difficult for us to admit the extent to which these traits exist within our lives because our egos are reluctant to admit to these faults. As Paul Tournier said, "We never see anything in this world except what we are inwardly prepared to see."[7] Competent school administrators move past the ego's defenses and make an inventory of derailing traits. They recognize that they must minimize the power of their derailers. We minimize the power of the derailers in our lives by recognizing them. Minimize the power of the derailers in your life by prioritizing those you identified from the list. Select the top three derailers and take action to reduce the risk to you and others from their negative impact. For example, suppose that your primary derailer is that others perceive you as being aloof. The desired action would be to *move against* your innate desires toward aloofness. In essence, the perfect antidote to a derailer is to do the exact opposite. Use every opportunity to demonstrate your willingness to become involved.

Discovering your personality type

We now understand why it is important to understand our personality type. Knowing our personality type provides us with key insights into our motivations. It lets us know why we are attracted to certain courses of action and avoid others. It lets us discover the details of our identity.

Many psychologists have set up classification systems to identify the various personality traits. Carl Jung, the famed psychologist, developed a system that contrasted eight dimensions and sixteen personality types. These eight dimensions are the basis of the Myers-Briggs personality assessment.[8] We may be outgoing (extroverted) or reserved (introverted). We may respond to a situation based on a gut feeling (intuitive) or we may want to collect and analyze data before we respond (sensing). When faced with working with other people we may want to involve them in the process (feeling) or we may want to process the issues in our solitude before acting (thinking). When it comes time to make a decision, we may make a decision immediately (judging), or we may want to continually analyze data, seeking more information and delaying the decision until we are assured of positive consequences (perceiving). The Myers-Briggs personality assessment yields sixteen different personality types. These personality types are greatly influenced by the environment.

Other personality classifications are equally complex. One useful grouping reduces the complexity of discovering personality types from the Myers-Briggs sixteen to three basic types. This grouping is based on the work of Karen Horney.[9] The *Personality Style Indicator* (PSI)[10] is based on Horney's personality theories. It provides us with an effective and efficient way of identifying our personality patterns. The PSI takes about thirty minutes to complete. Take the PSI now to determine your primary personality style. There are no right or wrong answers to the statements. You must answer every question if you want an accurate assessment.

THE PERSONALITY STYLE INDICATOR

Directions: The *Personality Style Indicator* enables you to identify your primary way of responding to most situations. By recognizing a primary way of responding to a situation, you become aware of the increased number of actions you may choose from in that situation. To accurately assess your primary way of responding, please select one of the two responses following the question: "If given the choice of the two following responses, which response is more indicative of how I would act?" When both responses are indicative of your behavior, select the one with which you most identify. You must choose one response to get an accurate score. Ignore the numbers to the right of each response.

In each of the following situations, if given the choice of the two following responses, which response is more indicative of how I would act?

1. (a) I like to receive direction. 1
   (b) I like to be in charge. 2

2. (a) I am a better follower. 1
   (b) I prefer to be left alone. 3

3. (a) I feel better when I know someone else is watching out for my best interests. 1
   (b) I can handle whatever comes my way. 2

4. (a) I feel safer in an organization where the boss takes care of the employees. 1
   (b) I'm self-sufficient; no one really has to help me. 3

5. (a) I go out of my way to help people. 1
   (b) I help others if it is in my best interest. 2

6. (a) You've got to cooperate with others if you're going to help them. 1
   (b) I really don't like to get caught up in the affairs of other people. 3

7. (a) I figure that the world is a pretty safe place. 1
   (b) The way I look at it, you have to outsmart others to survive. 2

8. (a) Basically, I believe that people should be trusted. 1
   (b) If I had the choice, I'd avoid people wherever possible. 3

9. (a) I may have my share of disagreements, but I don't carry a grudge. 1
   (b) If you don't agree with me, I'll confront you over the issues. 2

10. (a) You have to learn to get along with people; we need each other. 1
    (b) I can take or leave being with people. 3

11. (a) I like to share ideas or whatever I have if it helps others. 1
    (b) First come first serve, that's the way I've figured it out. 2

12. (a) Our purpose in life is to help others the best we can. 1
    (b) If you want me to help you, don't expect it to last forever. 3

13. (a) I enjoy a healthy discussion, especially when we challenge each other's ideas. 2
    (b) I like to build consensus. 1

14. (a) You figure other people out by challenging them. 2
    (b) I really don't care what other people are thinking. 3

15. (a) I love to win. 2
    (b) I don't mind winning, but I don't want to hurt anyone's feelings in the process. 1

16. (a) When I compete, I get to measure myself against others. 2
    (b) Competing with others is a waste of time. 3

17. (a) I get a lot of energy when I am angry. 2
    (b) I don't like to get angry; I'd rather work out our differences. 1

18. (a) I'm not afraid to express my anger. 2
    (b) I'd prefer not to argue, but I'll stay with you if I am pushed. 3

19. (a) The bottom line is that you can count on me to tell you the truth, even if it hurts. 2
    (b) If it is too painful, I'll temper any criticism that I have of you. 1

20. (a) I'll tell you what is really happening whether or not you want to hear it. 2
    (b) I know what's going on, but prefer to keep it to myself. 3

21. (a) Everything is a game in which you have to outsmart the other. 2
    (b) You catch more flies with honey than with a flyswatter. 1

22. (a) I like to be in competitive situations; I can outmaneuver most people. 2
    (b) I don't really need others, I have myself. 3

23. (a) I'm good at setting direction; I generally know what needs to be done. 2
    (b) I may know what needs to be done, but I like to listen to others. 1

24. (a) Giving orders is natural for me. 2
    (b) I don't like giving orders and I don't like taking orders. 3

25. (a) I love my space. 3
    (b) I like to be with people to keep an eye on them. 2

26. (a) My personal privacy is critical to me. 3
    (b) I hate being left alone. 1

27. (a) I usually find a way to be late to meetings and other engagements. 3
    (b) I'm prompt—no one is getting a jump on me. 2

28. (a) Sometimes I'm late for a meeting just so I won't have to stay in it as long as normal. 3
    (b) It is important to be on time for a meeting because of my responsibility to others. 1

29. (a) I consider myself different from most people in terms of my ideas and attitudes about life. 3
    (b) I figure that we're all the same; we're in for all we can get. 2

30. (a) Sometimes I feel like I just don't fit in with others. 3
    (b) The more I look at life, the more I am assured that we're in this thing together. 1

31. (a) I'll work harder for you if you don't tell me what to do. 3
    (b) If you tell me what to do, I'll confront you and let you know where you're wrong. 2

32. (a) I protect my independence whenever I can. 3
    (b) You have to cooperate in the world if you want to survive. 1

33. (a) My idea of a good time is to listen to quiet music in the solitude of my home. 3
    (b) My idea of a good time is to be on the golf course competing with my friends. 2

34. (a) It would be a great world if we all left each other alone. 3
    (b) I like to get a party going where everybody is having a great time. 1

35. (a) I have a few close friends at best. 3
    (b) I have many powerful friends. 2

36. (a) You don't need many friends to get along in this world. 3
    (b) I have many friends, they are there in case I need them. 1

Now that you've completed the PSI, it is time to discover your personality. Count the responses associated with each number (1–2–3).

1 (T) =

2 (A) =

3 (O) =

Count responses that you have that are associated with each number. The number with the largest amount of responses indicates your dominant personality style. Each person has personality characteristics associated with each of the three areas. However, it is the rare person who will not have a dominant area. Scoring patterns generally fall into the following categories: A strongly dominant area will have a score from 20–24. A moderately dominant area will have a score from 15–20. It is common to have two strong areas. We usually have a dominant area that defines our personality. However, when we find that our dominant area is not working, we automatically switch to our next useful area. The following table describes each personality type.

Personality Style Characteristics

1. T *Personality Type*	2. A *Personality Type*	3. O *Personality Type*
Brief Description: The *T* personality type constantly moves toward other people. They are friendly, trusting, and willing to assist others. They rapidly come to the aid of those they consider in need. They give primacy to the needs of others. They are excellent team members, enjoy collaboration and social settings.	**Brief Description:** The *A* personality type constantly moves against people. They are challenging, demanding, assertive, and enjoy the give and take of debate. They have a strong need to achieve and consequently have a strong ambition drive. They are efficiency experts and enjoy the use of power.	**Brief Description:** The *O* personality type constantly moves away from people. They enjoy working alone. They need their space. They are independent and see themselves as self-sufficient. They have a difficult time with meetings and often will withhold information unless asked. They refrain from revealing themselves to others. Unlike the *A*, they do not seek power or achievement. Unlike the *T*, they do not seek social inclusion.
T *Personality Traits*	A *Personality Traits*	O *Personality Traits*
Likes to be helpful.	Likes to be recognized.	Likes privacy.
Likes to be needed.	Likes prestige.	Likes to avoid competition.
Likes to be wanted.	Likes to make contacts.	Likes isolation.
Likes to be approved of by others.	Likes to gain new ideas.	Likes to be self-sufficient.
Likes to take directions or be guided.	Likes to compete.	Likes to resist rules.
Likes to be generous.	Likes to gain strategic advantage.	Likes to feel unique.
Likes to be appreciated.	Likes to have and use power.	Likes to be uninvolved.
Likes to be a friend.	Likes to be in charge.	Likes to resist advice.
Likes to seek common interests.	Likes to accept challenges.	Likes to rely on own intelligence.
Does not like rejection.	Does not like soft approaches.	Does not like intrusion.
Does not like criticism.	Does not like weakness in self or others.	Does not like being told what to do.

Our personality determines the traits we bring to decision making and leadership/management. Use what you've discovered about your personality to become more aware of your actions. There is no one best personality for a school administrator. Each personality type has strengths and weaknesses. The competent administrator, at his best, uses his awareness to ask what the situation/stimulus demands. If he is primarily a *T* personality, he will have to ask himself if the situation demands a *T* response. It may require an *A* or an *O* response. To the degree that he can match his response to the demands of the situation, he will be directing his personality to higher levels of competence. The *A* or *O* response is not his natural way to respond, but it may be the most accurate and appropriate way to respond. This is also true for those who have a predominant *A* or *O* personality type.

DECISION-MAKING STYLE

Decision making is at the heart of competence. Our competence is judged on the quality of the decisions we make as perceived by those who are affected by those decisions. A school administrator makes numerous decisions in a typical school day.[11] Some decisions are major and have long-term effects. Most decisions are minor and allow the school administrator to progress easily through the day. The sum of the quality of all decisions determines the school administrator's level of competence. Some decisions are more complex than others. The greater the consequences attached to the decision, the greater the weight attached to the decision. The school administrator does not have the same level of consequences when making a decision to allow a school dance as he does when he eliminates a popular program because of budget restrictions. There is more latitude in making decisions with limited consequences than there is in making decisions with major consequences. However, researchers have discovered that the pattern we use to make decisions is similar whether those decisions are minor or major.

Decision making is an integral part of competence. This is one difference that separates successful people from unsuccessful people. Yet, we seldom give significant thought to the decisions we make. Consider the students in your school. You can easily identify those who constantly have problems based on the poor quality of their decision making. Consider the teachers in your school. Good teachers consistently make quality decisions regarding instruction and students. Poor teachers consistently make poor decisions regarding instruction and students. Decision making seems to be an innate skill.

Decision making is linked to our personality type, thus providing it with this instinctual quality. In this way, our decision making defines our competence. Personality drives both decision making and leadership. Yet, decision making also exerts an influence on leadership. In many ways, this relationship is synergistic. Personality forms decision-making and leadership patterns. The results of decision making reinforce the personality and form leadership styles. The results of leadership reinforce both decision-making style and personality. In essence, the more we know about ourselves the more we can correct our actions and increase our levels of competence.

In the same way that we have a dominant personality type, we also have a preferred way that we make decisions. The style that we apply to decisions should be based on the context. However, it is more likely aligned to our personality. It is important to identify our decision-making style. Once we have identified our decision-making style we can become aware of other styles that can be applied in appropriate situations. The *Calabrese Decision-Making Style Indicator*[12] is an instrument that can help you to identify your primary decision-making style. Take time now to complete this instrument.

THE CALABRESE DECISION-MAKING STYLE INDICATOR

Directions: The *Calabrese Decision-Making Style Indicator* enables you to discover your decision-making style. Choose one of two responses to the statement "When making decisions" by selecting the response that most typifies your actions. In those cases where both responses are indicative of your behavior, choose the one response that *more strongly* resembles your decision-making action. You must respond to all statements to get an accurate assessment. Ignore the numbers to the right of each response.

In each of the following situations, when making decisions:

1. (a) I like to set priorities immediately. 2
   (b) I prefer to collect information before making priorities. 3

2. (a) I like to conceptualize the design before seeing the details. 2
   (b) I prefer to get people together to look at the problem. 1

3. (a) I like to experiment with different solutions. 2
   (b) I like to analyze what I am doing before moving ahead. 4

4. (a) I see myself as flexible in decision making. 2
   (b) I have a strong need to be in control. 3

5. (a) Sometimes I am ambivalent. 2
   (b) I act rapidly. 1

6. (a) I am spontaneous. 2
   (b) I like to ponder a wide range of alternatives. 4

7. (a) I have difficulty focusing on one solution. 2
   (b) I need plenty of details, facts, and figures. 3

8. (a) I tend to be indecisive. 2
   (b) I like to process information with others. 4

9. (a) I am creative. 3
   (b) I like to review data. 2

10. (a) I need some information but don't like to be overwhelmed by data. 2
    (b) I operate on an intuitive basis. 1

11. (a) I believe there is one best solution. 3
    (b) I believe that there are many equally good solutions. 4

12. (a) I like to be in charge. 3
    (b) I'm not worried about having control over the outcome. 2

13. (a) I go over every detail to be sure that I'm right. 3
    (b) I rely on my experience. 1

14. (a) I am aware of the values of my group. 3
    (b) I want to get things done; I worry about values later. 1

15. (a) I need to identify the problem. 3
    (b) I need to discover the hidden cause. 4

16. (a) I like to pull people together to brainstorm. 3
    (b) I like to work alone. 2

17. (a) I don't believe in "passing the buck." 3
    (b) I don't like to operate under pressure. 1

18. (a) I can usually find the right solution. 3
    (b) Time deadlines affect me. 4

19. (a) I ignore other information once I make a commitment. 3
    (b) I have a difficult time seeing the big picture. 2

20. (a) I like to get all of the credit. 3
    (b) I like to work with others and listen to their opinions. 4

21. (a) I get emotionally involved. 3
    (b) I try to separate my emotions from the decision. 1

22. (a) I am not afraid to decide. 1
    (b) I am people oriented. 3

23. (a) I can change my mind according to the context. 1
    (b) I like to think about the decision before making a commitment. 3

24. (a) I try to learn from my past mistakes. 1
    (b) I try to be patient. 4

25. (a) I am practical. 1
    (b) I am unemotional. 2

26. (a) I am impatient. 1
    (b) I like to process data from a variety of sources. 4

27. (a) I constantly think about how it will affect people. 1
    (b) I am more concerned with the organization than with people. 3

28. (a) I can look at five alternatives and pick the right one. 1
    (b) I logically try to resolve the issue. 2

29. (a) I don't get bogged down in impractical ideas. 1
    (b) I put my plan into action immediately. 2

30. (a) I am driven by specific goals. 1
    (b) I need to have criteria to evaluate my final decision. 4

31. (a) I initiate the decision-making process. 1
    (b) I can separate people from the problem. 4

32. (a) I find the complexity involved confusing. 4
    (b) I find the process straightforward and not confusing. 1

33. (a) I know I can find the right resources to help me. 4
    (b) I need specific data related to the problem I am trying to solve. 3

34. (a) I need to work with others. 2
    (b) I like to work alone. 3

35. (a) I like to analyze the situation. 4
    (b) I don't waste time analyzing what is wrong. 1

36. (a) I like to get people to agree on criteria before discussing the problem. 4
    (b) I like to bring people together to generate alternatives. 3

37. (a) I need time to completely think through the situation. 4
    (b) I believe you can do "too much" thinking. 2

38. (a) I don't like to be rushed. 4
    (b) I like to move quickly. 2

39. (a) I might be considered "wishy-washy" because I need to keep exploring alternatives. 4
    (b) I can make the correct decision quickly. 3

40. (a) Deadlines don't bother me. 4
    (b) I like to test my ideas before making a commitment. 2

41. (a) I like to hear people discuss possible alternatives. 4
    (b) I need to act quickly. 1

42. (a) People call me decisive. 1
    (b) People would say that I think things through. 4

43. (a) I can make a decision without much delay. 1
    (b) I need to observe and reflect on my experience. 3

44. (a) I can make an immediate decision without hesitation. 1
    (b) I am flexible and see the value in all alternatives. 2

45. (a) I like to generate choices. 2
    (b) I look for the one best choice. 3

46. (a) I find decision making difficult because of the validity of different solutions. 2
    (b) I like to spend a great deal of time discussing each option. 4

47. (a) I like to test alternatives before committing myself to a choice. 3
    (b) I can't waste my time in a drawn-out process. 1

48. (a) I like to use information to generate ideas to clarify my thoughts. 3
    (b) I can find the one clear choice. 2

49. (a) I need time to sit back and think about the issue. 4
    (b) I need to act decisively. 1

50. (a) I like to get people together to discuss the various alternatives. 4
    (b) I get confused from too much information. 2

Now that you've completed the *Calabrese Decision-Making Style Indicator* it is time to discover your decision-making style. Count the responses associated with each number (1–2–3–4). Place your totals next to the respective numbers.

1 =

2 =

3 =

4 =

The number of responses associated with each number indicates your dominant decision-making style. There is a wide range of scoring patterns. A strong dominant style will have a score greater than 15. A moderately dominant area will have a score from 8 to 15. It is common to have two strong decision-making style areas. You may also discover that you have no scores above 15. This means that you have yet to develop a dominant style or that you easily fluctuate from one style to another depending on the situation. There are specific characteristics associated with each of the four decision-making styles. Review these characteristics, summarized in the table that follows, and become aware of them as you make decisions.

Interpretation of the Calabrese Decision-Making Style Indicator

The *Calabrese Decision-Making Style Indicator* defines four different styles of decision making. Level four represents a collaborative, integrated approach to decision making. Level three is more decisive and less collaborative than level four. Level two represents a collaborative, non-decisive, and expedient approach to decision making. Level one is decisive, noncollaborative, and reactive in decision-making situations.

The four decision-making areas increase in levels of sophistication. For example, as the levels decrease, they decrease in sophistication. That is, the level 3 decision maker can generate more alternatives than the level 2 decision maker based on the collection and analysis of pertinent data, the generation of alternatives, and the weighting of alternatives against a set standard for the decision. In general, the higher the level of your decision-making style the more open you are to using each of the lower levels. The decision maker's choice of a primary decision-making style is a result of nature and nurture. It is a part of personality and it is a part of experience. The recognition of the primary style and an awareness of how that style helps or hinders the decision-making process is the first step in making better decisions and increasing competence.

Decision-Making Style Characteristics

Level 1	Level 2	Level 3	Level 4
Highly decisive.	Highly flexible.	Strong desire for perfection.	Integrates information and process.
Decisions are based on the values of performance, ease, expedience, uniformity, and immediate results.	Highly adaptable.	Driven by the values of authority, excellence, demanding methodology, order, and exactness.	Decision-making values center on discovery, knowledge, ingenuity, array, and inquiry.
Has a high level of confidence to make spot decisions.	Values are based on action, flexibility, expedience, choice, and precaution.	Immersed in the discovery process to target the correct problem.	Brings the best people in the environment together to focus on developing a wide array of solutions to a specific problem.
Maintains personal control over the decision context.	Desire to make decisions quickly is moderated by a compelling hope to make sure the decision fits the context.	Uses every resource to make sure the best alternative is selected.	Planning process includes an expansive database, consideration of long- and short-range aspects, and an adaptive ability.
Focuses on loyalty.	Surveys a greater variety of alternatives than the Level 1 decision maker.	Uses extensive planning.	Highly reflective and able to see the broad picture regarding the decisions that must be made.
Makes decisions to protect or extend the interests of the organization.	Willing to work with others in generating alternatives.	Detail oriented—analysis of decisions is logical and precise.	They operate with a high level of interpersonal trust regarding the sharing of information and ideas.

Decision-Making Style Characteristics (*continued*)

Level 1	Level 2	Level 3	Level 4
Uses heuristics to make instant decisions.	Views are short ranged and limits the use of data.	Integrates knowledge gained with personal experiences to find solutions.	Aware of the feelings of others and simultaneously of the need to process data.
Bored with long reports and prefers executive summaries.	Relies on personal or group intuition.	Wants to control the decision-making process and does not tolerate a decentralized process. Must be linked to the organization's authority structure.	Solutions embrace substance, implications are well thought out before implementation, and engage in a collaborative and cooperative process thoroughly investigating possible consequences.
Likely to tell a subordinate to summarize as succinctly as possible	Communication style encourages a great deal of discussion.	Involves others in the decision-making process only to the extent that they generate information relevant to the decision.	Highly tolerant of conflicting opinions and actually prefers a decision-making environment where diverse views are shared.
Communication style is results oriented and provides a single best solution.	Operates more effectively when the rules are flexible and those in authority allow a wider degree of latitude.	Focuses decision-making strategy on its impact on the organization as a whole.	Sends long reports and expects the same courtesy in return.
Uses power and can give directions quickly and efficiently.	Changes mind as the context changes.	Desires subordinates to bring different pieces to the problem.	Involves others in the decision-making process in terms of information gathering, solution generation, and openness to the creative solutions.
Highly effective in crisis situations.	Opts for a satisficing strategy as opposed to an optimizing strategy.	Operates in a hierarchical environment.	Takes time to make a final decision.

Compatibility of the Four Decision-Making Areas

	Level One	*Level Two*	*Level Three*	*Level Four*
Level One		Compatible	Compatible	Not Compatible
Level Two	Compatible		Not Compatible	Compatible
Level Three	Compatible	Not Compatible		Compatible
Level Four	Not Compatible	Compatible	Compatible	

Competent administrators understand the decision-making process. They are able to adapt their style to the situation. Their understanding of decision-making styles allows them to form teams based on compatibility, thus ensuring high levels of cooperation where attention is focused on the problem. No single decision-making style fits all situations. A competent decision maker is one who is open to understanding the demands of the decision context. As you become more open to the benefits of each decision-making level you increase the probability that you can integrate a nonprimary decision-making level into your primary style to make a successful decision.[13]

LEADERSHIP STYLE

Leadership style is driven by personality style. It is influenced directly by one's decision-making style. A school administrator's leadership style is woven throughout her work. It places her personal imprint on the school culture. Her success and ultimately her competence are based on how well she can shape the culture of the school community. If she can identify the existing school culture and lead it to higher levels of achievement, she will be successful. Her work will be an act of competence. However, if she fails to recognize the context, more than likely her efforts will fail regardless of her intellectual ability and previous experience.

The school context is the personality gestalt of the school community. When you previously identified your primary personality type, you noticed that it was one of three possible choices: *A, T,* or *O.* The personality types directly relate to the types of school contexts. The dominating personality type among members of the school community often determines the school context. This means that your school may have up to two-thirds of its members with a different personality style. This is the primary challenge to your leadership. Can you modify your personality style to align with the school context? Competent administrators understand this critical premise. This does not mean that you forfeit who you are—that would be impossible. It does mean that you recognize the most efficient way of communicating to your school community is to communicate in a language and context they understand. There are many measures of leadership. However, your competence in the school context will not be measured so much on a wide array of leadership traits as it will on your ability to demonstrate personal flexibility by working with the members of the school community and by recognizing the inherent nature of the school context.

Your task as a competent leader is to:

- Infuse the indifferent members with energy.
- Channel the energy of the antagonistic members toward cooperative, constructive action.
- Maintain the support and solidarity that already exists with cooperative members.

LEADERSHIP ASSESSMENT

The following leadership assessment estimates your current desire and ability to work with people who may have different ways of viewing the world. Before you take the following assessment, imagine that you are in a stress situation. In stress situations you are more likely to rely on patterned ways of acting. In each of the following ten statements you have three choices:

A—The statement represents how I generally respond under stress.

S—The statement represents how I sometimes respond under stress.

N—I never respond this way.

		A	S	N
1.	I lack tolerance for opinions that are different from mine.	A	S	N
2.	I suppress my anger when I deal with someone who is uncooperative.	A	S	N
3.	I withdraw when I am faced with strong opposition.	A	S	N
4.	I aggressively challenge those who are indifferent.	A	S	N
5.	I am willing to use those who are cooperative to get the job done.	A	S	N
6.	I will work with others only as far as they are willing to work with me.	A	S	N
7.	My job is clear; I do not tolerate anyone who gets in the way.	A	S	N
8.	I act congenially but I remember those who won't work with me.	A	S	N
9.	I will get even with anyone who challenges me.	A	S	N
10.	I live and let live and try to avoid problems.	A	S	N

If you had nine or more **N** scores, you work well with people. You understand how important it is to cooperate to get things done. If you scored less than nine, you need to review how you work with people. You need to identify personal strategies that are holding you back and replace them with strategies that are more effective. The school context is a dynamic environment. It is one that challenges every personality and decision-making style. Identifying the school context and applying the appropriate style to the context creates an environment that allows the school administrator to competently lead the school community.

COMPETENCE CHECK

Have you:

- ☐ Identified your personality style?
- ☐ Identified your decision-making style?
- ☐ Identified your leadership ability to work successfully with others?
- ☐ Identified your positive personality traits?
- ☐ Started to incorporate those positive personality traits that you do not now have into your personality?
- ☐ Identified derailing personality traits?
- ☐ Acted to eliminate the three top derailers that you associate with your behavior?
- ☐ Become more aware of your behavior to external stimuli?
- ☐ Adjusted your decision-making style to fit the context?
- ☐ Taken action steps to identify personal strategies that are holding you back from working more effectively with members of your school community?
- ☐ Identified your current school context as being cooperative, antagonistic, or indifferent?
- ☐ Acted to move your school context toward a cooperative context?

Were you able to place a ✓ in each of the boxes in the competency check? This is a crucial chapter in your quest for competence. It provides you with significant insight into your motivations, decision-making style, and willingness to demonstrate flexibility in working with others. The more that you understand yourself and others, the more you can recognize personal derailing strategies. Once these strategies are recognized you can act to replace them with positive, competence-building strategies.

NOTES

[1] Fromm, E. (1994). *The art of listening.* New York: Continuum (p. 46).

[2] Erikson, E. (1982). *The life cycle completed.* New York: W. W. Norton & Company (p. 73).

[3] Horney, K. (1945). *Our inner conflicts.* New York: W. W. Norton & Company.

[4] Simon, H. (1976). *Administrative behavior.* New York: The Free Press (p. 3).

[5] See positive characteristics listed in the following:

Bennis, W. (1998). Speed and complexity. *Executive Excellence. 15* (6), (pp. 3–4).

Magerison, C. (1993). Career choices and management development. *Management Development Review. 6* (4), (pp. 14–18).

Pollock, T. (1998). Attitudes that can help you get ahead. *Supervision. 59* (6), (p. 124).

[6] See derailing characteristics listed in the following:

Lombardo, M. and C. McCauley. (July, 1998). *The dynamics of management derailment.* Technical report 34. Center for Creative Leadership: Greensboro, N.C.

Van Velsor, E. & J. Leslie. (1995). Why executives derail: Perspectives across time and cultures. *Academy of Management Executive. 9* (4), (pp. 62–72).

Betof, E. & R. Harrison. (1996). Boards and the new leader dilemma. *Directors and Boards. 20* (3), (pp. 16, 18).

[7] Tournier, P. (1962). *Escape from loneliness.* Philadelphia: The Westminster Press (p. 173).

[8] See Kroeger, O. & J. Thuesen. (1988). *Type talk: the 16 personality types that determine how we live, love, and work.* New York: Dell Publishing.

[9] Horney, K. (1957). *The collected works of Karen Horney, Volume I.* New York: W.W. Norton & Company.

[10] Copyright 1996, Raymond L. Calabrese. This instrument may not be reproduced without the express written permission of Raymond L. Calabrese.

[11] Manasse, A. L. (1985). Improving conditions for principal effectiveness: Policy implications for research. *The Elementary School Journal. 85* (3), (pp. 439–462).

[12] Copyright 1996, Raymond L. Calabrese. This instrument may not be reproduced without the express written permission of Raymond L. Calabrese.

[13] The concepts presented in the *Calabrese Decision-Making Style Indicator* were adapted from the work of Phillip L. Hunsaker and Anthony J. Alessandra in their book *The art of managing people.* New York: Simon & Schuster (1986).

The Power of Feedback

In this chapter you will

- Understand the value of feedback.
- Understand how to create a personal model for 360°
  Administrator Feedback.[1]
- Understand how to use structured and unstructured
  feedback strategies.
- Understand how to use direct and indirect sources of
  feedback.
- Understand how to link feedback to well-established
  indicators of competence.
- Understand how to relate feedback to a personal
  assessment of competence.
- Understand how to assess feedback.
- Understand how to integrate feedback from an array
  of sources.
- Understand how to use integrated and analyzed
  feedback as part of a personal competence analysis.

UNDERSTANDING THE VALUE OF FEEDBACK

Feedback is critical to the improvement of performance. It is "information about past behavior, delivered in the present, which may influence future behavior."[2] Well-intentioned feedback focused on specific performance is a key to improving performance. It is the key to ongoing, sophisticated, and integrated competence. Feedback is the most effective means for understanding what is expected of us by our superordinates and subordinates. "Positive performance evaluations are contingent on the leader fulfilling the expectations of the performance evaluator. Because of this, it is valuable for the leader to know what those expectations are. One source of such information is feedback."[3] Feedback is usually linked to a performance appraisal. However, we can strategically use feedback prior to an appraisal to exceed superordinate and subordinate expectations. In this way, feedback is used for professional growth and is a major component of a cohesive professional growth plan. In this chapter, you will discover the power of feedback and learn how to use it to enhance your professional growth.

The following questions help to assess your current knowledge base regarding feedback.

	True	*False*	*I'm not sure*
1. Feedback regarding performance is important.			
2. Feedback should only come from a supervisor.			
3. Subordinates cannot give accurate feedback.			
4. Feedback is important—but only to a degree.			
5. Feedback is directly related to performance outcomes.			
6. Feedback requires a trusting environment.			
7. Feedback is time consuming.			
8. Adequate feedback is a result of one-on-one discussions.			
9. The source of feedback is critical.			

You answered nine statements regarding feedback. If I do not explain what your responses mean, you *will not* receive feedback. In a sense, your performance on the nine questions is essentially meaningless. Instead, you receive feedback as I explain each statement. Your response to the explanation of these nine statements is an indication of your attitude and understanding of feedback.

Feedback regarding performance is important. *True.* Inevitably we receive feedback. Our outcomes, to the degree that they are successful or unsuccessful, provide feedback. Yet, if feedback isn't structured, we seldom are aware that we are receiving feedback. For example, June Johnson, principal of Ellison Elementary School, is dissatisfied with her faculty meetings. She believes that the faculty lack motivation to contribute to these meetings. However, June does not prepare for the meetings. She puts an agenda together at the last minute. No one dares to give her feedback about her unprepared meetings. This frequently results in repeating past mistakes. When we are oblivious to what is happening we act like June Johnson. It is impossible to improve our performance because we are not open to available constructive feedback that will make us more effective. The more we seek and receive accurate feedback, the more likely we are to modify our current actions into accurate and appropriate performance.

Feedback should only come from a supervisor. *False*. The supervisor is just one part of a picture. There are many sources of feedback. Systematically collecting feedback from all appropriate sources is known as *360° feedback*. Using 360° feedback strategies implies that constructive data are collected from the entire circle of those in our environments who are in a position to observe our performance. As an administrator, you can receive feedback related to your performance from the following sources:

- **Supervisors**
- **Teachers**
- **Students**
- **Parents**
- **Colleagues (other school administrators)**
- **Staff (secretaries, custodians, cafeteria workers, etc.)**
- **Police liaisons**
- **Social service liaisons**

Church and Waclawski state: "Feedback from others, particularly with self perceptions, is clearly the wave of the future for leadership training and development efforts."[4] Each of the above groups is a part of your circle of feedback. Each group witnesses your performance with a specific lens and in a specific context. Members of these groups have specific special interests. As such, their view of your performance is limited. It can be accurately said that no single group has the full picture of your performance. Consequently, gaining accurate and appropriate feedback from a panolopy of sources requires a multirater feedback system. Wimer and Nowack state: "When done well, multirater feedback systems can lead to enormous positive change and enhance effectiveness at the individual, team and organizational levels."[5] When data from all groups are analyzed, the 360° Administrator Feedback instrument provides a composite picture of your performance as seen through the eyes of your work environment.

Subordinates cannot give accurate feedback. *False*. The feedback that an administrator receives from subordinates is highly accurate. It may not be the kind of feedback that the administrator desires. Yet, it reflects what the members of the administrator's organization see as reality. The important fact is that the feedback is accurate in the eyes of those giving the feedback. The perception of your performance is what counts. This perception may not be accurate, but it is helpful in making decisions as to how performance can be adjusted to alter damaging perceptions. For example, Mike Jackson, principal of Eagleston High School, received feedback that he was too "laid-back" in his approach. Mike felt that the feedback was inaccurate. However, in conversations with trusted friends he realized that it wasn't his approach to work, but the way he dressed. Mike came to school each day in an open-collar shirt. His dress was admittedly casual. Mike changed his dress. He began wearing suits. Within a month, he was receiving feedback that he no longer was using a laid-back approach, but one that was continually focused. Mike's approach to work hadn't changed—only his appearance. That change altered the perception of his faculty. The competent administrator takes feedback seriously.

Feedback is important—but only to a degree. *False.* All feedback is important. It is up to each person receiving the feedback to determine the accuracy of the feedback. If the feedback serves to stimulate reflection on how to become more competent, it has a high utilitarian value. The competent administrator recognizes that inherent in all feedback are valuable insights. These insights are filtered through the administrator's value system, integrated into a professional growth process, and separated from underlying motivations. The competent administrator seeks to learn from all feedback. The competent administrator moves away from a defensive posture.

Feedback is directly related to performance outcomes. *True.* The feedback the administrator receives is directly related to the administrator's performance. The people affected by the administrator's performance assess his performance each day on the basis of benefits they receive as a result of the performance. For example, if the administrator is highly organized, then his constituents benefit from excellent organizational skills. If the administrator is not well organized, then the constituents feel the pain associated with the lack of organization. If they receive low benefits, they see performance as less than acceptable. If they receive high benefits, they see the performance as highly acceptable. The outcome of the performance is tied to the benefits received.

Feedback requires a trusting environment. *True.* This statement is true if the feedback is to have a high degree of probability of being useful to the person receiving the feedback. In a trusting environment, the person receiving the feedback works with the person giving the feedback to identify how to improve performance. However, feedback is often given in a hostile environment. In a hostile environment, the people receiving the feedback often become defensive and defend their actions. In effect, they build a wall around themselves that prevents rather than encourages growth. Feedback has the power to help or to injure. When it is constructive and focused on professional growth rather than evaluation, its utilitarian value substantially increases.

Feedback is time consuming. *True.* Competent feedback takes time. However, the benefit received from the time and energy expended in gaining competent feedback more than compensates for the effort. Focus on the benefits and feedback efforts prove worthwhile. Feedback provides the following benefits:

- It provides a competency baseline from a variety of perspectives.[6]
- It provides the opportunity to develop a career plan.
- It provides enhanced self-esteem.
- It provides job security.
- It provides opportunities for professional growth.
- It provides links to organizational and community support that assists in attaining professional goals.

Adequate feedback is a result of one-on-one discussions. *False.* One-on-one discussions are valuable. However, they are a single source of feedback. Feedback comes in many forms: one-on-one discussions, skill assessment forms much like the ones taken in the previous chapter, analysis of outcomes of previous projects, assessments requested from a wide array of stakeholders, and personal comparisons to professional benchmarks, among others. The final decision as to the viability of feedback received from any person, group, or instrument rests with the person receiving feedback.

The source of feedback is critical if it is to be used. *True.* The source of feedback has to meet three criteria:

- **Credibility**
- **Relationship**
- **Integrity**

Those who provide feedback have to be *credible;* that is, the feedback they give has to be believed by the person receiving the feedback. The people providing feedback cannot allow personal biases to enter into their feedback. They cannot overlook issues because they like an administrator, nor can they exaggerate an issue because they dislike the person receiving feedback. They have to be believable.

Those who provide feedback have to be in a professional *relationship* with the person receiving the feedback. They are superiors, colleagues, subordinates, or other stakeholders. Each has a vested interest in the performance of the person receiving feedback. Each stakeholder experiences the consequences of the school administrator's actions. Each knows the quality of the action and its short- and long-term effects.

Those who provide feedback have to have *integrity.* Integrity means that those who provide feedback act in the best interests of the person receiving feedback. They provide feedback that is accurate and appropriate to the context. The feedback they provide is constructive and kept confidential. The person receiving feedback understands that all feedback, positive or critical, is meant to help when she senses that the person providing the feedback has integrity. Integrity-driven feedback is a catalyst for professional growth.

The feedback you received from your responses to the nine statements is a result of the interaction between you and me. This is a critical component of feedback. It is a synergistic approach between two people. You cannot receive feedback if you did not answer the nine statements. My explanation would mean nothing to you. If you answered the nine statements, then my explanations take on new meaning. You can assess your response to each statement in light of the information I provide to you and relate that information to your experience. If the information makes sense to you, you will integrate it into your experience and knowledge base. If it doesn't make sense, you will discard it or file it away for possible further use.

In Figure 4.1, feedback is identified as a mutual source of information. The performance action has to be perceived and received for it to qualify as feedback. The action can be directly on the person(s) providing feedback. Or, the person providing feedback can observe the action but be detached from the reception of the action. In either case, the person providing feedback has first-hand knowledge of the action or the action's effects. Once the person performing the action receives feedback, he has three alternatives: accept the feedback, reject the feedback, or accept only feedback that is aligned with his values, goals, or self-image. If the feedback is accepted, then the person is motivated to change current behaviors and embrace a behavior pattern more in line with the feedback that was received. If the feedback is rejected, the person continues on as is without behavior interruption. If the person accepts some aspects of the feedback, he modifies certain facets of behavior and continues with other facets of behavior. Which is the best approach? It depends on the utility of the feedback.

FIGURE 4.1   **Response to feedback**

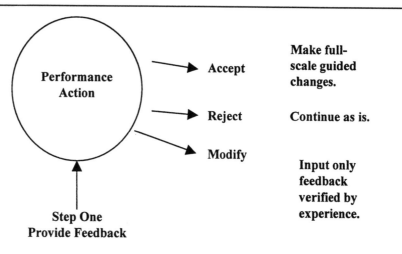

The utility of feedback is based on:

- **Accuracy**
- **Relevance**
- **Resources**
- **Ability**

Accuracy. The utility of feedback is directly related to the accuracy of the feedback. This means that the person providing the feedback has to correctly perceive the performance action and the performance outcomes. Often, feedback is of no utility because the person perceiving the action screens any action or outcome through a series of selective lenses. These selective lenses may be personal biases, prejudices, or ignorance. When the perception is accurate and free from screening, the performer of the action receives accurate feedback.

Relevance. The utility of feedback is directly related to the relevance of the feedback. The feedback has to be directly linked to the performance or the performance outcomes. If it is not linked, it is not relevant to the person receiving feedback. The more relevant the feedback, the more useful it becomes to the person receiving the feedback. Imagine desiring feedback regarding your communication skills and receiving feedback regarding budgeting skills. The feedback may be accurate and necessary, but it is not relevant. The more immediate the need, the greater the relevancy to the person receiving the feedback. Receiving feedback on a community meeting that took place three months ago is not as relevant as receiving feedback on the community meeting within twenty-four hours after its completion. This is especially true when a follow-up community meeting is scheduled to occur within a week. In this sense, relevancy is time related. Feedback, to be relevant, takes place close to the event that occurred.

Resources. The utility of feedback is directly related to the appropriate resources needed and the amount of resources available to gain the necessary competencies suggested by the feedback. Often, accurate and relevant feedback does not result in professional growth. The failure to use the feedback for professional growth is not a result of the lack of ability of the person receiving the feedback, but of the lack of resources to provide the necessary training indicated by the feedback. Resources allow the person to take advantage of the feedback to fuel the necessary changes and monitor coaching. For example, Lorin Jacklin, principal of Alpine High School, was criticized by her superintendent for poor time management. Lorin asked for suggestions, and the superintendent was unable to give specifics, but did offer to send her to a time management seminar. The superintendent provided the appropriate resources for Lorin to gain the necessary competence for her position. Lorin returned from the seminar and was able to turn her liability into a strength.

Ability. The utility of feedback is directly related to ability. A person may be well-intentioned, committed, and industrious, but if he does not have the aptitude to learn how to do a task he will not achieve the type of competence demanded by the role. It is important for each of us to accurately estimate our ability and to be cognizant of our aptitude. On one hand, we don't want to sell ourselves short. On the other hand, we don't want to jump in a river and discover we can't swim. Aptitude refers to our ability to learn a new task or to develop a talent. I enjoy writing and teaching. I do not enjoy creating computer programs. I have the intellectual capacity to learn the task. I do not have the emotional capacity to become a computer programmer. Therefore, my aptitude for computer programming is small in comparison with my aptitude for teaching and writing.

CREATING A PERSONAL MODEL FOR 360° ADMINISTRATOR FEEDBACK

The school administrator's role occurs in a politically dynamic environment (see Figure 4.2). It is a political environment because the school administrator is required to work with and through people to get things done. Leadership, management, and decision making all occur within this environment. This environment exists in all social organizations. The environment acts as a filter for the feedback the administrator receives. The political environment shapes the actions, attitudes, and values of its members. The competent school administrator recognizes the political dynamics within the school organization. Although the school administrator may be intelligent and technically skilled, if she does not acknowledge this environment she is doomed to failure. In this process, the politically naive school administrator alienates stakeholders and rapidly loses the support of superordinates. The loss of support compromises the school administrator's ability to compete for limited resources. This loss of support generates a loss of confidence in the school administrator from the school's stakeholders. This circular, destructive model, once in place, is difficult to stop. It often results in the school administrator being reassigned within the district or released from the contract.

The competent school administrator recognizes the political environment and proactively moves to manage the environment for organizational and personal benefit. One effective way to manage this environment is through the constructive application of the 360° Administrator Feedback instrument. Many organizations use a form of 360° feedback to improve employee performance. The reader will be able to recognize the wide variations of this form whenever "360°" appears with an accompanying phrase, such as the one used in this book, 360° Administrator Feedback. According to Center Point Systems, "360° performance feedback is the process of evaluating employee performance by soliciting specific job performance information from an employee's coworkers, managers, direct reports, and internal or external customers (where applicable). Also called multirater, multiperspective, and peer-to-peer

FIGURE 4.2   Feedback to manage a political environment

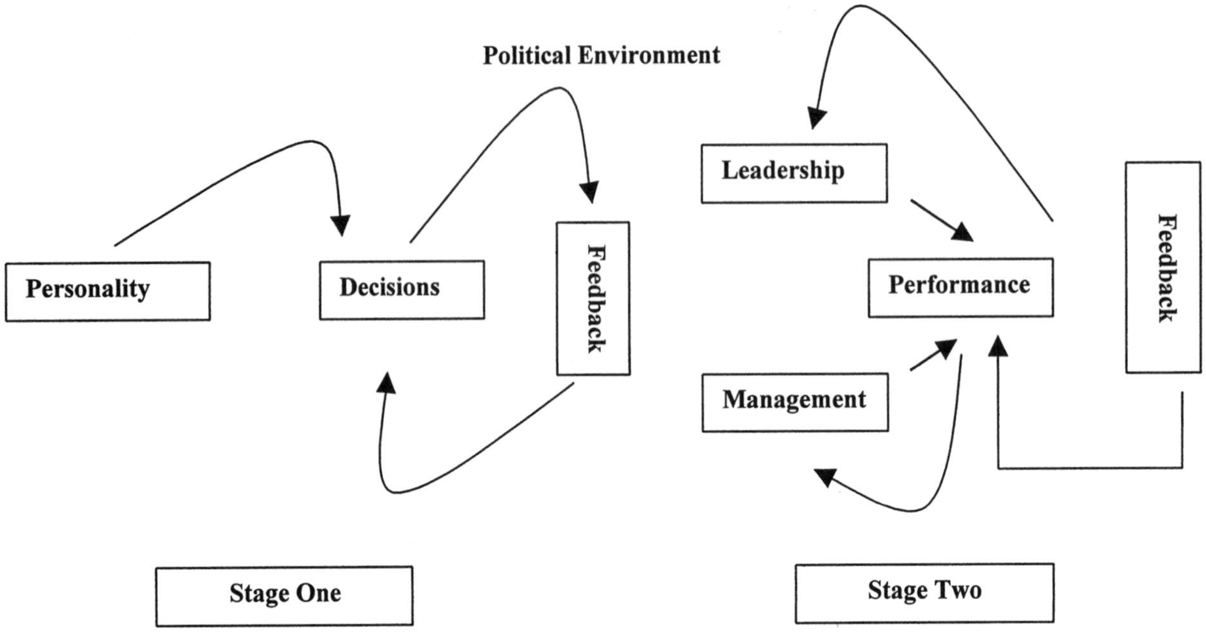

feedback, 360° feedback has been used extensively in corporate America for the past 10 years. The majority of Fortune 500 companies now use some form of multiperspective feedback as input to employee performance reviews. Managers, supervisors, and employees alike have found 360° feedback to be very effective in improving employee performance. Because feedback is gathered from multiple sources, employees find the results more compelling than traditional evaluations developed based on a single supervisor's or manager's perspective."[7]

The use of the 360° Administrator Feedback model occurs in two stages:

> **Stage One: Focus on the decision-making process and focus on the quality of decisions.**

> **Stage Two: Focus on specific leadership and management performance.**

Stage One: Focus on Decision Making

The quality of our decision making determines the quality of our professional lives. It is at the heart of the political environment. Martha Helson, principal of Thurston High School, thrives during a crisis. She makes instant decisions effectively. However, Martha uses the same process to make decisions when there is no crisis. As a result, she alienates people who feel that they should have been consulted prior to her decision. Martha could avoid this derailing behavior if she recognized that the decision-making process she uses directly impacts her political environment. As long as Martha makes quality decisions she will continue to maintain high levels of political support. However, once she makes a poor decision her support rapidly erodes. Martha's current decision-making process does not involve other people. This is a political liability. Martha is unaware of her decision-making impact on her stakeholders. She assumes that she is consulting them. However, her stakeholders have a different opinion. Martha makes decisions on well-entrenched patterns driven by her personality.

Our personality drives our decision making. Although we can't change our personalities, we can be aware that our personalities influence our decision making. Once we are aware of this influence, we can amend our decision-making practices. It is here that feedback is important. Meaningful feedback about decision making focuses on the decision-making process and the quality of our decisions.

The decision-making process

There are two dimensions to the decision-making process:

- The personal process we innately use to make decisions.
- The use of feedback to override our innate decision-making process and improve the quality of our decisions.

In the previous chapter you identified your primary decision-making style. Your style defines the personal process you use to make decisions. Your personal style may or may not be aligned with well-identified criteria associated with making quality decisions.[8] Each decision-making style expresses the process you use to make decisions. In Figure 4.2, feedback regarding how you make decisions allows you to modify your style and choose a style more aligned with making quality decisions. Continuous and accurate feedback related to decision making allows school administrators to overcome the filters embedded in their personalities. Refer to your decision-making style, which you identified with the *Calabrese Decision-Making Style Indicator*. Your type expresses the decision-making process you will most likely apply in a given situation. The feedback that you receive will be one indication as to the effectiveness of your primary style.

Stage Two: Focus on Specific Leadership and Management Performance

The first step in creating a personal model for 360° Administrator Feedback is to make the critical decision as to whom you ask for feedback. The people you ask will become the members of your *feedback team*. Your feedback team should consist of *superordinates, colleagues,* and *stakeholders*. Stakeholders include teachers, parents, students, staff, and community members. The number of people you place on your team depends on the time that you have available to analyze the data you collect. You should have people who represent each category of stakeholders. Involve students when they have the capacity and sophistication to understand the purpose of feedback. High school administrators are more likely than middle school or elementary school administrators to have a working relationship with students (e.g., class presidents, student council members, etc.). At a minimum, select at least one person who supervises your work, two colleagues who are familiar with your work, three people who report directly to you, and three people who are directly aware of your work, yet not formally associated with your organization. These nine people constitute your feedback team. Consult the following criteria in selecting your feedback team. Each person selected should meet all criteria.

Feedback team criteria

- **Identify people with whom you have frequent professional interactions.**
- **Identify people who have been working with you for at least six months.**
- **Identify people with integrity.**
- **Identify people whom you believe will take this process seriously.**

Send team members a letter explaining your request for their participation in the feedback process. The following is a sample letter that you can adapt for this purpose.

FEEDBACK LETTER

Dear Mr. Kane:

I enjoy my work as principal of Grayson High School. The faculty, staff, students, and parents are all part of my positive experience. I have spoken frequently to faculty about the need for continuous growth. Professional growth is important for me as well as for the faculty. As a result, I have made a commitment to develop a professional growth plan. In order to complete my professional growth plan I need your assistance. I need feedback on your observations of my performance as principal. The feedback that you provide focuses on my performance in the areas of leadership, management, and decision making. I am asking ten people to provide me with feedback. I selected you because of our frequent interactions since my appointment as principal, your integrity, and my belief that you will take this seriously.

The process is straightforward. In the near future you will receive forms from me to complete. Do not place any identifying marks on the forms and return them as soon as possible. Thank you in advance for your cooperation.

Sincerely,

Domains assessed

The 360° Administrator Feedback allows your feedback team to identify behaviors they have observed in your roles as leader, manager, and decision maker. Each of these domains operates in three primary contexts. Each context has primary aspects that stakeholders consider in relationship to your leadership, management, or decision-making behavior (see Figure 4.3). These contexts are:

- **People**
- **Politics**
- **Problems**

There is a flow between these contexts as the school administrator performs his duties throughout the course of the day. The 360° Administrator Feedback instrument isolates the focus on specific actions where stakeholder perception is high. The aggregation of these perceptions provides a wide array of data that looks at leadership, management, and decision making in three contexts and eighteen subcontexts.[9]

People. All leadership, management, and decision making occur with and through people. As a result, your competence is judged by the people in and associated with your organization. These are the stakeholders with a vested personal interest in your success. If you are successful, morale will be high, the organization will achieve its mission, and a high sense of cohesiveness will exist among members. There are

FIGURE 4.3   Context for the domains of leadership, management, and decision making

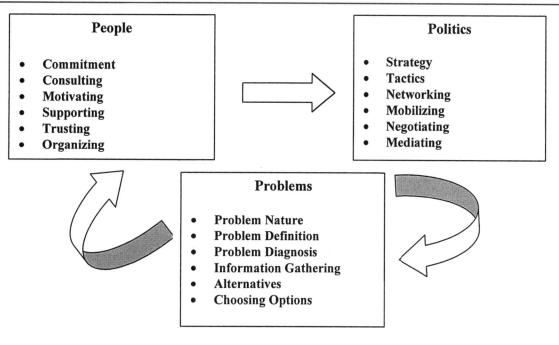

six indicators to competence in working effectively with people. These indicators include:

- **Commitment**
- **Consulting**
- **Motivating**
- **Supporting**
- **Trusting**
- **Organizing**

Commitment is the perception of stakeholders regarding the level of commitment they perceive you to have toward their interests. The higher the level of perceived commitment, the higher the loyalty of the stakeholders. A high level of commitment may be seen by teachers in the actions of a school administrator who aggressively argues with the school board not to reduce staff to preserve a tax rate. On the other hand, teachers may perceive a low level of commitment if the school administrator presents a plan to the school board on how staff can be reduced without eliminating services.

Researchers tell us that commitment by the administrator to the employees produces a high sense of positive self-regard toward the administrator. One study states:

> First and foremost, the manager who "got highest performance [GHP]" was described as a good pro-social manager who demonstrated active interest and concern for people (75% of behaviors of "high performance" bosses were in this category). The second most often cited category of behaviors of the boss who "got highest performance" were good cognitive processes, knowledgeable, expert, innovative (15% of managers specifically mentioned this cognitive expertise as eliciting their best performance). The ability and willingness of GHPs to teach their high cognitive skills is also a top characteristic of GHPs, but is included in the pro-social category. The third most often cited category of the manager who "got highest performance" was that he "challenged me," "set high performance standards," and had "high expectations" of any other single behavior of the GHP manager. No GHP managers were described as setting easy standards.[10]

Consulting is the perception of the stakeholders as to the school administrator's behavior in consulting vested parties *prior to* making a decision. In many cases, stakeholders want to be consulted in a meaningful way. That is, they want to have input into a decision before it is made. Their perceptions are highly individualized. At one end of the spectrum, some people are content with periodic notification of what is happening. At the other end of the spectrum, some people want to be part of a consensus-generating process. To the degree that these perceptions are met, the school administrator will be perceived to have a high consulting index.

Motivating is the stakeholders' perception of the school administrator as a charismatic, energetic force to cause people to act. A school administrator who is seen by stakeholders to be a high motivator is one who inspires others to succeed. Motivation may be perceived in words or actions. Actions may be directed toward a stakeholder or may be witnessed by the stakeholder. For example, one Massachusetts high school administrator inspired faculty by confronting an adolescent motorcycle gang. This administrator challenged fifty students on motorcycles to conform to school policy regarding taking motorcycles on school grounds. This challenge took place in plain view of the students, faculty, and staff of the school. He successfully challenged the students to conform to school policy. His behavior inspired teachers to challenge students to reach for higher standards of behavior. This was witnessed behavior. McDermott and O'Connor suggest that there are ten critical tactics that competent administrators want to **avoid** if they are to be effective motivators:

1. Ignore the achievements of others.
2. Assume you know what is important to others. Do not consult them, but if you do, ignore what they say, after promising to take it into account.
3. Take good results as the norm, but be extra sensitive and criticize any shortcomings.
4. Set standards that have no relevance to people's work. Make many small rules and enforce them arbitrarily.
5. If people are not sure how to do a task, just tell them to get on with it. Don't let them bother you with their problems.
6. Be condescending, or failing that, sarcastic, especially in public.
7. Engineer situations in which people develop a competitive fear of their colleagues.
8. Do not support people, but expect excellent results.
9. Take credit for others' successes and blame them for failure.
10. Do not tolerate failure, and make people anxious to cover their tracks. This will ensure a climate of blame and distrust, and encourage political infighting that will interfere with work.[11]

Supporting is the perception of the stakeholders that the school administrator stands with members in solidarity. Solidarity exists in any organization because "there are no solitary, free-living creatures: Every form of life is dependent on other forms."[12] The supporting school administrator recognizes this responsibility. Support may be perceived as material, emotional, or spiritual. A high support index indicates that stakeholders believe that the school administrator can be counted on to provide the appropriate resources when needed. Support is not often requested. However, there is an implicit belief in the stakeholder's mind that the school administrator understands when support is needed. Rewarding appropriate behavior is one way of demonstrating support for the staff. For example, the principal of Greenwood Middle

School annually recognized teachers whose students had the highest gain in scores on state achievement tests. The principal convinced the school board to reward the teachers with a $500 bonus. This kind of support for high performance recognized teachers who separated themselves from the norm. It is organizationally symbolic as well as personally satisfying for the person receiving the reward. A low support index indicates that stakeholders feel left out to fend for themselves. A low support index is indicative of high levels of alienation among stakeholders.

Trusting is the perception of the stakeholders that the school administrator has confidence in them. If their perception of the school administrator is one of high trust, they believe that he willingly delegates important tasks, has no need for constant oversight, and will not grab control over an important activity as pressure builds. Trusting emphasizes mutuality. When the school administrator trusts members of his organization, he is trusted by them. Trust is always an implicit factor in the strong organizational relationships that the competent school administrator forms. A low trust index indicates that stakeholders believe that the school administrator has little, if any, confidence in them to perform meaningful tasks.

Organizing is the perception of the stakeholders that the school administrator can organize them for success. They perceive the school administrator as the one who has the big picture. As stakeholders, their perception is limited. Their personal goals may be to organize their classes for instruction, whereas the school administrator must organize the school for instruction. The scope is significantly bigger. The school administrator who is perceived as having a high organizing index has the confidence of the faculty that the mechanical processes of the school will operate smoothly. A low organizing index indicates that the stakeholders believe the school administrator to be grounded in chaos, unable to make sense of her environment.

Politics is the action context. It is the context in which the school administrator works with and through people to accomplish personal and organizational goals. Politics is the art and science of governing. In this context, stakeholders view the school administrator with the high political index as one who operates in their best interests. The school administrator who is not able to produce benefits has a low political index. The successful, competent school administrator understands how to operate within the macro organization, avoid pitfalls, build constituent support, and remain psychologically and spiritually intact. There are six indicators to political competence:

- **Strategy**
- **Tactics**
- **Networking**
- **Mobilizing**
- **Negotiating**
- **Mediating**

Strategy is the planning of how to achieve organizational goals. It is well conceived, well designed, and effectively uses the resources available to the school administrator. A high strategy index, as perceived by stakeholders, means that they feel the school administrator has an overall plan to guide the school toward a known destination. On the other hand, a low strategy index, as perceived by stakeholders, indicates that they are unaware of any overarching plans. Rather, they see the school administrator as acting sporadically and chaotically.

Tactics are the action arm of strategy. Tactics are the applied actions that gain identified objectives. For example, Joe Mendoza, principal of Ellison High School, was challenged by the superintendent to raise achievement scores. Joe deployed a series of tactics to accomplish this task. He had teachers meet by academic areas to analyze current teaching strategies; parents offered input; students made curricular suggestions; and a staff development plan was put in place. Joe employed a wide range of tactics that resulted in significant organizational growth. A high tactics index means that stakeholders perceive that the tactics used by the school administrator are efficient, effective, and aligned with their values. A low tactics index, as reported by stakeholders, may mean that the tactics they observe violate their values, did not produce the intended results, or if they did work, did not work efficiently. The competent school administrator keeps each of these three aspects of tactics in mind.

Networking is the informal use of the political system to accomplish the school's mission. The school administrator with a high networking index is perceived as identifying key teachers, students, parents, community members, and other people in strategic political positions and making them a part of the school's overall mission. The use of networking often bypasses the formal political system. Here the school administrator explains a new program over a cup of coffee, lunch, or at a school basketball game. A low networking index suggests that the school administrator has not been able to identify the key figures or to effectively involve them in the informal political network.

Mobilizing is the school administrator's ability to bring the faculty together in a concerted effort to address a common cause. The school administrator with a high mobilizing index is perceived by stakeholders as being able to generate faculty enthusiasm, support, and action toward a common objective. Ann Holfield, principal of Brewer Middle School, wanted the school board to approve funding for a new reading program. Because Ann had carefully laid the groundwork with her faculty, she knew she could mobilize them into action. As a result, the entire faculty attended the school board meeting. One member after another spoke in favor of the program. The school board approved the necessary resources to fund the program. Mobilizing the community requires patience and work at the grassroots level. Mobilizing stakeholders toward a common cause is a political act that demands leadership. Stakeholders perceive the school administrator with a high mobilizing index as one who is capable of leading a common cause and supplying the energy to fuel the cause. A low mobilizing index indicates that stakeholders perceive the school administrator as unable to generate grassroots support for educational initiatives.

Negotiating is the school administrator's ability to work with others toward achieving a mutually satisfactory agreement. Nierenberg, in his classic book *The Art of Negotiating*, said, "Negotiation is a cooperative enterprise; common interests must be sought; negotiation is a behavioral process, not a game; in a good negotiation, everybody wins something."[13] Negotiating is central to the political process. The school administrator with a high negotiating index is perceived by stakeholders as able to produce satisfactory agreements with an array of groups and not lose sight of personal or group values. This school administrator always has an end in mind. The end is part of the school administrator's vision and the means becomes the mission. This enables the school administrator to bring different groups to the table that are committed to fulfilling the mission and vision. A low negotiating index indicates that stakeholders perceive the school administrator as unable to reconcile differences in order to achieve mutually beneficial agreements.

Mediating is the school administrator's ability to bring two opposing people or groups together to assist in resolving disputes. The school administrator with a high mediating index is perceived by stakeholders to be fair, just, open, patient, and willing to assist opposing groups to find common ground. A school administrator with a low mediating index chooses sides and is closed to the apparent needs of one of the parties involved in the dispute. Mediation skills are central to the political process because many stakeholders get entrenched in positions and are unable to understand the needs, desires, or interests of the other side.

Problems are the unifying context. Problems are the central thrust of leadership or management roles. The school administrator is hired to solve or prevent problems. Regardless of how competent the school administrator may be, problems occur. Problems often are the result of the interaction of *people* and *politics*. Glassman says, "The study of school administration is in most part the study of administrative behaviors that are problem based and problem driven."[14] How the school administrator resolves problems is a testimony to his leadership, management, and decision making. These problems may be large or small—as simple as getting the copy machine repaired, or as complex as leading a group of teachers who have decided to "work-to-rule" until the school board negotiates a higher salary. The competent school administrator can identify, solve, and prevent the recurrence of problems. There are six indicators to problem competence:[15]

- **Nature of the problem**
- **Problem definition**
- **Problem diagnosing**
- **Information gathering**
- **Alternatives**
- **Choosing options**

Nature of the problem is the school administrator's ability to recognize when a problem exists and its effect on the organization. A school administrator with a high nature-of-the-problem index indicates that stakeholders believe she can recognize problems before they reach a destabilizing state. For example, Carissa Lemply is principal of Quarry Elementary School. After attending state-sponsored meetings on instruction, Carissa realized that the state board of education was planning to set achievement goals for every school. Carissa involved her faculty in planning six months prior to the state board's announcement. Carissa was able to anticipate the problem. As a result, she prepared her faculty for the impending change. When faculty perceive that the school administrator understands the nature of the problem, they believe that the school administrator can put the problem into an appropriate context. On the other hand, the school administrator with a low nature-of-the-problem index is perceived by stakeholders as failing to recognize the existence of a problem and either over- or underreacts to the problem.

Problem definition is the school administrator's ability to place constraints on the problem and to accurately name the problem. A school administrator with a high problem-definition index can discern the depth, breadth, and scope of a problem. Molehills are not made into mountains. In effect, the high problem-definition index school administrator accurately manages problems. The low problem-definition index school administrator is never sure of the scope of the problem. For example, an assistant principal informed Jose Garza, principal of Chavez High School, that students were smoking pot in a third-floor lavatory. Jose told his assistant principal to shut all third-floor lavatories until further notice. This created a protest by students and a grievance from teachers. Jose acted arbitrarily. His judgment was inaccurate and his actions inappropriate. Inaccurate judgments increase the size and impact of the problem.

Problem diagnosing is the school administrator's ability to understand the cause and source of the problem. A school administrator with a high diagnosing index is perceived by stakeholders as being able to address the underlying source of the problem and prevent the problem from forming a reoccurring pattern. A low problem-diagnosing index indicates that stakeholders perceive the school administrator as a "firefighter" who constantly chases the symptoms of the problem and who is unable to identify the source of the problem.

Information gathering is the school administrator's ability to identify the necessary sources of information to adequately address the problem. It is impossible to gather all information. Too much information results in overload and potential paralysis of action. Competent administrators "... must be selective in what they attend to, that is, they can only attend to a subset of the available information in their environment."[16] A school administrator with a high information-gathering index is a rational decision maker. He is one who can select the appropriate information to make an effective and efficient decision. This school administrator withholds judgment until all facts are gathered. Solutions are driven by data rather than intuitive guesses. A low information-gathering index indicates that stakeholders perceive the school administrator to act reactively, without appropriate caution, and with a high level of emotion.

Alternative generation is the school administrator's ability to consider multiple options for resolving a problem. Each alternative is weighed against an objective standard. In the end, the alternative chosen by the competent school administrator is the result of careful consideration, information gathering, and a substantive brainstorming action with organization members. A school administrator with a high alternative-generation index is perceived as wise, as embracing an optimizing problem-solving strategy, and as giving stakeholder interests a priority. A low alternative-generation index indicates that stakeholders view the school administrator as jumping at a quick fix. This is known as a satisficing problem strategy. It takes considerably less time but it also produces far fewer appropriate solutions.

Weighing choices is the school administrator's ability to discern the quality of an alternative from among a wide array of possibilities. A high weighing-choices index indicates that the school administrator carefully sets a standard for the solution to the problem. The school administrator uses this standard to judge all alternatives. Any alternative that does not meet the standard is not considered an appropriate solution. A low weighing-choices index indicates that stakeholders perceive the school administrator as employing solutions without regards to a prospective solution's capacity to adequately resolve the problem.

Using the 360° Administrator Feedback

The 360° Administrator Feedback instrument allows the stakeholders you select to provide you with their perceptions of your leadership, management, and decision making in the three contexts. Make copies of the 360° Administrator Feedback and distribute a copy to each of the members of your feedback team.

360° ADMINISTRATOR FEEDBACK

Directions: The purpose of this questionnaire is to help school administrators learn more about their leadership, management, and decision-making patterns. You are asked to describe the leadership, management, and decision-making patterns of the person who requested that you complete this form. The feedback that you provide is used solely to help this person create a professional development plan. This person cannot do this without your candid responses. Make every attempt to ensure that your responses are accurate. Do not provide any marks or notations that identify you.

You will be given a series of statements regarding your school administrator. These are statements regarding behaviors that you may or may not have observed in your school administrator.

If your school administrator exhibits the behavior associated with these statements nearly every day, circle 4 (high frequency).

If your school administrator exhibits the behavior associated with these statements during the week but not daily, circle 3 (moderate frequency).

If your school administrator seldom exhibits the behavior associated with these statements, circle 2 (seldom).

If your school administrator never exhibits the behavior associated with these statements, circle 1 (never).

High Frequency	4
Moderate Frequency	3
Seldom Observed	2
Never Observed	1

The following statements refer to this person's relationships with people:

1. Stands by personal commitments.	4	3	2	1
2. Can be trusted to follow through.	4	3	2	1
3. Makes a promise and then keeps it.	4	3	2	1
4. Asks me for my opinion.	4	3	2	1
5. Consults with me on anything that may affect my job performance.	4	3	2	1
6. Involves me in the decision-making process.	4	3	2	1
7. Brings out the best in people.	4	3	2	1
8. Is an inspiration to many people in the school.	4	3	2	1
9. Encourages people to overcome challenges.	4	3	2	1
10. Can be counted on to help in times of trouble.	4	3	2	1
11. Provides people with the resources to get their jobs done.	4	3	2	1
12. Acts to mentor people.	4	3	2	1
13. Can be trusted.	4	3	2	1
14. Can be counted on to keep a confidence.	4	3	2	1
15. Will not betray the faculty or staff.	4	3	2	1
16. Is highly organized.	4	3	2	1

17. Is able to make sure the school
    runs smoothly.   4   3   2   1

18. Effectively coordinates faculty,
    students, and staff.   4   3   2   1

Subtotal People (Pp) _____

Average Score Pp (Subtotal divided by 4) ____

The following statements refer to this person's political skills in his or
her leadership role:

19. Has a long-range vision for the school.   4   3   2   1

20. Has a specific plan to meet school goals. 4   3   2   1

21. Has plans that make practical sense.   4   3   2   1

22. Is likely to know what to do in any
    situation.   4   3   2   1

23. Actions add to positive outcomes.   4   3   2   1

24. Actions are directly related to some
    greater plan.   4   3   2   1

25. Works effectively with faculty leaders.   4   3   2   1

26. Is respected by school board members.   4   3   2   1

27. Has a wide range of useful contacts
    to assist the school organization.   4   3   2   1

28. Can focus faculty attention on
    important issues.   4   3   2   1

29. Generates strong political support
    for educational causes.   4   3   2   1

30. Can unite faculty, students, and parents. 4   3   2   1

31. Is able to gain support for educational
    goals.   4   3   2   1

32. Works diligently to reconcile personal
    differences with faculty and staff.   4   3   2   1

33. Demonstrates an understanding of
    opposing points of view.   4   3   2   1

34. Can bring opposing sides to a peaceful
    solution.   4   3   2   1

35. Is fair to all parties in a dispute.   4   3   2   1

36. Gets opposing groups to discover
    common ground.   4   3   2   1

Subtotal Political Skills (Pt) _____

Average Score Pt (Subtotal divided by 4) ____

The following statements refer to this person's ability to solve problems:

37. Understands the problems the school faces.	4	3	2	1
38. Sees the depth and breadth of a problem.	4	3	2	1
39. Anticipates the potential short- and long-term consequences of problems.	4	3	2	1
40. Does not make a mountain out of a mole hill.	4	3	2	1
41. Focuses quickly on what needs to be done in a problem situation.	4	3	2	1
42. Precisely states the problem with little or no ambiguity.	4	3	2	1
43. Accurately identifies the symptoms of the problem.	4	3	2	1
44. Focuses quickly on the causes of problems.	4	3	2	1
45. Addresses the source of problems so that they do not recur.	4	3	2	1
46. Seeks to gather as much information as possible about a problem.	4	3	2	1
47. Precisely defines what information is pertinent to a problem.	4	3	2	1
48. Uses the information gathered to resolve an identified problem.	4	3	2	1
49. Identifies more than one possible solution to a problem.	4	3	2	1
50. Does not select the first viable alternative in solving problems.	4	3	2	1
51. Works with others to generate a list of possible solutions to problems.	4	3	2	1
52. Carefully weighs consequences before choosing a course of action.	4	3	2	1
53. Speaks about the standards a potential course of action must meet.	4	3	2	1
54. Only chooses act after carefully examining each potential course of action.	4	3	2	1

Subtotal Problems (Pb) _____

Average Score Pb (Subtotal divided by 4) ____

Total (Pp + Pt + Pb) ____

Recommendations

Directions: This part of the questionnaire asks you to make recommendations regarding the actions that you believe the person for whom you are completing this form should use. Read each description of each plan of action and circle the word that best describes your recommendation:

INCREASE the use of this action.
CONTINUE using this action as currently practiced.
DECREASE the use of this action.

I believe that this school administrator should:

1.	Make sure that every promise made is a promise kept.	*Increase*	*Continue*	*Decrease*
2.	Talk to people before acting, especially when it affects them.	*Increase*	*Continue*	*Decrease*
3.	Inspire the faculty through increased personal enthusiasm.	*Increase*	*Continue*	*Decrease*
4.	Provide more personal encouragement and support.	*Increase*	*Continue*	*Decrease*
5.	Delegate more and trust that the job will get done.	*Increase*	*Continue*	*Decrease*
6.	Concentrate more attention on organizing school programs and/or schedules.	*Increase*	*Continue*	*Decrease*
7.	Develop and communicate a vision and a set of goals for the school.	*Increase*	*Continue*	*Decrease*
8.	Become aware of the consequences of actions.	*Increase*	*Continue*	*Decrease*
9.	Connect with key faculty and community leaders.	*Increase*	*Continue*	*Decrease*
10.	Generate strong support among faculty and parents for key initiatives.	*Increase*	*Continue*	*Decrease*
11.	Be willing to negotiate differences.	*Increase*	*Continue*	*Decrease*
12.	Be fair and independent in dealing with two disputing parties.	*Increase*	*Continue*	*Decrease*
13.	Recognize problems before they become overwhelming.	*Increase*	*Continue*	*Decrease*
14.	Accurately assess the problem.	*Increase*	*Continue*	*Decrease*

15. Seek to identify and address the cause of a problem.   *Increase   Continue   Decrease*

16. Seek critical information prior to making decisions.   *Increase   Continue   Decrease*

17. Identify multiple alternatives before deciding which course of action to follow.   *Increase   Continue   Decrease*

18. Carefully select the best possible course of action to solve problems.   *Increase   Continue   Decrease*

You have completed the questionnaire. Please return this form, in the envelope provided, to the person listed below.

> Name
>
> Organization
>
> Street
>
> City   State   Zip Code

Gaining maximum use from the 360° Administrator Feedback

Maximum use is gained from the 360° Administrator Feedback by aggregating the feedback you receive from your identified stakeholders. The following table shows how one school administrator analyzed the feedback that he received.

360° Administrator Feedback

Name of Feedback Agent	People Area (Pp) (Average Score)	Politics Area (Pt) (Average Score)	Problem Area (Pb) (Average Score)
1. Supervisor	3.6	3.4	3.3
2. Colleague	3.7	3.8	3.7
3. Colleague	3.5	3.3	3.4
Average Score colleagues	*3.6*	*3.6*	*3.6*
4. Faculty	3.2	3.1	3.3
5. Faculty	2.8	2.9	2.7
6. Faculty	3.3	2.7	2.5
Average Score faculty	*3.1*	*2.9*	*2.8*
7. Community member	3.7	3.5	3.5
8. Community member	3.4	3.6	3.3
9. Community member	3.8	3.9	3.7
Average Score community members	*3.6*	*3.6*	*3.5*
Average Total (Sum column and divide by 9)	3.4	3.6	3.3

Range of Average Scores

| 1–1.9: Immediate attention needed. | 2–3.3: Planned areas for professional growth. | 3.4–4: Maintenance area. |

Recommendations

Sup. = Supervisor, Col. = Peer colleague, Fac. = Faculty member, Co. = Community member

I = Increase frequency   C = Continue frequency   D = Decrease frequency

Recommendation	Sup.	Col.	Col.	Fac.	Fac.	Fac.	Co.	Co.	Co.
1. Make sure that every promise made is a promise kept.	C	C	C	I	I	I	C	C	C
2. Talk to people before acting, especially when it affects them.	C	I	I	I	I	I	C	I	I
3. Inspire the faculty through increased personal enthusiasm.	C	C	C	I	C	I	C	C	C
4. Provide more personal encouragement and support.	I	I	I	I	I	I	I	I	I
5. Delegate more and trust that the job will get done.	I	C	C	D	D	D	C	C	C
6. Concentrate more attention on organizing school programs and/or schedules.	I	C	D	D	D	D	D	D	D
7. Develop and communicate a vision and set of goals for the school.	I	C	I	I	I	I	C	C	C
8. Become aware of the consequences of actions.	I	C	I	I	I	I	I	C	I
9. Connect with key faculty and community leaders.	C	C	C	I	I	I	C	I	I
10. Generate strong support between faculty and parents for key initiatives.	I	C	I	I	I	I	I	I	I
11. Be willing to negotiate differences.	C	I	I	I	I	I	I	I	I
12. Be fair and independent in dealing with two disputing parties.	C	C	C	I	I	I	C	C	I
13. Recognize problems before they become overwhelming.	I	I	I	I	I	I	I	I	I
14. Accurately assess the problem.	I	I	I	I	I	I	I	I	I
15. Seek to identify and address the cause of a problem.	I	I	I	I	I	I	I	I	I
16. Seek critical information prior to making decisions.	C	C	C	D	D	D	C	C	C
17. Identify multiple alternatives before deciding which course of action to follow.	I	C	C	C	D	D	C	C	C
18. Carefully select the best possible course of action to solve problems.	I	C	C	D	D	D	D	C	D

Matrix of Recommendations

Recommendation Refer to # above	Supervisor			Colleagues			Teachers			Community		
	I	C	D	I	C	D	I	C	D	I	C	D
Recommendation 1	0	1	0	0	2	0	3	0	0	0	3	0
Recommendation 2	0	1	0	2	0	0	3	0	0	2	1	0
Recommendation 3	0	1	0	0	2	0	2	1	0	0	3	0
Recommendation 4	1	0	0	2	0	0	3	0	0	3	0	0
Recommendation 5	1	0	0	0	2	0	0	0	3	0	3	0
Recommendation 6	1	0	0	0	1	1	0	0	3	0	0	3
Total—People (Pp)	*3*	*3*	*0*	*4*	*7*	*1*	*11*	*1*	*6*	*5*	*10*	*3*
Recommendation 7	1	0	0	1	1	0	3	0	0	0	3	0
Recommendation 8	1	0	0	1	1	0	3	0	0	2	1	0
Recommendation 9	0	1	0	0	2	0	3	0	0	2	1	0
Recommendation 10	1	0	0	1	1	0	3	0	0	3	0	0
Recommendation 11	0	1	0	2	0	0	3	0	0	3	0	0
Recommendation 12	0	1	0	0	2	0	3	0	0	1	2	0
Total—Politics (Pt)	*3*	*3*	*0*	*5*	*7*	*0*	*18*	*0*	*0*	*11*	*7*	*0*
Recommendation 13	1	0	0	2	0	0	3	0	0	3	0	0
Recommendation 14	1	0	0	2	0	0	3	0	0	3	0	0
Recommendation 15	1	0	0	2	0	0	3	0	0	3	0	0
Recommendation 16	0	1	0	0	2	0	0	0	3	0	3	0
Recommendation 17	1	0	0	0	2	0	0	1	2	0	3	0
Recommendation 18	1	0	0	0	2	0	0	0	3	0	1	2
Total—Problems (Pb)	*5*	*1*	*0*	*6*	*6*	*0*	*9*	*1*	*8*	*9*	*7*	*2*

Assessment of feedback

This school administrator was able to:

1. Identify how four categories of feedback team members view current competence levels.
2. Identify how each feedback team member perceived the school administrator's actions in 54 specific circumstances.
3. Receive recommendations from each feedback team member regarding increasing, maintaining, or decreasing specific behaviors.
4. Target behaviors and groups to modify or maintain.
5. Identify how four categories of feedback team members view current competence levels.

The school administrator, in this example, has a clear understanding of how feedback team members in four different areas perceive his current competence level. The school administrator's supervisor is satisfied with *people context competence* and *political context competence.* The supervisor believes the school administrator should improve in *problem context competence.* The school administrator's colleagues (other school administrators or assistant school administrators) see him as maintaining competence in all three areas. The faculty perceives that the school administrator can improve in each of the three areas. Community members perceive that he should maintain behavior in the people and political contexts and improve in the problem context.

The school administrator identifies how each feedback team member perceives his actions in fifty-four specific circumstances. The school administrator can quickly review each of fifty-four responses made by any of the feedback team members to gain specific perceptions. For example, if the school administrator wants to discover the behaviors the supervisor believes need to be addressed in the area of political competence, he finds that the supervisor scored a "2" on "Has a long-range vision for the school," a "2" on "Is respected by the school board," and a "1" on "Works effectively with faculty leaders." The school administrator may have a different belief than the supervisor. Yet, the supervisor's response can be used by the school administrator to become aware of his behaviors in this area and of his supervisor's perception of those behaviors. The nine feedback team members use this same process with each of the reports.

The school administrator receives recommendations from each of the stakeholders regarding increasing, maintaining, or decreasing specific behaviors. The school administrator assesses recommendations made by the nine feedback team members. Recommendations have direct application to the feedback team members' contexts. Teachers have perceptions far different from those of colleagues or supervisors. In this school administrator's case, teachers uniformly believe that the school administrator needs to increase evidence of competent behaviors in six political areas, three people areas, and three problem areas. Conversely, they perceive that behavior should be decreased in four different areas. The school administrator receiving this feedback refers to these recommendations. For example, recommendation five, "Delegate more and trust that the job will get done," received comments from the teachers which suggest they perceive that the school administrator may delegate too frequently. In this case, the school administrator uses this recommendation to heighten personal awareness of what is being delegated and to whom it is being delegated.

The school administrator targets behaviors and groups to modify or maintain behaviors. The scores and recommendations that the school administrator receives on the 360° Administrator Feedback allow him to target specific groups. Each group has a specific experiential and culturally determined perception of the ideal school administrator. The school administrator in this example matches or fails to match the idealized image that each person in each group has of him. The feedback the school administrator receives informs him of this match and the relationship that exists with each feedback team member's context. The school administrator uses the feedback to target behavioral changes with each context. If the school administrator is unsure of how to alter performance, then he seeks professional development in that area.

COMPETENCE CHECK

☐ Do you understand the value of feedback?

☐ Did you take the Understanding Feedback assessment?

☐ Do you understand the benefits that you receive from feedback?

☐ Do you remember the three critical criteria that feedback must meet to be effective?

☐ Did you understand Figure 4.2—Feedback to manage a political environment?

☐ Did you identify a core of stakeholders that will provide you with accurate feedback?

☐ Have you reviewed the 360° Administrator Feedback that stakeholders will complete?

☐ Do you understand how leadership, management, and decision making are interwoven into the people, political, and problem contexts?

☐ Do you understand the subdomains within each context?

☐ Have you chosen your stakeholders?

☐ Have you informed your stakeholders in person and by letter of what you intend to do?

☐ Do you understand how to analyze your feedback?

Were you able to place a ✓ in each of the boxes in the competence check? This chapter gives you the tools to collect critical perceptual data regarding your performance. The data may not be fully accurate. However, the data is accurate in the eyes of the beholders, those people most influenced by your performance. Using their feedback to inform your behavior is a major step toward becoming more competent. It is a blending of substance with image. The synergy between the two allows you to communicate your competence to your stakeholders.

NOTES

[1] Copyright 1999 by Raymond L. Calabrese. The *360° Administrator Feedback* may be used by the reader solely for personal development and not copied for workshop or other use without the express written permission of Raymond L. Calabrese.

[2] Seashore, C., & E. Seashore. (1992). *The art of giving and receiving feedback.* North Attleborough, MA: Douglas Charles Press.

[3] Salam, S., J. Cox, & H. Sims. (1997). In the eye of the beholder: How leadership relates to 360-degree performance ratings. *Group & Organization Management. 22* (2), (p. 208).

[4] Church, A., & J. Waclawski. (1998). Making multrater feedback systems work. *Quality Process. 31* (4), pages 81–89 (p. 82).

[5] Wimer, S. and K. Nowack. (1998). 13 common mistakes using 360-degree feedback. *Training and Development. 52* (5), pages 69–80 (p. 69).

[6] Dalton, M. (1998). Using 360-degree feedback successfully. *Leadership in action. 18* (1), (pp. 2–11).

[7] What is 360° Performance Feedback and Why Should I Use It? [Online]. Available: *http://www.centerpointsystems.com/360frameset.htm.* Accessed: February 6, 1999.

[8] See Irving Janis and Leon Mann's seminal work on decision making, *Decision-making: A psychological analysis of conflict, choice, and commitment,* New York: The Free Press (1977) for the specific criteria used to make a quality decision.

[9] The 18 subcontext indicators are adapted from Yuki, G., S. Wall, & Lepsinger (1990). *Preliminary report on validation of the managerial practices survey.* In K. Clark & M. Clark (Eds.), *Measures of leadership,* West Orange, NY: Leadership Library of America, Inc.; Lipshitz, R., & B. Nevo. (1992). *Who is a good manager? Leadership & Organization Development Journal, 13* (6), (pp. 3–9); and Peters, T. (1987). *Thriving on chaos.* New York: Harper and Row.

[10] Elbing, C., & A. Elbing. (1991). *Do aggressive managers get high performances?* New York: Scott Forsman (p. 63).

[11] McDermott, I., & J. O'Connor. (1996). *Practical NLP for managers.* Brookfield, VT: Gower (pp. 126–127).

[12] Lewis Thomas in E. Boyer & A. Levine's (1981) *A quest for common learning.* Princeton, NJ: The Carnegie Foundation for the Advancement of Teaching.

[13] Nierenberg, G. (1968). *The art of negotiating.* New York: Barnes and Noble (p. 29).

[14] Glassman, N. (1994). *Making better decisions about school problems.* Thousand Oaks, CA: Sage (p. 8).

[15] See G. Huber (1980). *Managerial decision-making.* New York: Scott Forsman and Company; and I. Janis. (1983). *Short term counseling.* New Haven, CT: Yale University Press.

[16] Phelps, R., R. Pliske, & S. Mutter. (1987). Improving decision-making: A cognitive approach. In J. Zeidner's (Ed.), *Human productivity enhancement,* Vol. 2. New York: Praeger (p. 303).

Identifying Career Derailers and Career Catalysts

In this chapter you will

- Identify potential professional derailers.
- Identify how to avoid potential derailing situations.
- Identify your capacity for effective action.
- Identify your potential for professional growth.
- Identify values, behaviors, and attitudes that derail professional growth.
- Identify values, behaviors, and attitudes that promote a highly successful professional career.
- Adapt the psychology of success to your professional career.

POTENTIAL PROFESSIONAL DERAILERS

Professional competence suffers when the school administrator is derailed. One study found that derailed school administrators were those: "who had typically run up a string of successes early on and were viewed as technical geniuses or tenacious problem solvers. Yet as they moved up in their organizations and job demands changed, some early strengths became weaknesses and some early weaknesses began to matter. The most common reasons for derailment were specific performance problems, insensitivity to others, failure to delegate or build a team, and overdependence on a single advocate or mentor."[1] Derailment occurs in the context of one's role or in the context of one's career. It occurs in the context of one's role when the school administrator, for unexplained reasons, suddenly loses the confidence of the faculty, students, parents, and community. The school administrator did not plan for this to happen. A set of events, seemingly unrelated, stymie the administrator's efforts to achieve personal, professional, and organizational goals. At best, she is running in place. At worst, her career is derailed.

Derailment is a time when the school administrator finds that "everything is going wrong." Former friends become adversaries, and superordinates who acted as protectors become distant. There is a paranoid feeling that she is the object of everyone's conversation. As this cycle takes on energy, the school administrator becomes increasingly isolated. She limits contact to one or two trusted allies, remains distant from the main body of the organization, and develops a mentality of "them against us." This scene is repeated in all organizations, public or private, social or political. What is clear is that when these events happen, the school administrator's career is in danger.

Michael Lombardo and Cynthia McCauley speak of derailment as ". . . involuntary and punitive. Derailment occurs when a manager who was expected to go higher in the organization and who was judged to have the ability to do so is fired, demoted, or plateaued below expected levels of achievement."[2] Derailment happens as frequently in educational contexts as it does in the private sector. For example, Karen Garcia was appointed principal of John Adams High School, in a large urban environment. She was viewed as a rising star. She was a breath of fresh air to the faculty, students, and parents. Within months, Karen became estranged from many of the faculty. Within a year, parents demanded her ouster. Karen was transferred to an elementary school. Karen blames special interest groups. Yet, she is unable to explain what happened and why it happened.

Derailment is a factor in all professional careers. It is not openly discussed, yet each professional has either had personal experience of being derailed or observed it happening to colleagues. It happens when an assistant school administrator becomes "stuck" in the job. It happens to school administrators who are fired or reassigned. It happens to superintendents whose contracts are "bought out" by the school board. In every case of derailment, it was not the intent of the derailed person to meet this fate. In fact, most people, if asked, would tell us that they are competent and that the blame for their derailment lies external to themselves. This is a defensive reaction. During derailment it is difficult to reflect on personal actions and much easier to project blame onto others. The truth is, derailment is a preventable condition if we are aware of our derailing behaviors, willing to substitute positive behaviors for derailing behaviors, and willing to take personal responsibility for our actions. Before we can act, we need to know the primary causes of career derailment.

The Six Primary Causes of Derailment

Derailment of professional careers has six primary causes:[3]

- **Difficulties working with others.**
- **Problems selecting and shaping a staff.**
- **Problems in moving from micro to macro levels.**
- **Lack of completion.**
- **Overdependence on a power/protection source.**
- **Disagreements with superiors on strategy and tactics.**

Difficulties working with others. This is the primary derailer for many school administrators. When the school administrator was hired, the faculty and community saw characteristics they believed important to their school community. The school administrator and school community entered a "honeymoon period." This honeymoon period is often short-lived once the school year begins. The intensity of the school day brings inordinate pressures from every conceivable angle. Internal faculty disputes, student discipline, parent and teacher disputes that spill over to the school board, and the daily pressures of motivating the faculty to increase student academic performance add to the stress felt by the school administrator. Under stress, the school administrator often adopts a communication style that alienates the faculty, students, and parents. This style is frequently authoritative, nonconsulting, and intimidating, for example, "My way or the highway."

As this situation develops, the administrator becomes more isolated. More time is spent in the office with the door closed. More time is spent on the telephone with external supporters. Moreover, more time is spent ruminating over the "evil" members of the staff. A circle-the-wagons mentality takes shape. The administrator's supporters become fewer and less vocal, causing further isolation. The administrator's primary response is to use power, because goodwill no longer exists to get members of the school community to cooperate. The pain felt by the administrator is also shared among the faculty. The only way to heal the pain is for the administrator to leave.

John Ramos explains it this way: "There are no simple answers."[4] He states that there are at least six reasons why people have difficulty working with others. These reasons include: inflexibility of management style; arrogance or abrasiveness; lack of good judgment or decision making; lack of a diverse work experience history; lack of loyalty; or a lack of motivation for a job. Each of the areas mentioned by Ramos focuses on the administrator's inability to work with others as a primary source of derailment.

Do you want to prevent derailment? You have no choice but to work effectively and efficiently with people. It is how the competent school administrator gets his job done. Fortunately, there are reversal strategies that we can employ to improve our working relationships. Take the following *self-check assessment*. Identify and implement any reversal strategies that may prevent professional career derailment.

Self-Check for Difficulties in Working with Others

Self-Check	*Reversal Strategy*
Are you isolated? **YES NO**	If Yes, become involved with your staff. Meet regularly with them.
Do you feel that the faculty is not supportive? **YES NO**	If Yes, commit to supporting faculty initiatives, become more flexible in working with faculty.
Do you need to "tell people what to do"? **YES NO**	If Yes, resist the impulse to direct. Ask for feedback and discover people's motivation.
Do you intimidate your staff? **YES NO**	If Yes, evaluate your tone of voice, posture, and gesturing. You may need to soften your approach.
If your faculty could vote on a school administrator, would you be elected? **YES NO**	If No, then consider why they would not choose you. Work to shore up support.

Problems selecting and shaping a staff. The staff the administrator selects and the staff's professional growth are critical to the administrator's success. The administrator is closely identified with the work of his staff. When the staff performs well, the administrator is praised. When the staff performs poorly, the administrator is criticized. Seldom is the staff transferred. Usually, the administrator is fired, transferred, or encouraged to seek another job.

Selecting and shaping the staff are critical to the administrator's success. James McAlister suggests: "Leaders are able to accomplish work by choosing the right people for important responsibilities, who are trained well and who work together effectively. This rarely happens by accident. Effective leaders are deliberate about surrounding themselves with others who are dedicated to the mission and vision of the organization and who are skilled at achieving desired results."[5] Selection of the right people may be the single most important decision that any administrator makes.

The selection decision helps to define school culture and values. In making this decision, the administrator needs to have a well-developed vision of desired qualities in prospective new members. The administrator identifies the qualities important in a faculty member and then matches these qualities to new hires. New hires are socialized by the staff into the staff culture. The administrator has to develop the staff by shaping, molding, and moving the staff in new, positive directions. School administrators who do not understand how to develop a faculty become the victim of staff resistance. For example, Joe Lengle, the new principal of Fenby High School, announced at his first full faculty meeting that he was going to significantly increase staff evaluation to improve faculty performance. The faculty was threatened; Joe left three years later. Joe didn't understand how to develop a faculty. He believed that he could use evaluation methods to pressure or coerce faculty members into fitting his personal model.

In essence, the derailing administrator primarily lacks focus on the selection of faculty, staff, and advisors. This is compounded by the derailing administrator's lack of understanding of the importance of developing these people. Ironically, one of the most effective ways to shape an organization is through the selection process. When careful attention is diverted from this process, the administrator allows other forces to determine staff growth.

The administrator has little latitude in selecting staff members. Selection is generally limited to replacing those who retire, transfer, or resign. Yet, each selection slowly changes the culture of the staff. Since changing the staff through selection is a long-term process, the competent administrator needs to focus on shaping the current staff. In a rapidly changing world, failure to emphasize staff growth leads to derailment. Fortunately, there are reversal strategies that you can employ to improve your selection and development of faculty. Take the following *self-check assessment*. Identify and implement any reversal strategies that may prevent career derailment.

Self-Check for Difficulties in Selecting and Shaping a Staff

Self-Check	*Reversal Strategy*
Do you build strong teams? **YES NO**	If No, commit to creating strong work teams.
Do you have an objective, written standard to use to guide your hiring process? **YES NO**	If No, develop goals and objectives with your faculty for each new hire.
Are you able to get your faculty to work effectively in teams? **YES NO**	If No, work with the faculty on learning how to "play effectively together."
Is the range of those you empower too narrow? **YES NO**	If Yes, become more open to diversity of culture, ethnicity, gender, ideas, and strengths.
Is there a high degree of mutual respect between you and your faculty? **YES NO**	If No, commit to work toward greater civility in communication among members. Establish "safe climates" for meetings.

Problems in moving from micro to macro levels. Imagine a teacher being appointed as assistant principal. Imagine an assistant principal being appointed to principal. Alternatively, imagine a middle school administrator being appointed as a high school administrator in a school twice as large as the middle school. Imagine an elementary school administrator being appointed superintendent of schools. These are typical career ladder routes for educators. Each step of the career ladder requires a change of perspective. The newly elected assistant principal can no longer view the school through the eyes of a teacher. The newly elected principal can no longer view the school through the eyes of an assistant principal. The newly elected superintendent can no longer view the school district through the eyes of a principal.

Each succeeding level requires a new vision. Each succeeding level requires a new strategic level. Each strategic level requires the ability to handle new levels of complexity. The competence that a person uses to move up the career ladder takes on greater scrutiny at each level. It takes on greater complexity because more stakeholders are involved, more resources are at stake, and it is more public and open to criticism. Derailed people are unable to effectively manage wide ranges of complexity.

Jim Tufola aspired to be a school administrator. Jim was an outstanding teacher. His school administrator recognized his potential, and encouraged him to get a master's degree and administrative certification. Jim was quickly appointed as an assistant principal. That appointment occurred twenty-five years ago. Jim was unable to make the transition from teacher to assistant principal. He continued to think and act like an outstanding teacher. His behavior was no longer valued by teachers or administrators. They had different role expectations. Jim was never fired, but he was never promoted. He became angry each time he was passed over for promotion. Jim was unable to make the transition from teacher to assistant principal. Derailed people quickly lose support of their superiors. Superiors try to find ways to hide or eliminate the person who could not make the transition.

Do you want to avoid the difficulties inherent in making the transition from a micro to a macro level? Do you find it difficult or anxiety producing to think of the next level? What about your current level? Have you successfully made the transition? Can you see the big picture as required by your position? The competent school administrator has no choice but to make this transition. Success in the previous position leads to promotion. However, the vision that was held in the previous position must be discarded for a new and broader vision. Fortunately, there are reversal strategies to improve your ability to move from a micro to macro vision. Take the following *self-check assessment*. Identify and implement any reversal strategies that may prevent professional career derailment.

Self-Check for Difficulties in Making Career Transitions

Self-Check	Reversal Strategy
Do you still think as if you were in the former position? **YES NO**	If Yes, identify other successful school administrators and meet with them. Ask them to share their vision of their school.
Are you able to get a true grasp of the depth and breadth of your role? **YES NO**	If No, commit yourself to an intensive period of education. You want to reconstruct your mental image of the school administrator's role.
Are you able to see your role through the eyes of your supervisor? **YES NO**	If No, meet with your supervisor or mentor. Discover what it is about your role that the supervisor desires to see happen. Understand the why of this perspective. Concentrate on that focus.
Have you moved micro managing to a global view? **YES NO**	If No, make a list of how you operate. Identify each tactic and strategy as either micro or macro. If the tactic or strategy is somewhere in the middle, indicate the direction it is taking.
Have you developed tactics and strategies that are aligned with your new role? **YES NO**	If No, then identify the tactics and strategies that are essential for your role. Seek advice and guidance from appropriate knowledgeable people.

Lack of completion. School administrators frequently become derailed because their visions are too scattered. They have grand ideas and are filled with enthusiasm. Unfortunately, many of these school administrators with great ideas quickly lose interest in the tedium required to take the ideas from conception to completion. They feel bored and go off to generate other fantastic ideas. They leave the task of completion to their staffs. Soon their stakeholders see through their "ideas." Stakeholders start to separate from this kind of school administrator. Then the school administrator is left with no one willing to work on a project. The school does not improve because faculty withhold commitment, the administrator lacks focus, and there is no discipline to stay with a project until it is completed. This school administrator is derailed by an inability to control, contain, and manage his excitement. Completion or follow-up is crucial to success. "Many otherwise capable managers fall down at this crucial point. They think clearly, plan well and delegate intelligently. Then they relax, only to be surprised when things do not work out as planned. Follow-up is an essential part of being an effective manager."[6]

Do you have difficulties in following through or completing projects? Does your sense of creativity and enthusiasm wane after you initiate a project? Many highly creative and enthusiastic school administrators can rally faculty to buy into creative projects. However, these same school administrators, once they get the ball rolling, leave the projects. They do not realize that their energy, creativity, and charisma moved the projects from a conceptual to an action stage. The competent school administrator recognizes that she must suppress the desire to move beyond a project until it has been successfully implemented. Even after successful implementation, the highly competent school administrator monitors the initiative, ensuring its continued success.

Perhaps you've had difficulty completing projects. This does not have to be a derailing strategy. Fortunately, there are reversal strategies you can employ to improve your ability to follow projects through to completion. Take the following *self-check assessment*. Identify and implement any reversal strategies that may prevent career derailment.

Self-Check for Possible Difficulties in Completing Projects

Self-Check	*Reversal Strategy*
Are you easily excited with new ideas? **YES NO**	If Yes, slow down! Evaluate each idea. Identify the time and planning you need to bring the idea to fruition.
Do you easily become bored once you initiate a new project? **YES NO**	If Yes, discipline yourself to stay with the project from initiation to completion. Model this behavior for your assistant school administrators and teachers.
Do you pay attention to detail? **YES NO**	If No, enlist a colleague who does pay attention to detail and who agrees to keep you apprised of important details that need to be covered.
Do you like to make a big production about your ideas? **YES NO**	If Yes, recognize that the bigger the production the greater the expectations. Downplay your ideas and expectations. Let the results speak for themselves.
If your faculty voted on your ability to follow-up, would you get a vote of confidence? **YES NO**	If No, then follow-up on every item, from discipline referrals, to calls to parents. Make your follow-up timely and substantive.

Overdependence on a power/protection source. The school administrator who overrelies on a single external source for support and protection creates a widespread perception of personal weakness. This school administrator has the potential of being derailed by both superiors and subordinates. The school administrator's superior does not want to take on additional problems. Subordinates desire their leader to be strong and self-reliant. Both groups believe that the school administrator was hired, in part, to be an independent problem solver.

Marcia Clarmon's story helps to illustrate this derailment factor. Marcia was the principal of Jackson Middle School. She is a perfectionist. She wants everything to be right. Her zeal for perfection resulted in the school schedule being perfect, halls neat, and faculty meetings precise. However, Marcia was afraid of making a move without consulting the superintendent. The superintendent lost confidence in Marcia and transferred her to a small elementary school. Marcia failed to realize that her superintendent was not interested in being her mentor. The superintendent wanted a job to be done. Marcia was unable to do the job without constantly conferring with the superintendent. She displayed a lack of self-confidence. Her superintendent was resentful because she felt Marcia was taking up valuable time.

The school administrator who displays a strong sense of independence demonstrates a personal sense of self-confidence. As long as the school administrator's actions are consistent with the direction of the school district, the superior views the school administrator as positive. One caveat to keep in mind: independence of action does not mean lack of communication. Effective and competent school administrators understand how important it is to meaningfully communicate with supervisors as well as subordinates. Meaningful communication keeps people informed and seeks appropriate input. When communication with a supervisor is limited to asking permission, the school administrator loses the confidence of his subordinates as well as his supervisor. A general feeling develops that the administrator is unable to formulate a vision without first checking with her supervisor. Subordinates need and desire a leader whose self-confidence is contagious.

Are you overreliant on your supervisor or other power source? Do you find it difficult to take initiative without gaining prior approval? Wisdom is often found in being cautious, but are you too cautious and sometimes paralyzed? How do you see yourself? How do others see you? The competent school administrator has no choice but to act confidently. Leadership demands self-confidence. Weak administrators create an overly cautious environment in which everyone scurries for protection. This produces an environment in which there is a lack of initiative. Followers develop resentment toward a school administrator who is unable to take personal responsibility for the direction of his organization. Inevitably, the followers begin to speak directly to the school administrator's supervisor. They know that is where the school administrator will head for advice and permission. Fortunately, there are reversal strategies to improve your ability to develop greater self-confidence and move from a dependency position. Take the following *self-check assessment*. Identify and implement any reversal strategies that may prevent career derailment.

Self-Check for Overdependence on Sources of Power or Protection

Self-Check	*Reversal Strategy*
Do you consult with your superior often? **YES NO**	If Yes, check the reasons for your consultation. Do you want to advise or inform? Seek advice only when necessary and appropriate.
If there is a disagreement with faculty, do you seek protection from your supervisor? **YES NO**	If Yes, try to work out the problems before they come to the attention of your superior. In only rare circumstances should you rely on the power source for protection.
Are you afraid to fail? **YES NO**	If Yes, realize that the fear of failure is immobilizing. View failures as learning moments. Begin to treat your faculty in the same way.
Does your faculty identify you with your supervisor? **YES NO**	If Yes, begin to create a "healthy distance" from your supervisor. It is time to have a separate identity.
If your faculty could vote on your independence as school administrator, would they view you as highly independent? **YES NO**	If No, begin to take stands that demonstrate your wisdom and political independence.

Disagreements with superiors on strategy and tactics. School administrators who derail often do not understand how to disagree or how far to carry a disagreement with their superiors. On one hand, few superiors want to be around "yes people." They want different opinions. They want to be challenged. The competent administrator understands this role and offers insights to supervisors without attacking or belittling ideas. The derailing administrator loses sight of the balance between disagreement and loyalty. He does not know when to stop disagreeing and when to fall in line behind the supervisor's strategic plan and tactics. This often occurs because the school administrator has not identified core values. These core values help the administrator draw the line. An administrator without a core value system does not know where to draw the line and easily misinterprets a disagreement over strategy as a moral issue.

Do you have difficulties in understanding how to disagree with your superordinates? Do you find it difficult to challenge your superordinate? Do you find yourself locked in a death struggle with your superordinate over issues that others would consider minor? Competent administrators can forcefully disagree with their superordinates and simultaneously maintain productive and constructive working relationships. Competent administrators are clear that they are on the same team as their superordinates and want the team to succeed. Because they understand values, they are in a position to understand whether an issue is one of a confrontation over personal values or simply a disagreement over strategy. When it is the latter, they are able to give their best advice and work to make a superordinate's strategy successful. There are reversal strategies to improve your ability to transcend disagreements. Take the following *self-check assessment*. Identify and implement any reversal strategies that may prevent career derailment.

Self-Check for Difficulties in Disagreements with Supervisors

Self-Check	*Reversal Strategy*
Are you able to present different alternatives to problems to your supervisor? **YES NO**	If No, present different alternatives to your supervisor as part of a general approach to problem solving.
Are you afraid of disagreeing with your supervisor? **YES NO**	If Yes, identify the causes of your fears. It may be that all authority figures cause anxiety. Read self-help books, speak to a professional counselor.
Do you know when to "back-off" in a disagreement with your supervisor? **YES NO**	If No, follow the directions of others at the meeting. Learn to develop a sense of timing and transition.
Can you identify three essential core values? **YES NO**	If No, read sources on how to do this process. A reflective act requires time and privacy.[7]
If your superintendent could vote on your ability to balance your disagreement over an issue with your willingness to offer support on this issue, how would the superintendent vote? **YES** (can make the transition) **NO** (can't make the transition)	If No, then speak with your superintendent. Ask how far you are allowed to go. Find out the signals that the superintendent sends that marks the transition. If you are unable to speak to superintendent, speak to a trusted colleague.

STRENGTHS OF HIGH PERFORMERS

Competence happens! Competent people find ways to solve problems, reconcile differences, unite people in a common cause, and provide increasing benefits to their organizations. Competence stands out like a shining lamp on a dark night. It cannot be hidden. Even if the competent person wanted to work in anonymity, her competence would soon be discovered by other people. Competent people seem to avoid the derailing patterns of their contemporaries. Where colleagues derail, the competent person seems to recognize the traps and easily avoids making the same critical, career derailing mistakes.

Differences between Competent High Achievers and the Derailing Underachiever

There are significant differences between competent high achievers and the derailing underachiever in all professions. One could argue that these differences are as much nature as they are nurture. That is, they may be as much a part of the constitution of the person as they are taught. In fact, if they are taught, those who already have a high competence potential have a higher readiness state to acquire new knowledge that leads to higher levels of competence. On the other hand, the derailing person desires to learn, but does not know how to apply what is learned. The knowledge is present; the correct and accurate application of the knowledge is missing. Ted Pollock feels that the difference between high achievers and those who never reach their potential can be found in four simple factors: High achievers have a realistic outlook on what they can achieve. They have a positive outlook in terms of self-expectancy. They have an innate habit of challenging or questioning how things are done. And, they are flexible; they have the capacity and willingness to change whenever necessary.[8]

Marian Marzlo is an example of an underachiever who is on the road to derailment. She is the principal of Toomey High School. Marian received a doctorate in instructional leadership that has given her an understanding of what must happen in the classroom. Although Marian seems to have all of the appropriate skills and training, teachers resist her leadership. Marian has participated in numerous leadership workshops. She also reads all kinds of leadership books. However, her efforts have proved fruitless. Her relationship with her supervisor is becoming increasingly strained because of continued teacher grievances. These differences are significant. Marian is unable to translate her knowledge into appropriate action. She does not have the whole formula.

The following five characteristics highlight the differences between nonderailing administrators and derailing administrators. Each explanation of the differential characteristics is followed by a self-analysis and *prescription for growth* (℞). Use these five self-assessments and prescriptions to eliminate personal aspects that potentially contribute to professional derailment.

Difference One: The use of time
Competent high achievers use time differently than derailing people. Hyrum Smith, CEO of Franklin Quest, says, "Controlling our lives means controlling our time, and controlling our time means controlling

the events in our lives. . . . Focusing on controlling the events of our lives makes all the difference."[9] Competent high achievers and derailing people have the same amount of time available: each has twenty-four hours in a day, one hundred sixty-eight hours in a week. These time boundaries cannot be expanded or contracted. The constructive use of the time available makes a major difference in who succeeds and who does not succeed.

The competent high achiever is driven by a clear vision that emanates from well-developed core values. The clarity of vision and mission enables the competent high achiever to resist external pressures to alter focus or priorities. The use of time is made efficient by the knowledgeable application of written goals. The following chart expresses the different ways time is used.[10]

Competent High Achiever	*Underachieving Derailer*
Focus on important, short-term issues.	Focuses on nonimportant and nonurgent issues.
Focus on important, long-term issues.	Focuses on issues lacking impact.
Places high priority on issues that make a difference.	Unable to distinguish between issues that make a difference and issues that are irrelevant.
Recognizes opportunities.	Unable to recognize opportunities.
Able to say no to intrusions.	Unable to say no to intrusions.
Able to prioritize.	Unable to prioritize.
Time is tied to personal vision and mission.	No overarching sense of vision and mission—driven by the vision and mission of external forces.
Establishes yearly, monthly, weekly, and daily goals.	Does not operate with a formal set of goals.

How does your use of time measure up?

1. I find myself being interrupted and going from one activity to the other.

   Often   Sometimes   Seldom   Never

2. I focus on problem prevention through relationship building.

   Often   Sometimes   Seldom   Never

3. I know there are opportunities, but I can't take advantage of them.

   Often   Sometimes   Seldom   Never

4. I can say no easily to those who want a piece of my time.

   Often   Sometimes   Seldom   Never

5. I make a list of priorities each day and generally complete the list.

   Often   Sometimes   Seldom   Never

6. I spend at least 80 percent of my time working to fulfill my vision and mission.

   Often   Sometimes   Seldom   Never

7. Each day I develop a set of written goals that fit into my weekly goals.

   Often   Sometimes   Seldom   Never

If you answered "Never" to one and three, and "Often" to two, four, five, six, and seven, you are one of the rare competent high achievers in the application of time. If your answers were different, you have room for growth. Examine the following *prescriptions for growth* (℞) and adapt them to your circumstances:

℞: **Identify personal patterns**. Our patterns of behavior are so deeply ingrained that we seldom are aware of our activity. How often have you logged on to the Internet and spent valuable time moving from one site to another. Each site is a little more interesting than the next. In the end, an hour or two disappear. What are the results of your time on the Internet? Has your search led you closer to accomplishing your vision? There are many "time distracters" in our lives. Identifying these time distracters is one way to gaining control over our life.

Action: Maintain a time journal for one week. List each activity, time spent, and results of the activity. Analyze your journal at the end of the week looking for patterns of behavior that pull you away from being a competent high achiever.

℞: **Set yearly, monthly, weekly, and daily written goals**. Goal setting and competence are highly correlated. When you put your goals in writing and review them daily, you set your subconscious mind to work to complete those goals. The time spent writing and reviewing goals will pay off in higher levels of competence and productivity.

Action: Write two major goals you want to accomplish within the year. Each month set monthly goals that contribute to the attainment of your yearly goals. Each week set weekly goals that contribute to the attainment of the monthly goals. Each day set daily goals that contribute to the attainment of weekly goals. Review your progress each week and move to eliminate behavior that keeps you from working on your goals.

℞: **Seize opportunities**. Opportunities are not predictable. They happen when least expected. Competent high achievers create opportunities as well as take advantage of opportunities that are presented to them. Competent high achievers are flexible. They realize that they have a brief window to take advantage of an opportunity. They rearrange priorities and move the newly discovered opportunity to the fast track.

Action: Identify your core values, vision, and mission. Be aware of opportunities that support your core values, vision, and mission. Also, seek to create opportunities from your existing environment. Delia Dixon, principal of Edwards Elementary School, provides an excellent model. Delia, along with the other school administrators in her community, is required to attend all school board meetings. Delia lives thirty miles from the school district. On school board meeting nights, Delia remains at school. Delia created an opportunity by opening her office to the public from 5 P.M. to 7 P.M. The parents thought her idea was fantastic.

Difference Two: Building and restoring relationships

Competent high achievers recognize that success is grounded in the relationships they form with other people. They know that each interaction is an opportunity to form a constructive working relationship. They also realize that differences do occur and that these differences are often exaggerated. They do not let the relationship deteriorate. They immediately seek creative ways to heal and restore any breach in the relationship. They are able to do this because they are present- and future-tense people. Underachieving derailing people are past-tense individuals. They hang on to grievances. Relationships do not have a priority in their lives until a crisis occurs. Because they have not cultivated relationships, the assistance they seek may be a mile long but only an inch deep. The following chart expresses the differences in relationship building between competent high achievers and derailing people.[11]

Competent High Achiever	*Underachieving Derailer*
Works hard to understand others.	Wants to be understood by others.
Negotiates well with others.	Operates on a zero-sum basis.
Gains cooperation of peers.	Unable to gain peer cooperation.
Is able to forgive and forget.	Unable to forgive or forget.
Spends quality time with organization members.	Remains isolated and aloof.
Has a healthy sense of self-deprecating humor.	Cannot laugh at self.
Expresses gratitude to faculty and staff for work well done.	Takes people and their work for granted.
High degree of self-acceptance and tolerance of others.	Low degree of self-acceptance and tolerance.

How do you measure up to forging and restoring relationships?

1. I am committed to understanding what other people say to me in conversations.

   Often   Sometimes   Seldom   Never

2. When push comes to shove, it's my way or the highway.

   Often   Sometimes   Seldom   Never

3. I find it easy to get people to work with me.

   Often   Sometimes   Seldom   Never

4. Although I have been hurt, I can get it behind me and work well with others, even those who hurt me.

   Often   Sometimes   Seldom   Never

5. I don't waste my time socializing with the members of my organization during work hours.

   Often   Sometimes   Seldom   Never

6. I take every opportunity I can find to let people know how much I appreciate their work.

   Often   Sometimes   Seldom   Never

7. I have a high degree of tolerance—different lifestyles and personal habits don't bother me as long as people are doing their jobs.

   Often   Sometimes   Seldom   Never

If you answered "Never" to two and five, and "Often" to one, three, four, six, and seven, you are one of the rare competent high achievers in developing and restoring relationships. If your answers were different, you have room for growth. Examine the following *prescriptions for growth* and adapt them to your circumstances:

℞: **Make relationship building a priority**. The famed psychologist Carl Rogers often spoke of the importance of relationship. He spoke of being genuine in a relationship. Rogers suggested that being aware of personal feelings, being open to disclosing feelings and attitudes, accepting and liking others, and a willingness to offer warmth, safety, and respect to others, regardless of who they are or the values they hold, is how we become genuine.[12]

Action: Assess your attitude toward other people. Do you find yourself attracted to some people and avoiding others? The competent leader moves toward all people. Choose one person you avoid and commit to forming a professional relationship with this person.

℞: **Laugh at shortcomings**. People appreciate those who can laugh at personal shortcomings. When a leader expresses this trait, he allows other people to realize that their leader is human. When followers join the leader in laughing, they are learning to laugh at themselves. It brings people together. President Ronald Reagan often demonstrated this trait when discussing his age during his presidential campaigns.

Action: Find ways to laugh at yourself. Begin privately and then, when comfortable, laugh publicly at your faults.

℞: **Let the past disappear**. When people work together, disagreements are bound to happen. If disagreements don't occur, people are not being honest with each other. The proof of a healthy organization is not the absence of disagreements, but the ability to acknowledge differences and sustain efforts to transcend those differences. The only way to transcend differences is to let the past disappear and to focus on sustaining the present as a means of building the future.

Action: Identify a person in your organization with whom you have had strong disagreements in the past. Commit yourself to working with this person in spite of past differences. Each time you bring one more person into the loop, you increase your power exponentially.

Difference Three: Savvy

The competent high achiever is distinguished from the derailing person by the degree of savvy that she displays. Savvy literally means to understand or comprehend. In a political sense, it is the ability to walk into a new job and understand what has to be done. It is a deep, innate understanding of what makes the organization and the people within it tick. Some may refer to this trait as "common sense," and others as "perception." As Stephen Covey states:

> It seems that every senior executive, especially in the US, is sensing that the future will demand more of a global mind-set, skill-set, and character-set. The new breed of leader will be characterized by the following 7 habits: (1) They are inquisitive explorers. (2) They know how to bring people with different characteristics and from diverse cultures together. (3) They focus on the importance of character. (4) They are *savvy*, optimistic people who have eyes for opportunities. (5) Global travel increases awareness and appreciation of cultural differences. This causes them to be less judgmental. (6) They focus on the quality of the foreign experience more than just the quantity of it. (7) They seek closeness more through shared social, spiritual, intellectual, and economic interests than they do through political or cultural connections.[13]

Savvy is an ability to get things done because of an understanding of what needs to be done. Derailing people lack savvy. Alan Bothus, principal of Agawam High School, lacks savvy. Alan will schedule meetings for his faculty in advance and then, an hour before the meeting is scheduled to begin, cancel the meeting and call an emergency meeting of another group of people. Alan doesn't understand the need people have to schedule events in their lives. Derailing people are often overwhelmed by their roles and meander from task to task with little coherence between tasks. The following chart expresses the differences in savvy between competent high achievers and derailing people.[14]

Competent High Achiever	Underachieving Derailer
Understands organization members' needs.	Does not understand organization members' needs.
Sees organization's place in larger context.	Unable to see beyond contextual boundaries.
Understands the need for future positioning.	Only aware of the present.
Trusts intuitive sense as to what needs to be done.	Relies too heavily on data not informed by intuition.
Has a high degree of self-knowledge.	Little understanding of self.
Has a healthy "street sense."	Not able to respond accurately to oncoming stimuli.
Consciously constructs his or her environment.	Allows the environment to determine his or her identity.
High degree of self-trust and trust of others.	Low degree of trust of self or others.

How does your savvy measure up?

1. How often do you check to ensure that you understand the needs of organization members?

   Often   Sometimes   Seldom   Never

2. How often do you share your school's role in relationship to the district, region, state, nation, globe with your administrative team?

   Often   Sometimes   Seldom   Never

3. Are you frequently surprised by state education mandates?

   Often   Sometimes   Seldom   Never

4. Do you do a "gut check" before acting?

   Often   Sometimes   Seldom   Never

5. How often do you spend time gaining self-knowledge as to your values, behaviors, attitudes, etc.?

   Often   Sometimes   Seldom   Never

6. Do you have a "sixth sense" when walking through the school about what is right or wrong?

   Often   Sometimes   Seldom   Never

7. How often do you overreact to stimuli within your environment?

   Often   Sometimes   Seldom   Never

8. How often do you experience doubt about your decisions or willingness to delegate important tasks to others?

   Often   Sometimes   Seldom   Never

If you answered "Never" to three, seven, and eight, and "Often" to one, two, four, five, and six, you are one of the rare competent high achievers in applying savvy to your work site. If your answers were different, you have room for growth. Examine the following prescriptions for growth and adapt them to your circumstances:

℞: **Competent high achievers seldom make assumptions**. They are constantly searching the environment for data to help them make effective decisions. As they process new data, they make appropriate corrections in direction. Similarly, competent high achievers do not take faculty and staff wants and needs for granted. They consistently seek to understand these needs and are aware that these needs change as the organizational context changes.

Action: Conduct a small focus group of faculty—ask them to talk about their needs as teachers.[15] A focus group is an effective way to discover how people really feel about issues.

℞: **Competent high achievers are always in the process of development**. Earlier in this book, you took the *Personality Style Indicator* and the *Calabrese Decision-Making Style Indicator*. Each assessment provided you with insights into your personality. Continue this journey. Continue to search for your hidden motivations, biases, and worldview frames. This is a lifetime search. The more you discover about yourself, the more you learn to trust your intuition and basic instincts.

Action: Go to the self-help section of your local bookstore. Commit yourself to reading one book a month that focuses on an aspect of self-development. Follow your instincts on what you want to read.

℞: **Competent high achievers seldom doubt their decisions**. They act with certitude. They trust themselves and they trust other people. Once they make a decision they never look back; they put all of their energy and resources into making sure their decision is effective. Derailing people waiver in decision making. They are afraid to risk and move into unknown territory where the outcome is uncertain. Their doubt is associated with a lack of confidence in themselves. This is also expressed in their lack of trust of other people.

Action: Practice making decisions with certitude. Gather data surrounding the decision context, generate a set of alternatives, weigh the advantages and disadvantages of each alternative, and then choose. Never look back. Diana Berg, an international business consultant, tells us, "There are no simple, logical steps to achieve success. We sometimes fail to capitalize on opportunities while we search for the mythical right way to accomplish something. Give yourself permission to begin without having a perfect plan."[16] The need for surety that the decision is perfect can paralyze us.

Difference Four: Systems thinking

The competent high achiever is distinguished from the derailing person in the way that he thinks about the world, problems, people, and the context within which his school organization operates. Tom Jackson, superintendent of Little Springs Independent School District, operates by the "principle of 200." He says that everyone knows at least 200 people. If he treats one parent without respect, it is as if he treated the 200 people the parent knows without respect. These 200 in turn each tell 200 more.[17] Soon, the entire community believes he is contemptuous toward parents. He understands the complexity of systems and the impact of interactions.

The competent high achiever not only has a bigger picture of the environment, but also understands that each person in the environment is a product of an expanding series of interactions. This is part of *systems thinking.* Senge says, "At the heart of the learning organization is a shift of mind—from seeing ourselves as separate from the world to connected to the world, from seeing problems as caused by someone or something 'out there' to seeing how our own actions create the problems we experience."[18] These interactions occur within and external to the school context. Identifying these forces and understanding how they cause a person to behave is central to competence.

The competent high achiever, once able to identify and understand these interactions, can begin to work within the environment to alter the interactions that occur. In contrast, the derailing person doesn't see or understand the wide range of interactions that are occurring. Consequently, this person is not able to effectively influence the environment to move toward constructive change. The following chart expresses the differences in *systems thinking* between competent high achievers and derailing people.[19]

Competent High Achiever	*Underachieving Derailer*
Understands the complexity of organizations.	Sees the organization as a simple organism.
Recognizes that each object in the organization is impacted by numerous internal and external interactions.	Understands only limited interactions that are framed by rigid boundaries.
Recognizes that feedback about the environment is critical to its understanding.	Does not seek feedback to form understanding.
Recognizes that small changes produce large results.	Continually focuses on trying to achieve unrealistic results.
Recognizes that systems resist change.	Moves rapidly into change mode without consideration of systems' response to change.
Views past "solutions" as part of current problems.	Does not consider past solutions as part of current problems.
Recognizes that moving too fast actually slows organizational growth.	Plows ahead with no concept of the rate of speed of change or growth.
Is able to identify positive and negative feedback loops.	Lacks understanding of the existence of positive and negative feedback loops.

How does your systems thinking measure up?

1. I often think of the school as one small organization that is influenced by a variety of forces.

   Often   Sometimes   Seldom   Never

2. I see the school as a set of grades/departments that act independently of each other.

   Often   Sometimes   Seldom   Never

3. I seek continuous feedback from a variety of sources.

   Often   Sometimes   Seldom   Never

4. I try to do one small thing at a time and do it well.

   Often   Sometimes   Seldom   Never

5. Although people are resistant to change, I push them into change.

   Often   Sometimes   Seldom   Never

6. I try to understand the past to get a grip on what is causing current problems.

Often   Sometimes   Seldom   Never

7. I can't move slowly—I am impatient. I want to get things done.

Often   Sometimes   Seldom   Never

8. I recognize that feedback is positive and negative. Each type informs my decisions.

Often   Sometimes   Seldom   Never

If you answered "Never" to two, five, and seven, and "Often" to one, three, four, six, and eight, you are one of the rare competent high achievers in understanding and applying the principles of systems thinking. If your answers were different, you have room for growth. Examine the following *prescriptions for growth* and adapt them to your circumstances:

℞: **Become trained to be a systems thinker**. You may not have been trained to be a systems thinker. Don't feel alone—most university programs that prepare school administrators fail in this task. Competent high achievers are not stymied by the gaps in their training or the weaknesses of other people. They move ahead. Take responsibility for becoming a systems thinker and introduce the concept to your faculty and staff.

Action: Begin by reading Peter Senge's *The Fifth Discipline*. Incorporate the concepts of systems thinking into your personal behavior. Make your organization a *learning organization*. You can connect to MIT's Learning Organization web site to access articles by Schein, Senge, and others. The web site is located at *http://learning.mit.edu/*.

℞: **Make your school an interactive, interdependent unit**. Each action by a faculty member impacts all faculty members. Each action by the school administrator impacts all faculty and students. Each faculty member is dependent on other faculty members to do his job. Each person in the system relies on everyone else in the system if the system is to operate effectively.

Action: Make a feedback loop of the interactions that you have with faculty, staff, students, and parents (see Figure 5.1). Extend the feedback loop so that you can see the interrelated nature of the problems you are facing. The feedback loop in Figure 5.1 refers to a feedback cycle initiated by the principal at a faculty meeting. Identifying feedback loops enables the school administrator to communicate more effectively by identifying where miscommunication gaps occur.

℞: **Make change a part of your personal and organizational life**. Change cannot be resisted. Even if we remain static, we are changing. The competent high achiever recognizes that change is inevitable and that she has a responsibility to direct change in a positive and constructive direction. The competent high achiever recognizes that change occurs

FIGURE 5.1   **Feedback loop**

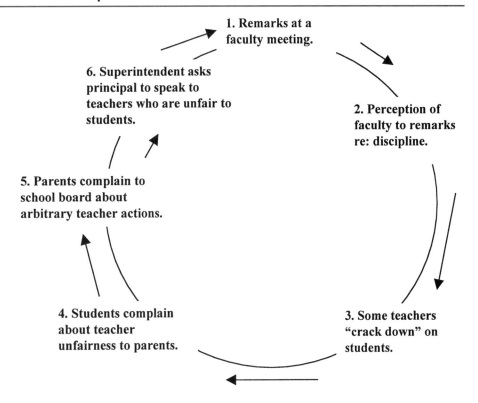

1. Remarks at a faculty meeting.

2. Perception of faculty to remarks re: discipline.

3. Some teachers "crack down" on students.

4. Students complain about teacher unfairness to parents.

5. Parents complain to school board about arbitrary teacher actions.

6. Superintendent asks principal to speak to teachers who are unfair to students.

best when it is hardly noticed. This is the principle of the *Just Noticeable Difference* (JND). The JND is 2.8 percent. This is also known as *Weber's Law.*[20] When the rate of change is no more than 2.8 percent, people are not cognizant that change is occurring. When the rate increases over 2.8 percent, people begin to pay attention. Change is inevitable, but the rate can be managed.

Action: Identify an important change that needs to take place in your school. Map out the change so that the rate of change is never more than 2.8 percent. As long as the rate of change does not exceed 2.8 percent, change will not be noticed or painful. Strategically plan the change to occur so that each increment of change has a minimum of two to three weeks to become rooted in the organization.

Difference Five: Balance

Competent high achievers are distinguished from derailers in the ways that they apply balance to their lives. Competent high achievers see themselves as more than their careers. They realize that they have family and friends who deeply enrich their lives. They also recognize that a life of continuous work creates the seeds for burnout, heart attacks, and isolation. They know that they are complex beings. They have physical, emotional, psychological, and spiritual needs as well as career needs. Each of these needs synergistically reacts with all other needs. The capacity to perform well at work is related directly to personal relationships outside of work, physical fitness, and one's spiritual life. Competent high achievers realize that when they go to work they don't change bodies or personalities. They are the same people with the same problems they had when they left their homes a few minutes earlier. Derailing people often forget all other needs except what occurs at work. Therefore, they neglect other important aspects of themselves. Loehr, author of *Toughness Training for Life*, states: "The best single measure of the balance of stress and recovery in your life is pure positive energy: fun. As the amount of negative stress in your life increases, your sense of fun and joy tends to decrease . . . Fun means excitement and arousal (energy expenditure) without physical or psychological pain (negative stress)."[21]

Joe Spanks, superintendent of schools, gives us an example of a life out of balance. He recently had his annual physical. Joe complained of back pain, headaches, and sexual problems with his wife. The doctor asked him how many hours he was working a week. Joe paused and said seventy to ninety hours a week. Joe's work had lost its fun. It was a time of tension, and his relationships with others were emotionally dry. Joe compensated by working harder and found himself trapped in a cycle whose only reward was increased stress and fatigue.

The following chart expresses the differences between competent high achievers and derailing people in the area of balance.

Competent High Achiever	*Underachieving Derailer*
Operates with a sense of balance in life.	Is driven and is unable to compensate.
Recognizes that other members of the faculty and staff need balance in their lives.	Assumes that all others must be equally committed and driven toward the organization.
Has a wide range of social contacts away from professional life.	Has limited social contacts away from professional circles.
Takes time to exercise regularly.	Cannot find time to exercise—too busy consumed with work.
Develops a sense of personal spirituality, e.g., connects with God, nature, universe.	Seldom considers spirituality important. Focuses totally on work.
Is able to leave work at work.	Carries work problems home and allows them to dominate the conversation.
Recognizes through awareness of mind and body when it is time to seek relaxation.	Unaware of signals being sent by mind or body. Operates on automatic pilot.
Operates in the zone of optimum stress (neither bored nor anxious).	Constantly has wide attitude swings from boredom to high anxiety.

How does your sense of balance measure up?

1. I feel that work is my life.

   Often   Sometimes   Seldom   Never

2. I encourage my faculty and staff to maintain a balance between work and home.

   Often   Sometimes   Seldom   Never

3. I seek to maintain a wide range of social contacts away from work.

   Often   Sometimes   Seldom   Never

4. I find time to exercise regularly.

   Often   Sometimes   Seldom   Never

5. I find work to be invigorating.

   Often   Sometimes   Seldom   Never

6. I take work home with me.

   Often   Sometimes   Seldom   Never

7. I listen to my body and mind and respond appropriately to signals related to stress.

   Often   Sometimes   Seldom   Never

8. I'm either fully involved in an activity or bored.

   Often   Sometimes   Seldom   Never

If you answered "Never" to one, five, six, and eight, and "Often" to two, three, four, and seven, you are one of the rare competent high achievers who has developed a sense of balance in life. If your answers were different, you have room for growth. Examine the following *prescriptions for growth* and adapt them to your circumstances:

℞: **Learn to achieve balance**. Balance is difficult to achieve in contemporary society. Yet, balance in life is a cornerstone to personal and professional competence. It is easy to get out of balance. Pressures exerted in work seductively destroy balance. Balance needs vigilance if it is to be maintained. Competent high achievers are vigilant to maintain balance in their lives. They are flexible and recognize there are days when balance is impossible. However, it is the direction toward balance that is important. They plan for balance with the same rigor that they plan for a new strategic initiative. They recognize that being out of balance hampers their creativity. Peter Senge, author of the best-seller *The Fifth Discipline,* claimed that the basic ideas for his book came during a period of meditation. The derailing person, on the other hand, has no concept of balance. This person sees little, if any, value in balance.

Action: Act now. Design a life of balance. Plan time for work. Discover ways to make your work fun. Rather than looking at the problems of work as crises, look at them as challenges. Plan time for reflection or prayer. Plan time to be present for the significant people in your life. Plan time to exercise. Plan time to read something other than work-related material. Moreover, plan time to enjoy a relaxing and nutritious meal. The basis for recovery from stress is to make sure that you are getting proper rest, nutrition, and exercise.

℞: **Be aware of the varying levels of stress in your life**. Stress accumulates in small increments. We take on increasing amounts of stress unknowingly. In this process, our bodies and minds adapt to increased levels of stress. The increased levels of stress are usually handled effectively over short periods. When stress is prolonged, it takes a physical and mental toll, resulting in frayed relationships, deteriorating health, and poor decisions. Competent high achievers are aware of their stress levels. They manage their stress levels in much the same way that they manage their organizations: they maintain a balance. Hans Seyle, the famed stress researcher, called this homeostasis. The derailing person has no concept of stress management and continues to plunge ahead, generating higher and higher levels of stress until a breakdown occurs.

Action: Identify all of the stressors in your life. Once you have identified these stressors, identify the stressors you cannot control and those you can control. Of the stressors that you can control, identify the conditions that you can change. Eliminate all unnecessary stressors from your life. Paula Medina, principal of Crowley High School, considers herself a workaholic. Although a workaholic, Paula rigorously tries to maintain balance in her life. When Paula feels she is under heavy stress, she makes a list of all the projects she has going. She prioritizes these projects. To qualify as a top priority project, a project must impact a large portion of the school, be a serious issue, and have long-term implications. If a project is not a top priority, she drops it. As she drops these projects, her stress level also drops.

℞: **Take control of your emotions**. It is impossible for the school administrator to operate in a pressureless environment. The school administrator's job is filled with pressure. In many ways, it is similar to the emergency room surgeon. There are periods of quiet, yet when a trauma victim is brought into the emergency room there is tension, pressure, and stress. A person's life is at stake. The surgeon does not react to the stimuli. Instead, the surgeon manages his emotions so that full focus is on saving the victim's life. The competent high achiever operates in much the same way. He is able to become detached from the emotions that swirl through a high-tension, pressure-filled environment. The derailing person allows his emotions to control his actions. He is buffeted by pressures on every side. His inability to detach from the emotional energy of the environment deteriorates his judgment.

FIGURE 5.2   **The Relaxation Response**

Step One: Choose a focusing word (This is a personal choice such as peace, love, shalom, etc.).

Step Two: Sit quietly in a relaxed position (home or office).

Step Three: Close your eyes.

Step Four: Focus on each muscle group and relax those muscles one at a time.

Step Five: Concentrate on breathing in a slow rhythm and repeating your focusing word.

Step Six: Stay relaxed, even if thoughts enter your mind, don't resist or criticize yourself. Acknowledge the thoughts and return to concentrating on your breathing.

Step Seven: Continue this practice for ten to twenty minutes.

Step Eight: Practice the relaxation response each day.

Action: One effective way to stay focused and to be removed from the pressures of the environment is to have a clear and steady mind. Dr. Herbert Benson suggests eliciting the relaxation response as a means of quieting the mind and becoming focused (see Figure 5.2).[22]

Adapting the Psychology of High Achievement

Competent high achievers have a formula for success.[23] Success isn't a matter of chance—it is planned. High achievers expect to succeed and apply the principles of success to their actions. These principles of success enhance their competence. Adapt this formula to your life and watch your level of competence rise along with your level of achievement.

Principle One: High achievers operate with a set of written goals. This principle was discussed earlier. Make it a part of your daily life.

Principle Two: High achievers distinguish themselves with their attitude. It is not a coincidence that high achievers are optimistic. This attitude brings a "can-do" sense of optimism to every task. This attitude is embedded in the roots of American culture. It carries a sense of invulnerability and invincibility in the face of multiple obstacles. This attitude also has a compassionate side and moves toward people so that all actions have a high degree of ecological benefit. These actions benefit the high achiever's entire environment.

Principle Three: Focus on differences. Examine the differences between the competent high achievers and the derailing people. Focus on moving all behaviors and actions to the left side of the ledger. You don't have to be a derailer. Make a conscious choice to become a high achiever.

Principle Four: Accept responsibility for yourself. Becoming a competent high achiever is not a birthright, nor is it bestowed externally. It is internally driven. It is acquired by people who accept full responsibility for their lives. They realize that the only thing they can control is their personal response to their environment. When this response follows the principles outlined in this chapter, these people consciously accept personal responsibility to competently contribute to their organizations. They do not blame, accuse, and attribute fault to anyone. They continually move forward in a positive, constructive manner.

Principle Five: Focus on the critical aspects of competence. The "80–20" or "Pareto" principle suggests that we should concentrate 80 percent of our energy on the 20 percent of tasks that make a difference.[24] This principle of focus is ingrained in all competent high achievers. They detach themselves from the distractions that take the attention of the derailing person. Determine which tasks, items, or people belong in the critical 20 percent and then apply the principle of focus.

Principle Six: Work hard and work smart. There is no substitute for hard work. Competent high achievers understand that hard work is a part of life. They embrace hard work. However, competent high achievers also work smart. They look for areas of synthesis, integration, and cooperation. They do not reinvent the wheel. They realize that others who have preceded them have provided a path to follow. They use this path as a starting point for their career journeys.

Principle Seven: Bridge Builders. Competent high achievers are bridge builders. They recognize that any success they achieve is the result of the assistance of countless numbers of people. They build bridges to people. They realize that some of these people will be unpleasant and try to derail them. However, they never burn a bridge. Rather than focus on burning bridges, they build new bridges, continuously expanding their networks.

COMPETENCE CHECK

Do you understand:

- ☐ The primary causes of derailment?
- ☐ The reversal strategies necessary to eliminate the potential for derailment?
- ☐ The differences between competent high achievers and derailing people?
- ☐ How to use time effectively?

☐ How to apply the prescriptions suggested in this chapter to your career?

☐ How to create powerful, constructive relationships?

☐ How to restore relationships to a constructive state?

☐ How to apply the notion of savvy to your work environment?

☐ The principles inherent in systems thinking?

☐ How to apply the principles of balance to your life?

☐ The relaxation principle?

☐ The formula for high achievement?

☐ How to put balance in your life?

Were you able to place a ✓ in each of the boxes in the competence check? This chapter can be a turning point for you. It provides you with a systematic process to identify potential derailing strategies. Once these derailing strategies are identified, you have a formula to reverse these limiting strategies and turn them into competent high achieving strengths. As you optimize your high achievement potential and limit any potential derailers, you benefit yourself and your organization. You are ready to act. The next chapter, on goal setting, provides you with the tools to take each of the competent high achiever characteristics and incorporate them into your personal and professional life.

NOTES

[1] Van Velsor, E., & J. Brittain. (1995). Why executives derail: perspectives across time and cultures. *Academy of Management Executive. 9* (4), (p. 63).

[2] Lombardo, M., & C. McCauley. (July, 1988). *The dynamics of management derailment.* Technical report Number 34. Greensboro, NC: The Center for Creative Leadership (p. 1).

[3] See Lombardo & McCauley (July, 1988), (p. 3).

[4] Ramos, J. (1994). Why executives derail. *Across the board. 31* (10), (p. 17).

[5] McAlister, J. (1992). Work habits that can derail your career. *Supervisory Management. 37* (9), (p. 7).

[6] Pollock, T. (1998). Crucial management skill: follow-up. *Supervision. 59* (6), (p. 24).

[7] See Calabrese, R., G. Short, & S. Zepeda. (1996). *Hands-on leadership tools for school administrators.* Larchmont, NY: Eye on Education, for a value identification process for school administrators.

[8] Pollock, T. (1998). Attitudes that can help you get ahead. *Supervision. 59* (6), (p. 24).

[9] Smith, H. (1994). 10 natural laws. *Executive Excellence. 11* (1), (p. 6).

[10] The chart applies the insights of Stephen Covey's *The seven habits of highly effective people.* Simon and Schuster: New York (1990).

[11] See John Powell's *Will the real me please stand up?* Valencia, CA: Tabor Publishing (1985), for practical guidelines to improve communication.

[12] Rogers, C. (1956). *On becoming a person.* Austin, TX: Hogg Foundation.

[13] Covey, Stephen. (1997). Seven habits of global executives. *Executive Excellence. 14* (12), (p. 3).

[14] See Warren Bennis's *On becoming a leader.* Reading, MA: Addison-Wesley (1989), for an excellent examination on the intuition/savvy side of the leader.

[15] See R. Calabrese, G. Short, & S. Zepeda's *Hands-on leadership tools for school administrators.* Larchmont, NY: Eye on Education (1995), for information on how to conduct a focus group in an educational setting.

[16] Berg, D. (1996). Keys to self-designed success. *Journal for Quality & Participation. 19* (2), (p. 81).

[17] See Joe Girard's (1981) *How to sell anything to anybody.* New York: Warner.

[18] Senge, P. (1990). *The fifth discipline.* New York: Doubleday (p. 12).

[19] See Jay Forrester & Peter Senge's "Tests for building confidence in system dynamics models." In A. A. Legasto Jr. (Ed.), *System dynamics: Studies in the management sciences* (pp. 209–228). New York: North-Holland.

[20] Dawes, R. (1988). *Rational choice in an uncertain world.* New York: Harcourt, Brace, Jovanovich.

[21] Loehr, J. (1993). *Toughness training for life.* New York: A Plume Book (p. 59).

[22] Adapted from H. Benson & E. Stuart's *The wellness book.* New York: Simon & Schuster (1992) (pp. 45–46).

[23] Adapted from R. Dobbins & B. Pettman. (1992). *The psychology of success, Equal Opportunities International, 11,* (1), (pp. 12–16).

[24] Van De Vliet, A. (1997). Beat the time bandits. *Management Today* (pp. 90–92).

Using Goal Setting for Professional Advantage

CHAPTER
SIX

In this chapter you will

- Understand how to use goal setting to increase your competence.
- Understand the inherent power of goal setting.
- Understand how to link goal setting to professional growth.
- Understand the benefits of goal setting.
- Understand how to apply the SMART process to goals.
- Understand the characteristics of effective goals.
- Understand how to link personal goals to organizational goals.
- Understand the importance of developing a personal mission statement.
- Understand how to apply time management skills to your goals.
- Understand how to write a goal-driven personal action plan.

GOAL SETTING: THE DRIVING FORCE BEHIND PROFESSIONAL SUCCESS

Goal setting is a liberating tool in professional growth and success. It empowers our achievement and ambition drives. Most successful people operate with a formal set of goals. "Extensive research shows consistent patterns in the work lives of so-called goal seekers. These people exhibit confidence; they are action-minded and expect to win. In fact, they habitually select activities where they have a chance of winning. They also have a tendency to make career, education, and work decisions without seeking help or advice. They feel a strong need to tackle tough goals and achieve them, not just well but with excellence. They set long and short range goals for themselves and plan their lives ahead. They don't describe themselves as lucky; instead, they believe they make their own luck."[1] They understand that goal setting creates the mental focus necessary to accomplish great tasks.

Without goal setting, our efforts are filled with a sense of ambiguity, lack direction, and have little coherence. We are torn apart by the swirling winds that surround us. The school administrator who does not use goal setting runs from one task to another but accomplishes little, whereas the school administrator who is goal focused understands how to put time and energy to the most productive use. The latter accomplishes much and her achievements are noteworthy. Attaining increased levels of competence requires an understanding and correct application of goal setting. Pierce indicates four reasons why we need to make systematic goal setting a major priority:

1. Goals keep us focused on what we want to accomplish.
2. Goals make our work exciting.
3. Goal completion adds to our self-esteem.
4. Goal-oriented people naturally model other successful people.[2]

There is a significant amount of research on the viability of goal setting. Yet, with all that we know about goal setting, few people follow through. Roughly 2 percent of people write and review goals daily. This small group of people is less prone to stress, has higher levels of concentration, exhibits high levels of confidence, consistently outperforms others who do not use goals effectively, and is more often pleased with performance.[3] Others look to these people for leadership. They make the difference in organizations and society. The difference in performance is not in intelligence. The difference in performance is in the willingness to use well-developed, psychologically proven tools. Goal setting is one tool that can be applied to your quest for competence.

Competent people unleash the power of goals to increase their competence. They are not satisfied with their present status. They recognize that to live is to grow and change. They use goals to set the direction and pace of growth and change. They use goals to take control of their personal and professional lives. They recognize that using goals constructively unleashes powerful psychological forces to accomplish positive ends. This creates personal and public benefit.

There are three types of power inherent in goals:

- **Focusing power**
- **Motivation power**
- **Satisfaction power**

Human beings innately have the capacity to employ each of the goal power attributes. Our human nature has an innate primal force that defines us as natural goal seekers. Understanding and harnessing this primal force allows us to use the power of goals for positive and constructive ends in personal, organizational, and communal contexts.

Focusing power. Goals provide us with *focusing power.* Focusing power allows us to place full concentration on a major priority. People without focusing power cannot concentrate. They find themselves confronted with competing priorities. These competing priorities constantly challenge for primacy. For example, John Hussins, principal of Oakwood High School, felt that increasing parental involvement in his school would be a benefit for teachers, students, and the community. John committed himself to increasing parent involvement. By November, John became bored with the project and turned his attention to an anti-drug program. By April, John became bored with the anti-drug program and began thinking about an anti-gang program. In the end, John lost credibility with his constituents because he was unable to stay focused and prevent other, often worthwhile, projects from scattering his focus. When we are unable to set and hold priorities, we shift focus to whatever commands our immediate attention.

Focusing power enables us to:

- **Prioritize competing goals.**
- **Focus attention on one major goal.**
- **Pay attention to the detail necessary to organize and achieve a major goal.**

Using focusing power harnesses our mental energy and uses it with maximum efficiency. This enhances our time management skills and gives us control over how we choose to use this resource.

Motivation power. Goals provide us with *motivation power.* Bob Pack of Design Benefit Plans says, "Motivation is what separates the winners from the also-rans."[4] Goals give us the impetus to act. They take our potential energy and translate it into kinetic energy. Goals are our catalyst for action. The more explicit and specific our goals, the greater their motivational power. Imagine the difference in these two goals: One person states that his goal is to succeed in life. Another person says that her goal is to be a highly competent, successful school administrator. Which goal is likely to be filled with motivation power? It is the goal that motivates the person toward a specific action.

Goals become sources of motivation power when they:

- **Act as a catalyst for action.**
- **Enhance self-esteem.**
- **Create a satisfaction–dissatisfaction dichotomy.**

Goals are motivational in that they serve as a catalyst for action. When competent people set realistic goals, their goals spur them into action. When we have great ideas, these ideas have only the potential for translation into action. They need a catalyst. It is much like having a fireplace full of wood on a cold winter's night without any matches. Something is needed to start the fire. A human being who has a goal to keep warm strikes a match and lights the kindling wood, the first step in the process of heating the home. The goal to keep warm served as the catalyst for action and transformed a potent, yet dormant fireplace into activity.

Goals enhance our motivation because motivation in psychologically healthy people is tied directly to positive self-esteem. Virginia Satir, the psychologist, says, "Self-esteem is the ability to value one's self and to treat oneself with dignity, love, and reality. . . . Integrity, honesty, responsibility, compassion, love, and competence—all flow easily from people whose self-esteem is high."[5] Whenever we accomplish a task, we have a rush of adrenaline. We increase our feelings of self-worth. We recognize that we are competent and capable of attaining a sought-after goal. When we increase our self-esteem through achieving realistic goals, we motivate ourselves to set new and higher goals. A self-fulfilling circle builds on each success. When we fail to attain a goal, a prior history of success frames the failure as only a temporary setback.

Satisfaction power. Goals serve as a motivational tool when they create a satisfaction–dissatisfaction dichotomy. The greater the dichotomy, the greater the motivation to achieve the goal. Satisfaction is tied to pleasure. Healthy, competent people move toward pleasure and avoid the dissatisfaction associated with pain. Tony Robbins, the motivational expert, says: "One thing is clear to me: human beings are not random creatures; everything we do, we do for a reason. We may not be aware of the reason consciously, but there is undoubtedly a single driving force behind all human behaviors. This force influences every facet of our lives, from our relationships and finances to our bodies and brains. What is the force that is controlling you even now and will continue to do so for the rest of your life? Pain and pleasure! Everything you and I do, we do either out of our need to avoid pain or our desire to gain pleasure."[6] When competent people set goals that are tied to gaining personal satisfaction and pleasure, they are more likely to attain these goals because the achievement of the goals provides a heartfelt source of pleasure.

Jane Hill, principal of Mill Valley High School, was asked by her superintendent to prepare a report on student achievement. Jane initially saw this as tedious work. She found countless, less important tasks to take its place. In essence, Jane avoided doing the task because it was painful. One day, in speaking with her mentor, she was counseled to frame ways to make this task pleasurable. Jane began to view the report as a way to communicate the high achievement levels of her students. She finished the report in twenty-four hours. Jane was able to move her reference point from dissatisfaction to satisfaction. Consequently, she was able to motivate herself to accomplish her task. The greater the potential satisfaction, the greater the motivation to accomplish the task.

Starting Point

Goal setting has a direct link to competence. Ironically, because the notion of goal setting is nearly universal, many people believe they know all there is to know about this process. In my experience in working with school administrators, teachers, parents, graduate students, and university colleagues, I find that most know about goals, but few understand the use of goals. Even fewer apply goals to their lives. "In 1953 researchers polled the graduating class of Yale University and found that 3% of the graduates practiced goal setting and had a set of clearly defined written goals. In 1973 researchers went back and visited the class of '53 and found that the 3% of the graduates who had clear and written goals had amassed a fortune worth more than the other 97% combined."[7]

Use the following survey to determine your readiness to include goal setting as part of your approach to becoming more competent.

READINESS FOR GOAL SETTING

1. I sometimes feel that I am running in place.	YES	NO
2. I feel that I have not reached my potential.	YES	NO
3. I want to improve the quality of my performance.	YES	NO
4. I would like to have more motivation over longer periods of time.	YES	NO
5. I want to contribute more to my organization.	YES	NO
6. I want to create a balance between my personal and professional life.	YES	NO
7. I want to link what I'm doing to my life purpose.	YES	NO
8. I want to gain control of my time.	YES	NO
9. I want to create a positive legacy in my work and family.	YES	NO
10. I jump from one task to another without completing either task.	YES	NO
11. I need direction in my life.	YES	NO

If you answered YES to seven or more statements, you are ready to make goal setting an important part of your life and allow it to drive your quest for greater professional competence. Goal setting will allow you to rid yourself of the feeling that you are running in place. It will allow you to set incremental steps so you can measure progress using small goals to accomplish a larger goal. As you attain these goals, your self-esteem will increase as you realize that you are using more and more of your potential. You will have a sense that you have control over your life and, in many ways, are the mastermind of your destiny.

Goal setting reduces meandering between two points and encourages us to use a more direct approach. When we use goals, we become more efficient. As we become more efficient, we become more competent. Competence does not expend unnecessary energy. Conversely, one of the primary ways of becoming more efficient is to become more competent. Roger Hilton, superintendent of schools, Hindsfall Independent School District, set a two-year goal of raising student achievement scores. Dr. Hilton set a series of small goals: understanding the basic components of student achievement, contacting and visiting high-performing districts, and organizing the district for success. Dr. Hilton used goal setting to make substantial academic changes in his district. His use of goals made him more focused. The more focused he became, the more efficient his efforts. Simultaneously, he integrated his current competence with newly acquired competencies in the areas of student achievement.

Using goals effectively makes us more competent because we focus on performance. Our performance directly affects our organization and the people within our organization. Each goal that we set also carries a sense of mutuality. That is, it promotes a sense of personal competence, achievement, and benefit for others affected by the goal. The members of the organization begin to model the behavior of the competent leader and assimilate goals into their daily work. Tom Peters said, "The single most effective way to get employees to enthusiastically embrace your goal-setting program is for you, the manager, to set and achieve challenging goals for yourself."[8] In this way, the user of goals becomes a model for others in the organization. They see the goal-driven, competent actions of their leader and begin to assume those same traits.

Goal setting, while unleashing one's personal potency, does much more. It enables the competent person to maintain a balance in life and to reduce the risk of burnout and other stress-related symptoms. In the same way that goals are used to efficiently lead to professional competence, they also lead to personal competence by enhancing relationships, contributing to the community, and finding ways to relax and renew one's life.

Those who discover and apply the potential in goal setting observe that they gain control over their time. They are no longer prisoners of the clock, but make time work for them. Competent people understand that each person has the same amount of time available, yet competence is often distinguished by how each person uses that amount of time. Hyrum Smith, CEO of Franklin Quest, tells us: "The trouble with time management instruction is that it focuses only on getting things done more efficiently. No one ever tells you to ask yourself, 'Why am I doing this?' or 'Should I really be doing this?' or, 'Do I want to do this?' And unless you are consistently making the opportunity to accomplish things that are important or meaningful to you, being better organized will only fill up your time and make you more frustrated."[9] One person drifts from one issue to another, spending too much time in one place and not enough time in another place. While another person, laserlike, goes directly to the critical issue, resolves the issue, and moves on in an effortless motion. There is a sense of grace in action that the goal-driven, competent person displays.

The goal-driven, competent person has other significant advantages over the person who does not use goals. The goal-driven, competent person is likely to leave a greater positive legacy that has wide-ranging impact. In the end, people want to believe that their lives have meaning. Victor Frankl states: "Our meaning of life differs from man to man, from day to day and from hour to hour. What matters, therefore, is not the meaning of life in general but the specific meaning of a person's life at a given moment. . . . Everyone has a specific vocation or mission in life to carry out a concrete assignment, which demands fulfillment. Therein he cannot be replaced, nor can his life be repeated"[10] It is the drive toward meaning that motivates us to become competent. Using goals effectively creates a personal sense of meaning, and allows the competent person to leave a constructive legacy that is value based and grounded in mutuality.

GOAL-SETTING TECHNIQUES AND APPLICATIONS

The constructive use of goals involves a process integrated with a focused approach. Goals are not randomly selected. They are not based on a to-do list. Goals serve a clear career and personal purpose. To liberate the power of goals, we need to follow a precise formula. This formula identifies seven stages to effective goal setting (see Figure 6.1):

> **Stage One: Goals are formulated.**
>
> **Stage Two: Goals are aligned.**
>
> **Stage Three: Goals are written and made public.**
>
> **Stage Four: Goals are committed to action.**
>
> **Stage Five: Performance is reviewed.**
>
> **Stage Six: Goals are adjusted.**
>
> **Stage Seven: Return to stage four.**

Stage One: Goals are formulated. Effective goals grow out of our value system. They visibly express our inner selves. José Blandina, principal of East Laredo Middle School, is driven by a set of values to contribute to the community where he was born and raised. José had numerous professional opportunities. However, José chose his current position because it is the barrio school he attended as a child. His goal to improve the education of the children at this school is driven by his value system. He has not forgotten his roots, and because of deep

FIGURE 6.1   Goal-setting Stages

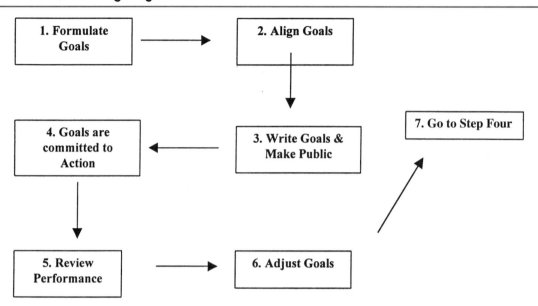

connections to his parents, family, and community, he chose to bring his leadership skills to this school. As he worked to transform this school, José formulated personal competence-driven goals aligned to the district's goals. José's competencies have to be adapted to the specific needs of this school. José identified high-priority areas: instruction, gangs, teacher development, and parent involvement. José was not satisfied with student achievement. Consequently, he formulated the following competence-driven goal:

> *I will identify successful instructional models aimed at Hispanic middle school students.*

The knowledge that José gains from pursing this goal will directly influence his teachers, students, and community. It is important that José's competence-driven goals provide personal, professional, and organizational benefit.

Stage Two: Goals are aligned. Effective competence-driven goals are aligned. Aligned goals unite different organizational levels. In this sense, superordinates view the subordinate's goals as supporting the organization's mission. Subordinates view their leader's goals as both inspiring and liberating. In essence, effectively aligned goals bring people together rather than serve as a source of division. Aligned goals share common values and are mutually beneficial. The competent professional takes responsibility for proper alignment of goals. When we align goals, we add to the synergy within the system. The competent person can direct a wide array of system resources to facilitate goal accomplishment. When goals are not aligned within the system, competition rather than cooperation develops. Different groups compete to achieve different ends. Members of these competing groups sabotage attempts by their perceived competitors in an effort to "win." In effect, when goals are not aligned, a zero-sum context is developed. A zero-sum context is an environment that only recognizes winning or losing or being wrong or right. The context does not promote competence. However, goal alignment promotes both competence and collaboration.

Goal alignment functions in a 360° pattern. It operates vertically in that the competent school administrator makes sure that personal goals are aligned with those of the district. It operates horizontally in that the competent school administrator makes sure that school goals are aligned with the hopes and desires of the surrounding community. It is aligned in an angular fashion in that the competent school administrator's goals are aligned with teachers' goals at each grade level and within each academic discipline. The greater the alignment of goals the more success the competent school administrator can expect.

Stage Three: Goals are written and made public. There is a big difference between an unexpressed goal and an expressed goal. The unexpressed goal, although well intentioned and signifying the deep desires of the person, lacks the three types of goal-driven power because the goal is not written or made public. Competent professionals express their goals in writing. "The human mind is a goal-seeking device. It wants to work toward giving you what you want, but first you must give it a clear picture of exactly what that is. Do not be hesitant to write down the description in great detail. . . . Not only is it beneficial to write down your goals, but you should keep them in a place where you can look at them often."[11] When the school administrator expresses his goals in writing, he can quickly refer to those goals during the day. The school administrator can more easily modify those goals.

In addition, the school administrator can refer to the written goals as a source of motivation. Even when goals are written, they lack their full potential if they are not publicly divulged. The more public the goal, the greater the personal commitment to see that the goal is achieved. The vast majority of change programs encourage participants to share their change goals with supportive people. When we publicly share our goals, we put our self-image on the line. Competent professionals realize that a competent person thrives under pressure and uses pressure as a source of motivation. They use their knowledge of 360° contacts to share their goals publicly. This public commitment keeps them focused on the primary task.

Stage Four: Goals are committed to action. Effective goals move from potency to action. The competent professional's desire to achieve a goal causes mental and physical action-steps to move toward the goal. Competent people realize that action matters. In moving from inertia to action, a series of psychological and physical processes takes place. The mind begins to separate distractions; adrenaline starts to flow into the blood stream. A single step, slowly taken, encourages further steps. During these initial steps, the competent professional continually adjusts to the environment through the reception of feedback. Adjusting to feedback provides an increase of confidence.

It does not matter what you do to start toward your goal. All that matters is that you start. Alexia Johnson provides a good example of moving toward action. She felt dissatisfied with her child's school. She felt that discipline and academic standards should be higher. At first, Alexia was overwhelmed at the thought of changing a school. She took the first step and set up a meeting at her home for the school administrator, teachers, two board members, and four other parents. This meeting led to the development of a task force to develop recommendations for improved discipline and higher academic standards. Alexia's children now attend a school that has become a model in her district. Commit the abstract to action as Alexia did and watch constructive changes occur.

Stage Five: Performance is reviewed. Competent professionals regularly review their performance. Through the cyclic review of performance, they determine how to adjust and adapt strategies to efficiently and effectively reach their goals. They know that all performance, if it is to improve, must be monitored. Otherwise, they risk practicing an incorrect technique to the point where it becomes an ingrained habit. The more ingrained the mental process, the more difficult it is change. Try this simple test. Are you right-handed or left-handed? Today, try eating with your nondominant hand. Try brushing your teeth with your nondominant hand. You can do it, but it will be difficult. You have had years of practice training your dominant hand to respond. It is difficult to change ingrained practices. However, in spite of the difficulty, we have the capability to change. If we are to change, we must continually be aware of our performance and have a willingness to substitute a new constructive behavior for the old regressive behavior.

When we monitor our performance, we coach ourselves in modifying unproductive strategies. We monitor our performance by seeking feedback from trusted colleagues and advisors. We also seek feedback from other sources who witness our efforts. Feedback can be *informal* or *formal*. Informal feedback includes the brief encounters that we may have in hallways, at lunch, or at a social gathering. Formal feedback focuses on specific needs assessments centered on goal outcomes. It identifies specific people who have the capacity to make critical, constructive judgments regarding our performance. Both types of feedback are essential. Warren Bennis, a strong advocate of feedback, says that executives can keep pace with the rapidly changing world by seeking feedback: "Arrange within your team, group, or family some form of 'reflective backtalk.' I learned this lesson when talking to one CEO who said: 'I talk to my spouse for reflective backtalk, and I use her as a mirror. She acts as a psychological safety net.' We all need to reflect on our experience, particularly negative experience, with someone we trust."[12]

Stage Six: Goals are adjusted. Once performance is reviewed and strategies altered, competent professionals examine their goals. They understand that goals must be flexible and adapt to the influence of new data. As progress is made toward the goal, the competent professional gains experience and knowledge. This new experience and knowledge leads to greater insights. These insights frequently result in a different or modified vision. As the vision is modified, the mission and goals also have to be modified.

Imagine that you are on vacation with your family. You and your family are planning to drive from Chicago to Cape Cod. The goal is clear. The route is clear. As you and your family begin your vacation, the weather bureau announces that a hurricane is forming and threatens the East Coast. As you move closer to your goal, the weather bureau warns that the hurricane will strike Cape Cod. The family stops for lunch, re-examines their vacation goals, and chooses to vacation in the Blue Ridge Mountains of Virginia, far away from the hurricane. It is the intent of the goal that is important. Vacationing at Cape Cod or vacationing in the Blue Ridge Mountains provides the same end. The competent professional continually demonstrates flexibility in the pursuit of goals. Flexibility is continually influenced by a stream of incoming information. If a new goal is adopted, then return to stage four and continue the process.

Creating Effective Goals

There is a method for creating effective goals. Using this method enables you to use the goal-setting process to maximize professional competence growth. Many goal-setting experts recommend the SMART approach to creating goals.[13] The SMART acronym is an easy way to evaluate each of the goals you set to make sure that the goal is effectively stated. Each goal must have all of the following SMART characteristics:

S = Specificity

M = Measurability

A = Attainability

R = Relevancy

T = Time dimension

Specificity. Goals need to be specific. Your competence-driven goals need to have a specific, identifiable skill, knowledge base, or object you want to acquire. Competent professionals understand the need for specificity. Specificity implies narrowness of focus. It encourages concentrated action. Notice the difference between the following two goals set by two different Anglo school administrators in a largely Latino community:

Specific goal: I will learn five Spanish greetings.

Nonspecific goal: I will learn to speak Spanish.

The nonspecific goal is laudable, but it is overwhelming. What does it mean to learn a new language? How long will it take? The well-intentioned school administrator will start strongly and slowly see his motivation ebb. The task is too formidable. However, the school administrator setting the specific goal knows exactly what he wants to accomplish. The rule of specificity requires us to focus precisely on what we want to accomplish. The more specific we are in our goal setting, the more likely we are to achieve that goal.

Measurability. Goals need to be measurable. When we make our goals measurable, we know whether or not we have attained them. Measurability significantly contributes to personal motivation in goal attainment. It requires a predetermined standard to inform us when we have attained our goal. Establishing measurability takes careful planning. It requires that the goal be stated in specific outcomes. Competency demands measurability. Notice the difference in the goals set by the following two school administrators:

> **Measurable goal**: I will observe five classes this week.

> **Nonmeasurable goal**: I will do classroom observations.

The nonmeasurable goal demonstrates the intention of the school administrator to do classroom observations. However, this school administrator has not set a measurable goal. What does the school administrator mean by "doing classroom observations"? It is subjective and therefore cannot be measured. On the other hand, the school administrator who set the measurable goal of observing five classes during the week will know by the end of the week how well he performed. He will know whether he met or exceeded the goal.

Attainability. The competent person sets attainable goals. The ability to identify attainable goals marks a significant difference between those who demonstrate competence and those who do not. The grasping for unattainable goals is a trait of underachievers. I regularly see this difference in university students. Underachievers, when assigned a paper, choose a topic beyond their grasp. They have a wonderful idea, but they do not have the knowledge of how to attain their goal. Competent students, conversely, identify a challenging and attainable target for the theme of their paper. A speaker on goal setting related an experiment in which researchers had subjects toss clothespins into buckets. The subjects were able to move the bucket as close or as far away as they desired. The researchers were able to identify three groups of subjects. One group moved the bucket to the other side of the room, as far away as possible. They were not able to toss the clothespins into the bucket accurately. Another group placed the bucket at their feet; they were able to drop every clothespin into the bucket. A third group moved the bucket just far enough away that it was attainable, yet the outcome was in doubt. In examining the achievement records of these subjects, researchers discovered that the third group had the highest record of achievement. They challenged themselves and yet made sure that their goal was attainable. Consider the difference in attainability of the goals of the following two school administrators:

Attainable goal: This week I will read one professional article a day related to school discipline.

Nonattainable goal: I will review the literature related to school discipline.

The school administrator who set the nonattainable goal has bitten off more than he can chew. The school administrator did not understand the depth and breadth of the material that exists related to school discipline. He may go to the university library and take out ten books. It is likely that these ten books will sit on his desk until the books are due at the library. The books will not be read. On the other hand, the school administrator who set the attainable goal is likely to effectively manage time and read a seven-page article related to school discipline. It is an attainable goal. It is a goal that can be achieved within one week.

Relevancy. Effective goals are relevant. They are applicable to the issues that the competent professional finds in the work environment. They make sense to the person who is making the goal. Relevant goals are the link to the goal maker's professional growth. Relevancy is a separator between competent professionals and those who are not yet competent. The competent professional intuitively understands the importance of establishing goals linked to context and environmental demands. This demonstrates a deep sense of efficiency. There is little, if any, extraneous movement. Work, learning, planning, and goal setting act harmoniously toward one common mission: to promote professional growth and competence and provide benefit to the competent professional's circle of influence. Consider the difference in relevancy of the goals of the following two school administrators:

Relevant goal: I will identify five effective alternatives to suspension models.

Irrelevant goal: I will contact community leaders to get their thoughts about education.

The school administrator who selected the irrelevant goal is not connecting the goal to an application at the school or in her professional growth plan. She is hoping that the right connections are made. On the other hand, the school administrator who set the relevant goal understands that the community demands effective alternatives to suspension. This school administrator will identify five effective models, increasing her knowledge base, expertise, and leadership. The competent school administrator maintains a weblike construction between the needs of the environment and her goals.

Time dimension. Effective goals are placed in a time dimension. Assigning a time frame to a goal serves two primary functions. One, it motivates the goal setter to complete the goal. The goal setter is constantly reminded of an impending deadline. As a result, it eliminates procrastination. Two, it aids in organization. The goal setter, by adding a time frame to goal attainment, allocates appropriate resources efficiently to acquire the goal. When goals are organized they complement rather than compete with each other. When we operate without goals or with ineffectively constructed goals, we often become victims of overload. Janis states: ". . . harassed decision makers, realizing that they are confronted with tasks too complicated to manage, suffer a further decline in cognitive functioning as a result of the anxiety generated by their awareness of the stressful situation."[14] If the goal setter creates too many goals that are moving forward simultaneously, a stress-filled environment that promotes failure is created. The goal setter has a choice and can structure goals so that his physical, emotional, and intellectual resources are equally applied to each goal. In this way the goal setter's resources are never depleted, they are consistently renewed. Consider the difference in applying the power of establishing time dimensions to goals of the following two school administrators:

> **Effective use of time dimensions**: I will conduct a focus group with parents of low-income students to discover their concerns regarding their children's achievement (Completion date: One week from today).

> **Ineffective use of time dimension**: I will conduct a focus group with parents.

The school administrator who used the time dimension ineffectively failed to set a time frame for completion of the goal. This school administrator is likely to procrastinate and fail to achieve this goal. The other school administrator understood the importance of the time dimension. This school administrator set a time limit of one week to accomplish this goal. It is likely that this school administrator will accomplish this goal. When a time dimension is used in goal setting, it reduces the risk of goal conflict. The former school administrator, when confronted with another challenge, will feel the pressure to move toward solution of the immediate issue rather than prioritizing issues. "The school administrator, once armed with the list of problems, needs to determine the priority of the problems. Many school administrators, especially those with less experience, have a tendency to solve problems in sequential order."[15]

Applying the Goal-Setting Process to Achieving Professional Competence

Effective goal setting unleashes potential and promotes competence. In order to make goal setting work for you, apply the following six steps:

Six Steps in Applying the Goal-Setting Process

1. Identify a personal mission.
2. Map the mission.
3. Identify priorities.

4. Apply the Pareto principle to professional and workplace competence needs.
5. Use time management skills.
6. Develop and implement personal action plans.

Identify a personal mission

Competent professionals have a strong sense of mission. Their sense of mission enables them to stay focused. One's mission is not a vague idea about the future. A compelling, clear, and specific mission provides the competent person with energy and direction. Having a mission provides a deep-rooted emotional lift that supports the surmounting of challenges. In this respect, identifying and completing a mission is crucial. To accept a mission means to act on faith in one's ability to conquer the unknown. Embracing a mission is a risk-taking adventure in which competence determines survival. Competent, mission-driven people are ". . . designed for struggle, for survival. Only fatal and final injuries neutralize that irrepressible striving toward the light . . . an older, deeply rooted, biologically and spiritually stubborn part of us continues to say yes to hoping, yes to striving, yes to life."[16] A personal mission has the following components:

- A mission provides a sense of calling.
- A mission is a journey.
- A mission is a unique assignment.

A mission provides a sense of calling. This sense of calling is internal and intuitive. It is almost a compulsion that one feels to do a certain task, take a certain job, or change direction in life. Once this inner voice is heard, there is no turning back from the mission. The mission becomes, in many ways, an obsession. It is the person's reason for being. People are called to all kinds of missions. Some women feel called to be computer programmers and others to be scientists. Some men are called to be psychologists and others to be school administrators. Identifying a personal mission is becoming aware of this internal call. The identification of this internal call releases the mission's power.

Angela Braden-Calzone spent twelve years as a middle school teacher in an affluent school district. One summer day Angela went to the city's poor West Side to buy fruit from a street vendor. As she drove through the streets, she felt a strong internal impulse to become a school administrator in a school on the West Side. This became her mission, and it made all the difference for Angela and the students in her school.

A mission is a journey. A mission is always a call away from the place we are at to a different place. This call can be internal when it is a personal sense of mission, or it can be an external call when a person is given a mission to complete. For example, a superintendent asks a principal to transfer from a highly effective school to a school with severe problems. The principal is "called" to "straighten out" the school. The principal is happy in his present setting. However, this principal welcomes the superintendent's mission and accepts the challenge. In essence, any embrace of a mission is a physical, psychological, intellectual, and spiritual movement toward a desired objective. It is a moving from one place to another.

A mission is a unique assignment. When a person accepts a mission, that mission becomes a unique assignment. It may be a personal mission or it may be a group mission. To the extent that others "buy into" the mission it becomes a group mission. Often, leaders take their mission and communicate it so effectively that the members of their organizations embrace the mission as their own. There are situations in which the leader and members have the same end in mind. Acquiring this end is the reason for the organization's existence. For example, all major league baseball teams want to win the World Series. Yet, the end is not the mission. It is the journey toward this end that is the mission. When the end is reached, the mission is completed. It is time for another mission. Jim Savon retired as superintendent of schools. The community deeply appreciated his efforts. Jim's replacement was a disaster and resigned seven months after taking the position. The school board asked Jim to come out of retirement until a new superintendent could be hired. Jim agreed and became the acting superintendent for four months. Jim had a new mission; he had to bring a sense of reconciliation to the district. There were hurt feelings, distrust, and anger. Jim was able to accomplish his mission by the time the next superintendent was hired.

Identify your personal mission

There are three facets to identifying a personal mission:

- Identifying values.
- Determining focus.
- Aligning tasks.

Identifying values. Unless we can identify our values, we are likely to go from one mission to another without feeling a deep sense of accomplishment. When personal values are directly linked to what we want to accomplish, we attach greater emotion to the mission. Therefore, our commitment is higher and our will to act greater. Follow the actions of Marcia Hanson, a school administrator, who went through this value discovery process.

Step One:

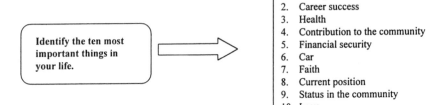

These ten values Marcia listed are those that she considers the most important to her personal happiness and professional satisfaction. The more Marcia integrates personal satisfaction the more competent she becomes. When we operate from a value base, we can operate in multiple spheres with little cognitive dissonance.

Step Two:

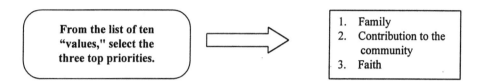

From the list of ten "values," select the three top priorities.

1. Family
2. Contribution to the community
3. Faith

Determining focus. It is an arduous process to choose among ten highly attractive alternatives. The difficulty lies in the desirability of each alternative. Yet, narrowing the list of alternatives to three is essential if Marcia is to be value centered. This winnowing process allows Marcia to identify the values that drive her life. It is important to be aware of your internal physical and emotional feelings. The following may help you in this process:

* Choose a value from your list.
* Take that value and place it against the other values on your list. Ask yourself which value is more important. Be aware of any emotional or physical feeling that you have as you make your choice.
* Repeat this process with each value until you identify the three most important values.

Awareness of these three values enables the school administrator to focus growth efforts and to align life tasks.

Aligning tasks. In Figure 6.2, the three primary values Marcia Hanson identified are surrounded by boundaries. The octagonal-shaped

FIGURE 6.2   Boundaries

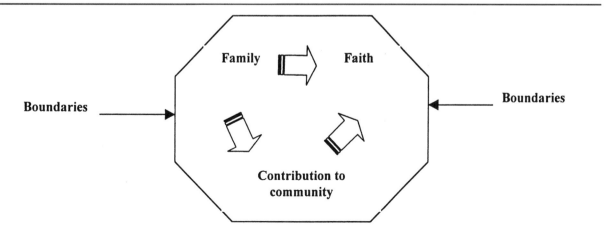

boundary represents the competent person's sense of identity. She is sure of herself. She knows what is important and what is not important. When confronted with competing options for her time, energy, and personal resources, she can reference these competing sources against her primary values. Any option that integrates the primary values is embraced. Any option that detracts from the primary values is discarded.

Marcia was asked by the president of the PTA to speak at the PTA's next meeting on Thursday evening. Marcia reviewed her schedule. She had a board meeting on Monday, a basketball game to supervise on Tuesday, and church on Wednesday. She politely declined and offered three other possibilities for potential speakers. She needed time to spend with her family and to rest. Marcia had a genuine offer from the PTA president. She weighed this against her primary values (see above values). Referencing her primary values made her decision much easier.

Identify your primary values before proceeding. Once you identify your three primary values, you can write your mission statement. Competent people have an explicit mission statement. The mission statement is flexible; it can and should change as you change. However, if sufficient reflective time is given to its development, it will be continually refined rather than radically changed.

Effective mission statements are:

- Precise.
- Focused.
- Explicitly or implicitly contain the person's primary values.

George Morrisey, a career consultant, says: "A statement of mission is probably the single most important strategic document you can have whether you are functioning in a Fortune 500 corporation, a small business, or as an individual professional. It provides clear guidance for all significant decisions. A mission statement describes the nature and concept of your business as well as your life. It also clarifies the conditions under which decisions will be made regarding your clients, products or services, and your fundamental philosophy, values, and principles."[17]

Mission statements do not waste time, energy, resources, or words. Mission statements reflect a sense of efficiency and precision. Each word conveys a sense of purpose. They are brief and to the point. The mission statement is focused. It is not obscured by a myriad of options or paths to follow. It provides a clear path, one that is well marked. The mission statement explicitly and implicitly conveys a set of values. These primary values fuel the mission statement and provide the competent person with a sense of ownership. And, as Nella Barkley, president of Crystal-Barkley Corporation states, a mission statement "is a broad and specific statement of direction that has the capacity to frame your activities for the rest of your life. . . . [It is] a rationale for both your personal and professional life."[18] A mission statement is critical to the person who desires to become increasingly competent. A personal road map is periodically consulted to make sure that all personal actions are coordinated to produce the desired result. Mission statements, like goals, need to be written and publicly expressed. Examine the following two mission statements:

> **Effective mission statement**: I will be a source of leadership, compassion, and integrity to my family, school, community, and church.

> **Ineffective mission statement**: My mission is to make my school a better place to learn by focusing on important instructional issues. Therefore, I will meet regularly with teachers, parents, and students to review instructional progress. The instructional progress of my school will be the best in the district. The school will be a model for other schools.

The school administrator who made the effective mission statement knows what he has to accomplish. He can ask himself if any action he took was driven by leadership, compassion, and integrity to the groups that he considers important. On the other hand, the school administrator who has the ineffective mission statement has lofty ideals, but expresses no values. The mission statement is not precise or focused. It is "politically correct" but will soon be forgotten by the school administrator and anyone else familiar with the statement.

Write your mission statement before proceeding:

_____

_____

_____

_____

_____

_____

You now have a personal mission statement. This personal mission statement will operate like a computer operating system. Although I am writing this chapter using word processing software, the operating system continues to operate in the background. It supports my efforts. In the same way, your mission statement supports all that you do. It is your operating system. It operates in the background. As it operates in the background, it sanctions highly public, time-limited missions that integrate with the features of the operating system. For example, the effective mission statement "I will be a source of leadership, compassion, and integrity to my family, school, community, and church," is the operating system for the following specific mission:

> *My immediate mission is to motivate the faculty to improve student performance on state achievement tests.*

This immediate mission statement is clear, there is no ambiguity. The school administrator knows precisely what to do. The competent professional functions with a continually operating mission that drives other, more visible, time-limited, and specific missions. The completion of each of these missions needs to be mapped.

Map the mission

Competent people know they need to consult a map before they take a journey. They begin by acknowledging their starting and ending points. This means they know their current location and their precise destination. They apply the goal-setting process to get from the starting point to the ending point. Each goal brings them closer to achieving their mission.

> **Starting point:** The composite school score on the previous year's state achievement test was the 51st percentile.

> **Specific mission:** My immediate mission is to motivate the faculty to improve student performance on the state achievement tests by two percentage points.

Establish the parameters for the mission. Each mission has a series of parameters that define the journey. If you are traveling from San Antonio, Texas, to Chicago, Illinois, during January, the potential weather defines the clothes that you will take for the journey. You will leave San Antonio, where the temperature is 60 degrees, and arrive in Chicago, where the temperature is –5 degrees. One parameter in this journey is the time of year that you are traveling, another is the length of stay in Chicago, and a third is the nature of your business. Each mission has essential parameters. Two essential parameters that are evident in nearly every mission include the time frame and the players involved in the mission.

- **The time frame**: The time frame can be rigid or flexible. External forces often dictate the degree of flexibility. Imagine that it is September and that the state achievement tests are in April. This time frame is seven months. The mission will be completed on the day students take the state achievement.
- **The players**: Each player brings specific strengths to the mission. Each player has a specific role with responsibility. The competent administrator understands the strengths and weaknesses of each player and uses these players effectively. The essential players in this mission are faculty, students, parents, and specific instructional leaders.

Identify priorities

Each mission has a series of priorities. For the trip from San Antonio to Chicago, the priorities may be clearing one's calendar, arranging travel tickets, lodging, and rental cars, or making professional contacts. Establishing priorities helps us to establish daily, weekly, monthly, and semester goals. The school administrator establishes the mission by communicating major priorities with faculty. Each major priority becomes an important goal. Each goal achieved becomes a step toward the achievement of the mission.

Planning is essential if these priorities are to be met. Competence requires planning. In planning for the mission, the competent school administrator anticipates events so that she is prepared for a wide array of contingencies. This means that the competent school administrator has a high degree of flexibility. Flexibility is more akin to adaptability than to wavering. The competent, flexible person knows where she is going. She has her sights focused on completing her mission. Events that are beyond her control require flexibility. Her ability to adapt to rapidly changing environments is a mark of her competence. Mary Samptor, principal of Johnson Elementary School, organized her school for a large-scale, outdoors environmental learning activity. Teachers planned this event for months. The day of the event the entire area was placed under a tornado watch. Mary quickly met with her teachers. They used the natural event that was unfolding to teach students about tornadoes, safety precautions, and so on. The day was a success because Mary and her staff were able to adapt to unpredictable events. Flexibility is directly related to competence.

Organizing the mission means setting goals in a sequential order so that each goal builds on the success of the previous goals. Imagine the construction of a new highway. It is impossible to construct a new highway (the mission) without a carefully constructed plan in which priorities are identified. The first priority may be the conceptualized design of the proposed highway. The second priority may be legislative support. The third priority may be acquiring the rights to the land to construct the highway. Each priority/goal is in sequence. Each priority/goal is part of the mapping of mission. To eliminate confusion over which priorities to choose, use the *Pareto principle.*

Apply the Pareto principle

Competent people use the Pareto principle consciously or unconsciously. Velury states: "In the world of problem solving, the Pareto principle is king. We all have experienced that 90 percent of the business comes from 10 percent of the customers, and that 80 percent of the complaints come from 20 percent of the customers."[19] The Pareto principle suggests that we should focus 80 percent of our energy on the 20 percent of activities that make a difference. If we can identify that 20 percent, we work effectively and efficiently. Competent people continuously refocus their energy to apply their work to those issues, items, people, and so on that make a difference, while those who want to be competent, but seem to make little progress, scatter their efforts over a wide array of issues. Figure 6.3 expresses how two different school administrators apply the Pareto principle.

Both school administrators desire to be competent. One school administrator spends the bulk of his time on activities that make a difference, activities that affect professional growth. The other school

FIGURE 6.3   Pareto Principle

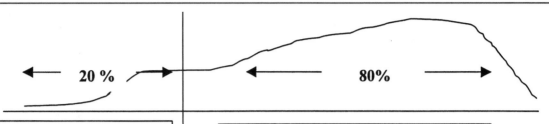

The Competent School Administrator:	The Ineffective school administrator:

The Competent School Administrator:

- Sets daily goals.
- Completes summary of week's activities for superintendent.
- Makes personal contact with essential faculty.
- Sets meeting with school board president.

The Ineffective school administrator:

- Opens mail.
- Searches the Internet for materials to help teachers.
- Develops needs assessments to send to teachers regarding back-to-school night.
- Makes contact with former professor to renew connection.

administrator, although well intentioned, drifts through the day without direction. Time is wasted on the Internet, paperwork is done that could be delegated, mail is opened and sorted, and tasks are completed that could be done by the secretary. This school administrator spends the bulk of his time concentrating on the 80 percent of activities that do not affect the school or professional growth. This administrator struggles to become competent because he lacks focus. He does not know how to manage his time to complete his mission.

Use time management skills

Time management skills are critical to the competent person's completion of mission. Hobbs defines time management as "the act of controlling events."[20] Time is purely democratic. Each person has the same amount of time each day. In that sense, all people on the earth are equal. How we use the time available to us helps to determine our competence. "The aim is to use more of our time rewardingly, doing the things which actually lead to results."[21] Covey, in *The Seven Habits of Highly Effective People*, presents a time management matrix.[22] He suggests we focus the majority of our efforts on tasks beneficial for others and ourselves. He calls these *Quadrant II tasks*. In essence, these are mission tasks:

- Prevention—contingency planning.
- Relationship building—vertical and horizontal.
- Recognizing and acting on new opportunities.
- Planning—mapping the mission.
- Recreation—personal renewal.

Covey suggests that effectiveness can be bolstered by focusing on Quadrant II tasks and integrating what he calls Quadrant I activities as part of an effective time management scheme. Quadrant I activities are compelling and meaningful. Quadrant I actions revolve around crises, pressing problems, and deadline-driven projects. Focusing on other activities robs us of the effective use of valuable time. Competent people frame the use of time around Quadrant II activities without neglecting those in Quadrant I.

Analyze your time management by using the *Time Management Analysis Matrix* that follows for three days. Be rigorous in maintaining this matrix. Analyze where you are spending your time. Focus on the critical 20 percent. Ask yourself if you are scattering your valuable assets. Once you determine how you use your time, you can regain control over your life by making decisions to use your time wisely. Remember that the application of your time has to be value driven. It is focused on accomplishing your mission. Make sure that each use of your time is value driven. Competence in many ways proportionally relates to the effective use of time and the relationship of each action to defined values. To the extent that we increase these proportions, we increase our competence.

Time Management Analysis Matrix

Activity	Time spent	Value driven	Describe short-term benefit	Describe long-term benefit	Check if no benefit
Met with parent returning daughter from suspension.	.75 hr	Yes	Student reinstated.	Mother is now cooperating with school.	
Surfed the Internet.	1.5 hrs.	No	None	Found two sites for further reference.	No real benefit.
Attended teacher team meeting.	1 hr.	Yes	Built relationships with teachers.	Gain confidence and trust.	

Develop and implement personal action plans

A personal action plan is the mechanism that liberates goal setting. Competent professionals use action plans to guide their professional lives. They understand that the best ideas remain impotent unless committed to action. Each mission the competent person undertakes needs an action plan. The action plan identifies:

- **The mission**: Identify the specific mission that you want to accomplish. Be specific as you describe your mission.
- **The goals**: List the long- and short-term goals needed to complete to your mission. Update your goals as you move closer to

your mission. The completion of each goal signifies a personal accomplishment and the need to establish a new goal. Do not rest on your achievement.

- **The time frame**: Place each goal within a time frame. The time frame identifies when you expect to complete the goal. Establishing a time frame keeps you on-task. Be flexible but be focused.
- **The resources**: Identify resources that you will need to accomplish your goals. These resources change as you modify your goals. Identify resources that facilitate movement toward the mission and goal achievement.
- **The strategies and tactics**: The strategies and tactics that you use are the specific planned actions that bring you closer to attaining your goals and completing your mission. Identify strategies and tactics that other people have used successfully in similar circumstances. Modify these strategies and tactics to fit your personality and work context.
- **The outcomes**: The outcomes are a source of personal motivation. List the benefits you expect to gain by completing the mission. The benefits you identify provide the personal leverage you need to succeed. Review your outcomes regularly to maintain a high level of motivation.

The following is an example of a professional action plan of a high school administrator whose mission was to earn a doctorate.

Action Plan

Mission	My specific competence mission is to begin doctoral studies.
Goals	
Long Term Goal 1	Completion of the doctorate.
Long Term Goal 2	Use dissertation to identify ways to increase student achievement.
Short Term Goal 1	Contact university for application forms/process.
Short Term Goal 2	Send in application and all related materials.
Short Term Goal 3	Register for and take GRE.
Time Frame	
Long Term Goal 1	This will be completed three years from the date of my acceptance.
Long Term Goal 2	This will be completed three years from the date of my acceptance.

Short Term Goal 1	This will be completed by the end of this week.
Short Term Goal 2	This will be completed by the end of this month.
Short Term Goal 3	Registration will be completed by the end of the week. The GRE will be taken at the earliest possible test date.
Strategies	
Strategy 1	Contact superintendent for recommendation and support.
Strategy 2	Make contact with former graduate advisor. Demonstrate interest in program.
Strategy 3	Make long-range career plans involving doctorate.
Strategy 4	Purchase GRE practice software—commit to 30 minutes practice per day.
Outcomes	
Outcome 1	Earned doctorate.
Outcome 2	Wider career mobility (e.g., superintendency or higher education).
Outcome 3	Publication from dissertation.
Outcome 4	Positively impact student achievement at my high school.
Outcome 5	Increase in salary.
Outcome 6	Increase in prestige.
Outcome 7	Earned respect from faculty and staff.

Action plans are flexible. Action plans do not control the maker. They serve as an awareness check for their designer. They are meant to be an aid, not a burden. The power of the action plan rests in its ability to keep the designer focused on the task. You can use action plans to increase competence by gaining specific skills and knowledge, attaining degrees and certification, and putting personal competence into action. They have unique organizing and focusing strengths. *Complete an action plan to increase your competence before proceeding.*

COMPETENCE CHECK

Have you:

☐ Identified your readiness for goal setting?

☐ Understood the seven stages to effective goal setting?

☐ Formulated your goals?

☐ Aligned your goals with those of your organization?

☐ Committed your goals to writing?

☐ Shared your goals with your supervisor and/or staff?

☐ Taken steps to implement your goals?

☐ Adjusted your goals?

☐ Applied the SMART process to your goals?

☐ Identified a personal and/or professional mission?

☐ Identified your personal primary values?

☐ Written your mission statement?

☐ Mapped your mission?

☐ Applied the Pareto principle to your mission?

☐ Analyzed your use of time?

☐ Committed yourself to using personal action plans to attain specific missions?

Were you able to place a ✓ in each of the boxes in the competence check? This chapter is critical in your quest to becoming more competent. Only 20 percent of professionals use goals. Moreover, only 10 percent of those who use goals actually commit them to writing. Using goals will make you more competent. However, goal setting alone will be an empty process if your goals are not driven by a value-based mission statement. Once you identify your personal mission, you can align your goals with your mission and produce personal and professional benefit for yourself and others. This process will increase your contribution to your school community and open professional doors for you. Competence is linked to the desire to succeed. It is linked to the desire to leave a beneficial legacy. Constructively using goal setting will unleash your inherent potential.

NOTES

[1] Hughes, C. (1965). Goal setting: Key to individual and organizational effectiveness. American Management Association (p. 39).

[2] Pierce, D. (1995). Setting effective goals and objectives in safety and health programs. *Occupational Hazards 57* (10), (p. 169).

[3] See Mind Tools, *gasou.edu/psychweb/mtsite/goalsett.html.* Cite Damon Burton (1983).

[4] Pack, B. (1995). Motivation: The fun part of management. *Managers Magazine. 70* (7), (p. 7).

[5] Satir, V. (1988). *The new peoplemaking.* Mountain View, CA: Science and Behavior Books (p. 22).

[6] Robbins, A. (1992). *Awaken the giant within.* New York: Fireside Books (p. 53).

[7] Tracy, B. (1998). *The power of written goals. www.gapmtn.com/goalsetting.html.*

[8] Peters, T. (1997). Setting goals for employees. *Incentive. 171* (5), (p. 61).

[9] Smith, H. (1994). 10 natural laws. *Executive Excellence. 11* (1), (p. 6).

[10] Frankl, V. (1984). *Man's search for meaning.* New York: Simon & Schuster (p. 113).

[11] Hopkins, T. (1994). *Low profile selling.* Scottsdale, AZ: Tom Hopkins Institute (pp. 201–202).

[12] Bennis, W. (1998). Speed and complexity. *Executive Excellence. 15* (6), (p. 3).

[13] See *classes.ag.uiuc.edu/FSHN350/self.html* as a source of the SMART technique.

[14] Janis, I. (1977). *Decision making.* New York: The Free Press (p. 17).

[15] Calabrese, R., G. Short, & S. Zepeda. (1996). *Hands-on leadership tools for school administrators.* Larchmont, NY: Eye on Education (p. 208).

[16] Gardner, J. (1970). *Recovery of confidence.* New York: W.W. Norton (p. 117).

[17] Morrisey, G. (1992). Creating your own career. *Executive Excellence. 9* (1), (p. 13).

[18] Nella Barkley quoted in Lancaster, H. (October 14, 1997). Managing your career. *Wall Street Journal.*

[19] Velury, J. (1997). Statistical thinking in problem solving. *IIE Solutions. 29* (10), (p. 31).

[20] Ladouceur, M. (1994). Four dimensions. *Executive Excellence. 11* (1), (p. 11).

[21] Van De Vliet, A. (1997). Beat the time bandits. *Management Today* (p. 91).

[22] Covey, S. (1990). *The seven habits of highly effective people.* New York: Simon & Schuster (p. 151).

The Formula for Success

In this chapter you will

- Understand how to transform competence into career success.
- Understand how to identify resources that will aid career growth.
- Understand how to build an image of competence.
- Understand how to nurture and sustain competence.
- Understand how to accelerate your career path.
- Understand how to create a network of professional support.
- Understand how to connect with appropriate career mentors.

THE FORMULA FOR CAREER SUCCESS

Throughout this book we have been talking about increasing your competence. Your increasing levels of competence add value to society when you translate your talents into action. Translating talent into action can be a difficult journey if no one has shared the road map with you. How often have you felt frustrated because people didn't recognize your ability? How often have you felt frustrated because you were not able to get your foot in the door? How often have you felt frustrated because your competence is assumed and not rewarded?

Most people experience frustration in landing the right position, one in which their skills are fully utilized. Often the frustration is compounded when we see others less talented, less competent, move rapidly into positions that we know are more suited to our capabilities. We may wonder how these people had doors opened for them. The fact is, they understand a crucial component of competency. They understand the formula for career success. In this chapter, you'll learn the formula for career success. Once you learn the formula, you can apply it to your career. You will be able to take your evolving competence to an environment in which it is applied and appreciated. Unlike the person who understands the formula and is not competent, you will be able to maintain your success. Competence and career-based strategies work together to provide personal and professional benefits that extend to the community.

Ingredient One: Optimism

Competent people are optimistic. They have a healthy sense of optimism expressed as a positive expectation for the future. Their sense of optimism does not deny reality, but embraces reality with an inner spirit of toughness. Competent people believe they have the resources to surmount any challenge. "Positive, optimistic thoughts give rise to good moods, and good moods foster positive thoughts, in a mutually supportive interplay that tends to make positive moods fairly stable. . . . Furthermore, an optimistic view of life events makes difficulties less stressful and less likely to produce illness."[1] We are not born optimistic or pessimistic. We develop these attitudes over the course of our lives. They are learned attitudes that we cultivate in our families, social networks, and life/school/work environments. In a very powerful way, they become the mental models we use to explain life. Good leaders know they have to communicate a sense of realistic optimism to their constituents. They know their constituents are constantly monitoring them for signs of hope or fear, confidence or anxiety. This same sense of optimism the competent leader expresses toward constituents emerges from an inner manifestation of a positive world view.

Optimistic leaders have a significantly different way of explaining events than those with pessimistic attitudes. This is called an *explanatory style*. According to Bloomfield and Cooper, an explanatory style is "the way you describe your difficult experiences to yourself and others."[2] Each of us has an explanatory style. Our explanatory style informs our anticipation of future events. How we anticipate the future determines, to a large degree, how we respond to turbulent episodes. These episodes are unpredictable. We have a choice of responding proactively or passively.

Josh Peters, principal of Greer High School, was meeting with his graduation team to make final preparations for the evening's graduation. He was called out of the office and informed that the senior class president committed suicide. Josh was shaken. He composed himself and immediately began to conceive of ways to respond compassionately to the family, begin the healing process at the school, and make graduation a healing and joy-filled celebration. Josh Peters demonstrated an optimistic attitude. When faced with a turbulent event, he responded constructively. He didn't allow the event to control his behavior. He felt the pain of this student's death. However, he knew that he could handle this situation. He recalled his past and knew that he had successfully faced crises. This would be no different. The difference between Josh and a pessimistic school administrator is clear. One anticipates his ability to handle the challenge; the other is unsure of the outcome of his actions. It is the optimistic attitude that breeds the mental toughness needed to reach the next level of success.

We can change our attitude, regardless of level, to a healthier, more optimistic level by incorporating some of the same strategies that world-class athletes use in their training programs. These strategies are also used to prepare leaders at every level. They are taught at leadership institutes for business executives. You can use these same strategies to your benefit:

Mental Toughness Strategies
- Have confidence in your abilities.
- You are what you read, speak, think, and eat.
- Use mental visualization.
- Trust your feelings.
- Maintain a tight focus.
- Use rest constructively.

Have confidence in your abilities. You know who you are and how far you have progressed in your career. You could not have come this far if you were not competent. It is because you are competent that you are reading this book. You desire to take your competence to a whole new level. The same skills that took you this far will be used by you to learn new skills, adapt to new contexts, and provide benefit to you and those who surround you. Take a moment and generate a list of every success that you have had in your life. Begin as early in your life as your memory allows. This is your confidence list. This is your optimist list.

You are what you read, speak, think, and eat. We've all heard the old computer cliché: "Garbage in, garbage out." This cliché applies to our quest for mental toughness and optimism. We can't be optimistic if we are filled with negative input. Negative input comes from the news, the naysayers that surround us, negative material that we read, media programs that deaden our senses, and the food that deprives our bodies of energy. When we practice optimism we think, speak, and act optimistically. This is not a denying of reality, but an embracing of reality. The pessimist says, "That's never been done before." The tough-minded optimist says, "This is going to be a tough challenge, but I'm game." We can use the rule of thumb that *actions inevitably follow attitude.* In the previous example, who do you think will most likely overcome the challenge, the pessimist or the optimist?

Use mental visualization. World-class athletes have refined the practice of visualization to an art. They use visualization to rehearse an event long before the event actually takes place. They see themselves, in their mind's eye, successfully completing each part of their future performance. It is as if they were actually participating. Researchers continuously demonstrate the efficacy of visualization. "A vivid mental picture is worth a thousand words. Images are much more powerful than words in stimulating emotion. . . . Your central nervous system can't tell the difference between something vividly imagined and something that actually happened."[3] You can use the same techniques to prepare yourself for career and professional success.

You can create visualizations to prepare you for any social or professional situation. Using imagery constructively will transform your career. Sports psychologists tell us: "Imagery is the process by which you can create, modify or strengthen pathways important to the coordination of your muscles, by training purely within your mind. Imagination is the driving force of imagery. Imagery rests on the important principle that you can exercise these parts of your brain with inputs from your imagination rather than from your senses: the parts of the brain that you train with imagery experience imagined and real inputs similarly, with the real inputs being merely more vividly experienced."[4] You can make imagery work for you. The key is to practice the visualization repeatedly until it becomes a part of you. If at any time during your visualization you feel that your mental image isn't exactly right, pause and correct it! This is your chance to get it right without penalty. Each time you practice your visualization it becomes easier. As it becomes easier, gradually increase the intensity of each of your senses. Add more and brighter colors to your image. Add sound, perhaps cheering and words of congratulations coming from many sources. Add the sensation of touch as you shake hands, feel your notes and your suit. Add the sense of smell, one that invigorates you in this scene. The more you bring each of your five senses to play in your visualization, the greater the emotional and lasting impact that the visualization has on your mind.

The following visualization "rehearses" you for an interview. You may want to have someone read the visualization to you or you may want to put it on tape.

Close your eyes and relax. Breathe deeply into your abdomen. Breathe deeply and slowly, drawing life-giving oxygen into your body. As you breathe deeply, begin to feel yourself gradually relax. As you breathe deeply, check each muscle group for possible tension. If you find a place of tension, recognize it and release it. Begin with your face and jaw, now move to your neck and shoulders—always releasing any tension that exists. Check your arms and hands. Relax your arms and loosen your fingers. Become aware of the muscles in your upper back and lower back and recognize and release any tension that is found in these areas. Move your attention to your hips and buttocks area, releasing tension. Concentrate your attention on your thighs, calves, and feet, recognizing and releasing any tension. You are now in a more relaxed state. You are now ready to begin your visualization. Imagine, in your mind's eye, that you are preparing for an interview for a new position, one with more responsibility, more opportunity to positively affect the lives of people. You see yourself in a waiting room eager to be called for your interview. Look at yourself, notice how professional you look in your clothes. They have never fit better. Your hair is perfect. Everything about your physical appearance expresses a strong sense of a confident person, a person filled with high personal self-esteem. You see yourself as relaxed and calm. You sit there breathing deeply, a peaceful look on your face. It is the look of a self-assured person. It is the look of a person who knows the depth and breadth of his capabilities. It is the look of a person who already knows the successful outcome.

In this scene a person enters and invites you to come into the interview room. You rise with energy and a wide smile on your face. You sense that this is the moment you have waited for. It is the moment you have prepared for all your life. It is your moment. Confidently, you move toward the room and enter. You quickly survey the room, noting the position of the chairs and table. You smile at each of the interviewers, and they can't help but return your smile. As you sit, you are aware of your posture. You are sitting straight, confidently, and with a sense of personal power. As the interview proceeds, it is as if you anticipated every question. You respond to question after question with confidence, knowledge, and ease. Often, you use the questions to explain in detail your approach to a situation, and as you do the members of the interviewing team smile, nod toward one another. It is as if they have been waiting for you. You are the answer to their hopes and aspirations for a leader to fill this important position.

As the interview concludes, you confidently move toward each member of the interviewing team. You look at them intently and shake their hands. They respond by telling you how grateful they are to have had you come for the interview. You know at that moment that you will be offered the position. You leave the room confidently, already thinking of what you will do in this position. Before you can leave the room, you are called back, and as you return the interviewing team is applauding you, each member is smiling, and the chairperson tells you that they will recommend you for hiring. You are clearly the best person for the job.

Visualization helps you condition your body and mind for success. The more competent you become at the process of visualization, the more powerful the tool. Take care as you practice visualization. Each of your images needs to be carefully chosen and constructed. Do not allow yourself to construct images that are detrimental to your emotional, physical, or professional well-being. Use your image construction to enhance each of those areas. The following components are essential to constructing an effective visualization:

- Imagine that you are at the place of your performance.
- Construct positive thoughts about what is taking place and the outcome.
- See yourself progressively becoming more relaxed.
- See yourself tightly focusing on the single objective that you want to attain.

- See yourself as master of your domain where you overcome obstacles.
- See yourself extending your emotional, physical, and cognitive capabilities to the limit.
- Identify that you have achieved your goal, sensing how your five senses respond to this achievement.

Trust your feelings. Optimistic and mentally tough people connect to their feelings. They have a well-cultivated intuitive side they use to make decisions. They don't make a decision, large or small, if it goes against their intuitive sense. Some people refer to this process as a "gut check." Our physical being is always interacting with our mental being, each informing the other. Even when our consciousness is unaware of this internal dialogue, it continues unabated throughout the day. When we access how we feel both physically and emotionally about an issue, we bring our subconscious mind closer to the surface. We can determine if the feelings are fear or anxiety. If they are fear, we don't have to succumb to the fear; we can question it and discover what is making us fearful. We can also sense when we are excited about an issue, or if we feel a sense of calm about an issue.

How many times have you experienced a sense of calm after making a decision? Each time that you did, your subconscious was telling you that you made the right decision. Becky Sandstrom, principal of Jaxson Elementary School, was asked by a neighboring district to apply to be the principal of their new middle school. Becky, at first, was thrilled; these people had heard of her reputation and wanted her as principal. After the initial thrill, Becky sensed a great deal of anxiety. She sought out her mentor at the university to discuss her anxiety. She realized that her anxiety was related to the prospect of change and not to her ability to do the job. Once she faced her fears, Becky had a deep sense of calm. She knew what she had to do. Becky applied for the position. She was subsequently hired as principal. She was as successful in this job as in her previous position.

The best way to access our true emotional and physical feelings is to become emotionally and physically quiet. Meditation, deep breathing, or a period of silence is helpful in this process. Once you quiet your mind and physical body, you become aware of the variety of emotions and physical feelings that you experience. Identify these feelings and question why you feel this way. Use this information to inform your professional and career decisions.

Maintain a tight focus. A tight focus enables us to rid ourselves of distractions and to focus on accomplishing our primary goals. Optimistic and mentally tough people are dedicated to personal mastery. Their sense of personal mastery allows them to identify what is indispensable and what can be discarded in their pursuit of professional and career goals. There is a sense of personal integration. A tight focus can be developed through practice. Jannot states: "Every day, practice focusing by gazing at the tip of the sweep second-hand of a clock, without allowing your internal voice to interrupt your concentration. The idea is to stop your mind and totally tune your eyes and ears to that one tiny thing. Do this for 15 seconds at first, then rest for 15 seconds."[5] This simple practice helps to develop a tight focus.

Use rest constructively. Optimism and mental toughness require constant nurturing. Rest is essential to maintain an optimistic attitude. All competent people have a sense of pacing to their activities. They know when it is time to exert themselves. They know when it is time to rest. They have adopted a rhythm in their lives. They apply this rhythm to all of their activities. This results in a high state of relaxed readiness. They are ready at any moment for exertion, yet, they refuse to expend energy foolishly. Rest is a critical part of physical, mental, and emotional recovery. James Loehr says, "Recovery is an important word and a vital concept. It means renewal of life and energy. Knowing how and when to recover may prove to be the most important skill in your life."[6]

Ingredient Two: Understanding What You Want to Create

All competent people begin with the end in mind. They have a clear picture or vision of the outcome of their efforts. Similarly, you need to have a clear picture of your career. Richard Koonce, career coach, says: "Have a mission. Do you have a mission in life? What do you feel passionate about? Are you able to harness this passion and use it to do your daily work? . . . Yet, having passion about your work is critical to career success and satisfaction."[7] What you feel passionate about becomes the focus of your work. In essence, if we are to be successful, we must find our heart in our work. Joseph Campbell said: "Follow your bliss. The heroic life is living the individual adventure. There is no security in following the call to adventure. Nothing is exciting if you know what the outcome is going to be. To refuse the call means stagnation. What you don't experience positively you will experience negatively. You enter the forest at the darkest point where there is no path. Where there is a way or path, it is someone else's path. You are not on your own path. If you follow someone else's way, you are not going to realize your potential."[8] Career success is tied directly to the meaning that our work provides. The more career meaning you discover, the more job satisfaction you will find. The more we feel job satisfaction, the greater our sense of career success. Our sense of job satisfaction and career success is often limited by myths. Be aware of these myths and transform them into new constructive myths to apply to your personal and professional life.

Myth 1: Belief of a limited work span. For a brief historical time, the work span of human beings was limited. It was seen as starting at sixteen and ending around sixty-five. This is no longer true. More people are finding work to be an important part of their lives. Considering breakthroughs in health care, nutrition, and physical activity, many people are physically, emotionally, and intellectually capable of work well into their nineties. We are capable of working throughout our entire adult lives. The key to extending work years is to discover what you really like to do and then to do it.

Myth 2: Belief of being destined to do a specific job. Competent people create their destinies. They recognize that mastery over one's destiny is determined more by inner control than by external control. Our limitations are generally self-imposed or inherited from well-intentioned others. Breaking this barrier is difficult, but it is done by thousands of people each year. We are responsible for our destiny. We can't blame circumstances. If we have the courage, we can take steps to create a new destiny.

Myth 3: Belief of needing the right experience for the job. Every person who wants to demonstrate competence at higher levels of responsibility faces this test. Competent people know that anyone experienced in a job at one time took that job without experience, and learned on the job. They know that it takes a leap of personal faith to cross the threshold of limited experience and try something new. They don't allow their lack of experience to intimidate them.

When we eliminate these myths we open a wide array of possibilities for our careers. We are no longer trapped into a step-by-step sequence that someone else identified as the path. We create our own path and timetable. Begin by imagining what you want to accomplish in your life. Visualize the contribution you desire to make to society. The position is the vehicle to making this contribution. Many vehicles can take you to your destination. Once you've identified your outcomes, then identify the various vehicles that contribute to those outcomes. Identify how to qualify for these positions and set a timetable for achieving your desired outcomes. At each step of the way, continually ask yourself, "What are the constructive, beneficial outcomes that I want to produce in this position that contribute to producing my life outcomes?" This will keep you on task.

Ingredient Three: Identification of Resources

We achieve professional and career success by closely integrating our lives with others. We have an interdependent society in which we support each other. There are valuable resources at our disposal if we know how to identify them. Once we identify these resources, we need to use them to our advantage. As we use this network of resources, we also contribute value to it. This network of resources will help you to get the positions in which you can use your competence for the benefit of society. It works synergistically. There is an unwritten principle that whatever assistance you receive you contribute to others who are also searching. This network of resources is simultaneously internal and external.

Internal resources

Emotional/psychological resources. Each of us has a personal emotional bank. This bank is a psychological reservoir that allows us to meet everyday challenges. When our bank is full and stable, we have a greater capacity to constructively channel our emotional energy. When our bank is unstable, we react inaccurately and inappropriately to external stimuli. Our emotional and psychological health has to be nurtured if we are to derive the greatest benefit. When we master our emotions, we strengthen our immune system, lessen the stress response, and make life's challenges work for us and not against us. Dr. Morton Orman suggests incorporating the following strategies into your lifestyle.[9] These strategies give you control over your emotions:

1. Accept change as a part of life and be prepared for it to affect you.
2. Do not be afraid to express your emotions in constructive ways. When you feel anger, sadness, or loss, express your emotions to others. The most effective way to express emotion is to use an "I" statement. "I feel angry." "I feel elated." In this way, we acknowledge the existence of the emotion and it is no longer in control.
3. Set realistic expectations for yourself and others. Learn to be kind to yourself. You will not save the world but you will make a difference if you are able to contribute your competence over a long period.
4. Stand firm against any form of emotional or physical abuse. You don't have to take it. Learn to express yourself assertively.
5. Create sacred time and space. Take time to recreate yourself. This is the place where you renew your spirit. You become invigorated for the challenges that lie ahead.
6. Connect with your social support family. This could be your family, significant other, or those emotionally close to you. You need each other. Together you can face life's challenges
7. Celebrate your successes. Life is stressful. It is wonderful when we overcome obstacles and succeed against all odds. Take time to celebrate your achievement with others who want you to succeed.

Financial resources. Financial resources are important to successfully pursue professional and career success. These resources allow us to go to school and earn essential degrees or credentials. They permit us to take time to renew, read, and reflect on our lives. Without adequate financial resources, our ability to translate our competence into meaningful professional and career success is limited. Often, adequate finances are linked to one's personal perspective. Right now, you have to decide on the importance of your career. Consider these three questions:

- Are you willing to invest in yourself and your future?
- How much are you willing to invest?
- If you had the opportunity to invest in a "surefire" stock with a guaranteed payback of 30 percent, would you invest?

Are you willing to invest in yourself and your future? You are your future! If you don't believe in yourself and your future, can you imagine anyone else being willing to invest in you and your competence? Investment requires sacrifice. Yet, the investment you make in yourself will be one of the most important investments you make in your life. Investing in your career means that you will invest in the right clothes to meet role expectations. I strongly recommend John Molloy's *New Dress for Success*.[10] Molloy, an international business consultant, has made a living helping people to be successful by dressing for success. Ellyn Bogdanoff says, "While dress does not guarantee success, it can assure failure. Your appearance can turn off your client and you may not even be aware of it."[11] Investing in yourself means that you purchase the proper tools to be successful. You need a quality "day planner." You need proper writing instruments. You need a computer with access to the Internet and appropriate software. You need to buy professional books for your home reference library. Investing in yourself means that you are willing to pay the extra tuition, workshop fees, and travel expenses for extended training if it is going to help your career development. Cutting back on fringe enjoyments in place of professional growth has the potential for large dividends.

How much are you willing to invest? Some people are willing to invest in themselves, but they set a limit on that investment. For example, they'll buy a suit of inferior quality rather than one of superior quality. They are unaware of the impression they create in the minds of their constituents by wearing an inferior suit. The old adage "You get what you pay for" is true in all aspects of our lives. If you choose something of inferior quality, you need to expect inferior performance. Similarly, there should be no reasonable limits on your willingness to invest in your career. Seek out the best and the best will come to you. Observing others teaches us of the validity of this statement. It takes a leap of personal faith in your future. It is a wonderful wager.

If you had the opportunity to invest in a "surefire" stock with a guaranteed payback of 30 percent, would you invest? Most people would borrow money to invest if they did not have the money on hand. Yet, the same people would not invest in themselves. Competent people realize that each time they invest in themselves they build the foundation for long-term, substantial payback. This expresses confidence in one's ability and hope in the future. It is the mark of a person who faces the future unafraid, unwavering, and full of confidence. This is the kind of person we want to include as a friend or colleague. Lisa Marshall is a good example of this behavior. Lisa sat at her desk and reflected on her career. She remembered how she and her husband sacrificed so that both could attend graduate school. The time, the stress, and the money were all problems. They survived. She remembered how they both took a cut in pay to move to a new location to take positions with much more promise. "What a journey," she thought. "Here I am superintendent of schools and my husband the Dean of the College of Education. The sacrifice was worth it."

Social support resources. Each of us needs a social support network. This network provides emotional and psychological support. The members of our social support network can be liberators or anchors. Anchors are people who are personally fearful and project their fears onto us. They sap our confidence. They find the dark side of every cloud. These are pessimistic people. Stay away from these people, if possible. They will not help your career. If you listen to them, you will adopt their fears, anxieties, and lack of motivation. On the other hand, there are liberators in our social support network. The liberators are people who give us permission to succeed. It is important to have people you respect, trust, and love give you permission to succeed. It is not that you need permission. You don't. They are giving psychological permission. Their permission tells you that they have faith in you to succeed. These liberators are also willing to show you the path and point you in the right direction. There are few of these people around. When you find one, listen to what she has to say. She is a trusted friend and an essential part of your social support network.

Time resources. Earlier we spoke about the democratic nature of time. Now we speak of time as a resource. Time is a resource if it is used and framed in a utilitarian way. Use the notion of time as a guide to plan your career. Time is a common currency through which we communicate to others. It is through this common currency that we chart our personal destinies. One thing is certain: time doesn't wait if we are not ready to act. If we are not ready at the right time, then an opportunity is forever lost. Hal Bodick sat on his front porch. Hal had retired two months earlier as principal of Howland Elementary School. Hal reflected on his life and wondered, what if he had taken that job as middle school principal when he was asked? What would have happened? He wondered, what if he had finished his doctoral studies when he was at the university? What would have happened? Hal continued to reflect, and then thought he might go to law school now that he had time. He looked up the telephone number and then thought, "I'll do it next year." Hal is a victim of "What if." That is part of his legacy. Competent people don't delay, they act. They use time as a valuable resource. They see their career paths as open-ended, with various transitions. Time is not limiting. It is a resource for planning and communicating.

Core resources. Core resources are our intangible strengths. These resources are not externally visible, yet they manifest themselves through our actions. When we hear someone say, "She is a strong woman," we don't think of the woman as a weight lifter. We think of her as displaying the capacity to overcome personal challenges. She is a woman who is unafraid of facing difficult situations. When we hear someone say, "He has integrity," we can't see his integrity. Yet, we know that the person is ethical, he keeps his word, and his actions match his words. His integrity is manifested through his actions. Competent people have internal resources that they count on when the going gets tough. These internal resources allow them to survive and dominate difficult times. Maslow identified these core resources and associated them with self-actualized people. He called these core resources *being values*. These being values represent the internal resources of competent people.

Being Values or Core Resources

Truth: Identified as honesty; reality; nakedness; simplicity; richness; essentiality; oughtness; beauty; pure; clean and unadulterated completeness.

Current Internal Resource: **YES**   **NO**

Goodness: Identified as rightness; desirability; oughtness, richness; wholeness; perfection; completion; uniqueness; honesty.

Current Internal Resource: **YES**   **NO**

Beauty: Identified as rightness; form; aliveness, simplicity; richness; wholeness; perfection; completion; uniqueness; honesty.

Current Internal Resource: **YES**   **NO**

Wholeness: Identified as unity integration; tendency to oneness; interconnectedness; simplicity; organization; structure; order, not dissociated; synergy; homonymous and integrative tendencies.

Current Internal Resource: **YES**   **NO**

Dichotomy: Identified as transcendence: acceptance, resolution, integration, or transcendence or dichotomies, polarities, opposites, contradictions, synergy i.e. transformation of oppositions into uniting antagonists into collaborating or mutually enhancing partners.

Current Internal Resource: **YES**   **NO**

Aliveness: Identified as process: not deadness; spontaneity; self-regulation; full functioning; changing and yet remaining the same; expressing self.

Current Internal Resource: **YES**   **NO**

Uniqueness: Identified as idiosyncrasy; individuality; noncomparability, novelty; suchness; nothing else like it.

Current Internal Resource: **YES**   **NO**

Perfection: Identified as nothing superfluous; nothing lacking; everything in its right place; unimprovable; just-rightness; just-so-ness, justice.

Current Internal Resource: **YES**   **NO**

Necessity: Identified as inevitability; it must be just that way; not changed in any slightest way; and it is good that it is that way.

Current Internal Resource: **YES**   **NO**

Completion: Identified as ending finality; justice; it's finished; no more missing or lacking; totality; fulfillment of destiny.

Current Internal Resource: **YES**   **NO**

Justice: Identified as fairness; oughtness; suitability; architectonic quality; necessity; inevitability.

Current Internal Resource: **YES**   **NO**

continued

Order: Lawfulness; rightness; nothing superfluous; perfectly arranged.   Current Internal Resource: **YES   NO**
Simplicity: Identified as honesty; nakedness; essentiality; abstract unmistakability; essential skeletal structure; the heart of the matter; bluntness; only that which is necessary; without ornament; nothing extra.   Current Internal Resource: **YES   NO**
Richness: Differentiation; complexity; intricacy; totality; nothing missing or hidden; all there, "nonimportance" everything is equally important; nothing is unimportant.   Current Internal Resource: **YES   NO**
Effortlessness: Ease; lack of strain, striving, or difficulty; grace; perfect and beautiful functioning.   Current Internal Resource: **YES   NO**
Playfulness: Fun; joy; amusement; gaiety; humor; exuberance; effortlessness.   Current Internal Resource: **YES   NO**
Self-sufficiency: Autonomy; independence; not needing anything or other than itself in order to be itself; self-determining; environment-transcendence; separateness; living by its own laws; identity.   Current Internal Resource: **YES   NO**

Examine Maslow's being values in this chart and identify those that are part of your internal resources. Identify ways to build this important resource by adding additional being values.[12]

External resources

External resources are comprised of people and information sources. Competent people assemble a wide array of external resources. They continually monitor these resources to fuel career success. The following are primary external resources to identify and cultivate. Remember that external resources come into existence only after we identify them and assimilate them into our career planning.

Mentors. A mentor is a person who takes a special interest in your professional growth. The mentor counsels, guides, coaches, provides access to previously hidden paths, discloses trade secrets, and opens up a vast network of potential relationships. The mentor's motive is unselfish. There is nothing in the mentoring process for the mentor, with the exception of the goodwill that mentoring generates. Kartje says, "Mentoring relationships are helping relationships usually focused on achievement. The primary dynamic of the mentoring relationship is the assistance and support provided to the protégé by the mentor."[13] In an ideal world, we can choose our mentors. However, it seldom works that way. Mentors choose those whom they want to mentor.

Joyce Carson, an assistant principal, desperately wanted to find a mentor. She cultivated her university professor, Dr. Mary Mason. Yet, Mary paid scant attention to Joyce. Joyce was upset and spoke to Dr. Mason. Dr. Mason told Joyce that she didn't have time for her. Joyce was crushed. She put her disappointment behind and focused on making her career work by herself. Six months later she reflected on how her superintendent had opened doors for her, given her training opportunities, and offered excellent advice. She had a mentor and didn't realize it until that moment. That is often how it is with mentors.

Even if the mentor desires to mentor, that person who is to be mentored has to desire it. In essence, a relationship is formed between the mentor and the person receiving the mentoring. The mentor offers, usually informally, the invitation to mentor. The person invited into the mentoring relationship looks at the invitation and decides whether to accept or to decline. Once this relationship is accepted, it operates most successfully when both parties are honest, forthright about their expectations, and communicate effectively. At best, it is a dance lesson in which the mentor teaches the protégé the steps to a new dance. The mentor realizes that the ultimate goal of any mentoring relationship is freedom from mentoring and ultimately surpassing the mentor in professional success.

The true mentor operates from a "no strings attached" position. Calabrese states: "The mentors I have known were all other-centered. Their view of life was inclusive and expansive. They seemed to transcend the tedium of the career choice that infects most of us. Mentoring is a core part of their lives because it identifies that which they feel is central to the meaning of their existence. It wasn't because I was anything or anyone special that they chose to help. It was simply because I was a human being who happened along their path and they chose to help."[14] Competent people continually cultivate mentors and serve as mentors. They know how to receive graciously and give without expecting a return. Identify people who are serving as your mentors. Determine how you can reinforce these relationships.

The following table represents the mentors that Jill Pearson, principal of Longmeadow Elementary school, identified. Create a similar chart for personal use.

Name of Mentor	*Position*	*Actions to Reinforce Relationship*
Joseph Peterson	Superintendent, Lake ISD	Invite to lunch weekly. Meet weekly in office to ask questions. Ask for books to read that are helpful.
Mary Snarski	Principal, Oliver High School	Call for advice regarding student state achievement test. Ask to review papers before submitting to university classes. Invite to lunch and dinner.

Friendship resources. Competent people create a wide web of professional friendships. They genuinely like people and like to be around people. Creating friendships is important for introverts as well as extroverts. If you have an *O* personality (see Chapter 3), then moving toward people may be difficult. This natural disposition does not have to limit you. Select people with whom you want to cultivate relationships. Use your natural sense of efficiency to limit your circle to those who add value to your career. If you are a *T* or an *A* personality, you like to be around people. Creating a network of friends is a natural extension of your personality. These friends serve as a personal support system and as information sources. They are the informal network that provides you with the details of a job, an upcoming but unannounced vacancy, and the potential challenges inherent in a position. Be careful how you select your friends. The kinds of friends who become resources have the following qualities:

- *They understand and communicate mutuality.* Mutuality implies a strong sense of giving to make a relationship work. When a spirit of mutuality exists, each person shares in the creative health of the relationship. It is a letting go of personal interests to understand and meet the needs of the other person in the relationship.
- *They understand and offer support.* Support in a friendship is social, emotional, and intellectual. Support is a form of camaraderie in which victories and defeats are shared. One is never alone at the top of the pinnacle or at the bottom of the hill. It provides a sense of security, a safety net.
- *They understand how to balance advice with patient listening.* It is difficult to refrain from offering advice, especially when a close friend is struggling. However, competent people, competent friends, understand the importance of being silently present and withholding advice until it is requested.
- *They understand commitment and its enduring sustainability.* True friendships are marked by sustainability. It is this sense of sustainability that causes the friendship to endure and survive the many challenges to its existence. Endurance is bred from commitment. Commitment generates sustainability.
- *They are inclusive in terms of the other's personality.* A friend is completely accepting of the other in the relationship. It is the sense of acceptance that allows the other to remove masks and present his true personality without guile. Honesty exists in this environment. Each knows the other with all of his faults.

Can you identify friends with these characteristics? If you can, you have an invaluable resource. This resource will contribute to your personal and professional growth. This resource will be the basis of support in your quest for greater competence.

Professional connection resources. Professional connections are an important resource. They are not necessarily friends. They are people who are acquainted with you as a professional. They recognize and appreciate your competence. It is because of your high level of competence that they have developed respect for you. Professional connections can be cultivated. Consider cultivating connections in the following venues:

- Within your school district.
- Within your state and national professional association.
- With faculty at the university.
- With administrators at the university.
- With members of your state education organization.
- With well-known consultants who provide services to your district.
- With state representatives and senators.
- With national organizations that have local groups such as Phi Delta Kappa.

Information resources. Information sources are important external resources. They provide you with information related to professional development, career opportunities, emerging paradigms in your field, and identification of people at the cutting edge in your profession. Adrian Peroli, principal of Haver Middle School, decided to seek a superintendent's position. She checked with the state school board, the university placement office, and the state department of education for possible openings. In addition, she used formal and informal networks to keep her apprised of events. Before Adrian applied, she carefully checked out each community through the World Wide Web and made several visits, informally interviewing people. She knew the issues, the community's values, and how her skills matched the community's needs. Adrian Peroli is now a superintendent of schools.

Information sources provide you with the tools to become increasingly competent. These sources have expanded in the last decade and continue to expand exponentially with the dramatic use of technology. At one time, the primary information resources were local newspapers and the public library. The Internet provides access to all types of data. The following web sites can be powerful sources of career and competence growth:

www.nassp.org: the National Association of Secondary School Principals.

www.ed.gov: the U.S. Department of Education. Besides being a source of excellent data, it also provides many excellent links.

www.aera.net: the American Educational Research Association. If you are interested in pursuing a career in higher education, become familiar with this organization.

www.chronicle.com: the Chronicle of Higher Education. The Chronicle of Higher Education provides listings of the majority of openings in higher education. Access to the job listings is free.

www.accesseric.org: ERIC is a primary source of information related to published materials in the education profession. This web site provides abstracts of most important education-related articles.

www.nwrel.org/national/regional-labs.html: regional educational laboratories. Each laboratory has a wealth of information related to the education profession as well as to professional growth. You can search all of the regional laboratories simultaneously by visiting *www.brown.lab.edu*.

www.edweek.org: Education Week provides you with a search capacity to reach their archives. Education Week is also a source of professional openings, especially those related to central office.

Ingredient Four: Writing a Plan of Action

You have assessed your primary internal and external resources. You know your strengths and weaknesses. Develop a plan of action to strengthen your internal and external resources. An effective plan of action looks like the following:

PLAN OF ACTION
JASON PETERMAN

External Resources

Strengths:

Mentors. I have two people who are serving as mentors: Dr. Maria Caberia, Chair of the Department of Educational Administration, City University; Dr. Mike Cadwell, Superintendent of Schools. Both have taken a personal interest in my career. I cultivate these relationships and have often sought their advice.

Information resources. I enjoy technology. I use the Internet regularly to discover information sites that drive my career. My use of the Internet is pointed. I do not waste time browsing. I have discovered four sites that identify vacancies in my professional field. In addition, I use the local university and city library career development centers. I feel I am on top of what is occurring in my profession.

Weaknesses:

Professional connections. I have two wonderful mentors, yet I have few, if any, professional connections. My excuse is that I don't have the time to "waste" making professional connections. I don't know anyone in my state organization, nor do I know my local representatives well enough to call them. It's time to start creating a web of professional connections.

Plan: I will identify the leaders in my state and regional school administrator's organization. I will make appointments to talk to them, to discover the issues they see as important to this region. Further, I will contact the state education agency and make appointments to talk to those in curriculum and testing divisions. I want my school to be on the cutting edge. These people will become a resource to me. Finally, I will join the local chapter of Phi Delta Kappa and begin to network with other members of this organization.

Friendships: It was hard for me to admit that I don't have many friends. In fact, I can't count more than three people that I consider friends. I am a self-reliant person. I've always figured that I've been strong enough to do it alone. I'm learning that this isn't the best way. I realize that I have to reach out and connect with others. I tend to be an introvert and a definite O-type personality.

Plan: I'm going to identify positive and productive people whom I can cultivate as friends. I will use the characteristics mentioned in this book to select my friends. I understand that mutuality is expected. I will be a friend to these people. I will start slowly, identifying one person per month and working to build a friendship with that person.

Internal Resources

Strengths:

Emotional/psychological. I am an emotionally strong person. I am not afraid to appropriately express my emotions. Expressing my emotions appropriately helps me to deal with stress in my life. I set realistic, yet stretching goals for myself. I know that life requires me to adapt or change, so I prepare myself for the changes that are part of life. Above all, I find time to exercise and rest each day. I don't know what I would do if I couldn't do my five miles each day.

Core resources. I have an inner strength that seems to be a natural part of me. I don't know where it comes from. It may be my faith commitment or it may be a part of my character, but it does exist. Last year, when four students were killed in a car accident, the school community was pleased with the compassionate way I responded to the students and parents. I overheard remarks speaking of my inner compassion, integrity, and strength.

Social support resources. I may not have many friends, but I do have strong social support. My spouse is supportive. I consider her my best friend. My parents have always been there for me and continue to be supportive. A long time ago they gave me the freedom I needed to pursue my personal goals. My social support group extends into my church. At church I have a sense of fellowship and feel that if I were in a crisis I would be able to count on the people to help me. In each of these areas, I can count on people to support me if necessary.

Weaknesses:

Financial resources. A close examination of my use of financial resources is embarrassing. I discovered that I don't invest in myself. In fact, I go "cheap" on myself. My professional clothes are satisfactory, but they don't pack the image that I want to project. My shoes—not wing tips—have holes in the soles and the heels are worn down. I don't have a quality planner. Moreover, I haven't taken a course since I finished my master's degree.

Plan: I am going to invest in myself. I know that "Rome was not built in a day," so I will start slowly and act consistently. My first investment is to buy the book *New Dress for Success.* Next, I am going to purchase a quality pair of professional-looking shoes. Each month I will invest in myself. By this time next year, I will acquire the tools of the trade. I will also dress in a way that is consistent with my goals and the professional image that I want to project.

Time resources: I could use time management skills. In many ways, my poor time management skills are linked to my unwillingness to invest in me. I haven't invested in an appropriate day planner. I didn't go to a time management seminar because of its cost. Many days I feel like I am running in place. I get a lot done, but I'm not sure if what I'm getting done is getting me closer to my desired job objective. There is always so much work to take home. My briefcase is always full of work, my desk overwhelming, and my to-do list crowded. I need to get control of my time.

Plan: I'm going to get control of my time. The first thing that I'm going to do is to re-read Covey's *Seven Habits of Highly Successful People.* Covey has a whole chapter devoted to time management. I remember reading, "If you're going to climb the ladder, make sure it is up against the right wall." I'm going to put my ladder up against the right wall. I'm going to invest in a good day planner and the time-management seminar that will tell me how to effectively use my day planner.

When you construct your plan of action, use the same format as Jason Peterman. Describe your strengths and weaknesses as he did. Develop a brief plan that specifies actions that you will take to address your weaknesses. Each week evaluate your progress to change your weaknesses into strengths.

Ingredient Five: Getting the Right Job

Step 1: The right frame
You've followed this book and worked through all of the assessments. You know your strengths and weaknesses. You know that competent people somehow find the right job. They find the job that fits their level and type of competence and one in which they can express their passion. The job and the person seem to attract each other. What do they know that you don't? They know how to open the door so that they present the most important product they have to those who are interested in that product. You are the important product to be presented. You are now focusing on a unique type of competence. It is personal marketing com-

petence. In contemporary American society, highly skilled individuals must understand and apply personal marketing competence if they are to have an opportunity to apply their professional competence. Personal marketing competence is often the separator between professionally competent people who get the right job and those who become frustrated and remain in the same position. It begins with the right mental frame.

Competent career climbers apply the right mental frame to seeking career opportunities. Because they apply the right mental frame, they know that they are able to move ahead of 80 percent of the population. They apply the Pareto principle by focusing 80 percent of their energy on the 20 percent of opportunities in which they will be most successful. Are you a competent career climber or a place-bound person? Analyze the differences between the two. Notice how people in each category below frame their careers.

The Right Frame

Competent Career Climbers	Place-Bound Persons
Goal focused.	Does not apply goals to career.
Applies the principle of career awareness.	Operates on the principle of arrival.
Views the hiring process as a relationship activity.	Views the hiring process as trying to prove competence.
Views the interview as an opportunity to help.	Views the interview as a personal contest with interviewers.
Not place or career bound.	Bound by place, career, and other inhibiting factors.

The competent career climber is goal focused. This is an important distinction. You have to know where you are going if you ever want to arrive at your destination. A person who has a career goal to be superintendent of schools has to start as a teacher. Having the goal of being a superintendent of schools gives this person the opportunity to shape the experiences that build toward achieving a superintendent of schools position. Each experience and assignment adds to the qualifications that she takes to the application process as she nears her goal. Those who are not goal focused hope that opportunity will strike. They wait and wait, usually to no avail.

The competent career climber applies the principle of career awareness. This person never arrives. He understands that he must demonstrate competence in his new position. All the while he is demonstrating competence, he has one eye on the next position. He is trying to understand what it takes to succeed in that position. With the other eye, he is making sure that he is successful in his current role. He knows that the easiest way to sabotage a career is to appear to be too ambitious. He also knows that any demonstration of lack of competence automatically stalls career growth. Consequently, he works hard and smart. He works hard because he knows that hard work always pays off. He works smart by focusing on projects that provide high visibility for his organization and the people in it. If his people are productive, successful and happy, he receives the greatest benefit.

The competent career climber views the hiring process as a relationship activity. The competent career climber understands that the hiring process is a relationship activity. She knows that she would not be called into an interview if the hiring team did not believe she was competent. She understands that the subconscious motivation is to answer two key questions: One, can this person really solve our problems? And two, will this person "fit" into our culture? Fit is the most important of the two factors. When the hiring group feels that it is a good "fit," they are ready to ask the person being interviewed to enter a long-range relationship. Those who, in the hiring process, best assure the hiring team that they answer these two questions are usually hired.

The competent career climber views the interview as an opportunity to help. One of the most effective ways to approach the hiring process is to consider it an opportunity to share knowledge. Competent people do this all the time. They seek every opportunity to help other people by sharing their vast storehouse of knowledge. The hiring process is no different. When you frame the hiring process as an opportunity to share your knowledge and to help the hiring organization, you take all of the pressure off yourself. If you get the job, fine. If you don't get the job, you leave knowing that you have helped the organization. The positive and constructive approach to career success is to always give more than you receive.

The competent career climber has no limits to mobility. The competent person realizes that opportunities don't grow on trees. He has to prospect for opportunities. When and where he finds an opportunity, he accepts the challenge and acts. He understands that all the fears associated with mobility are myths. He has seen through personal experience that children adjust and are usually better off because of a move, that it is not difficult to sell a home and purchase a new home, that they can remain close to loved ones and friends. He also realizes that he has one life to live. This life has a sense of destiny. He chooses to follow his destiny wherever it takes him.

Step 2: The right resume

Myth: *A great resume is no more than two pages long.*

Many competent people never get to express their competence because they don't get the position that is best suited to their level of competence. Instead, they become frustrated. One essential reason for their failure to get the right position is that they are never considered for hiring regardless of their competence. The lack of consideration is due usually to the quality of their resume and application package. *The one crucial mistake that most education job seekers make is to succumb to the myth of the brief resume.* The concise resume is effective in the private sector. However, the culture of the private sector and the culture of the public sector, especially educational organizations, are quite different. The reality of the education/social service cultures is that the larger the resume, the greater the opportunity for being asked to interview. The resume, in the educational context, is not a concise communication about your employment history. Rather, it is an extended narrative that demonstrates your competence through a thorough description of your professional career. The following guidelines take you through each component that belongs on your resume. Use the examples as models.

THE RESUME

Caution: Everything on your resume must be accurate. Act ethically and with integrity. People are fired for misrepresenting themselves on their resumes.

Do not put "resume" or "curriculum vitae" on the top of your resume. Everyone knows what you are submitting. The first entry is your name and address. This is usually placed on the left side of your paper. Opposite on the right side of the paper list your home and office telephone numbers. If you have an email address, it is appropriate to put it in this place.

Dr. Larry Smith	Office Phone: 210–555–1234
9432 Songbird Lane	Home Phone: 210–555–4321
San Antonio, TX 78444	email: lsmith@inter-net.com

Do not list a job objective. This is unnecessary information for those who are reviewing your resume. When you list a job objective on your resume, you limit yourself. It may not exactly match the job specifications. However, you may have qualities that the hiring team thinks are appropriate for the school district. A specific job objective such as "To become a high school administrator" may cause the team to file your application rather than contact you and ask if they can include your materials for the newly opened middle school position.

Education. *In this area, list your college or university degrees in chronological order. Use this category to inform people that you have the required training and certification to be successful at the advertised position. You also inform them that you have met state certification requirements.*

Education

Ed.D. The University of Massachusetts at Amherst, Amherst, Massachusetts, May 1991.

> Area of concentration: Instructional Leadership
> Massachusetts state certification as a K-12 school administrator and superintendent of schools.

M.Ed. Eastern Illinois University, Charleston, Illinois, May 1988.

> Area of concentration: Counseling and psychology
> Illinois State certification in counseling.

BA The University of Kentucky, Lexington, Kentucky, May 1979.

> Area of concentration: Secondary education, social studies, and mathematics.
> Kentucky State certification as a secondary school teacher of social studies and mathematics.

If you are currently pursuing a degree and have not yet officially completed the requirements for the degree, you can put the following entry on your resume:

M.Ed. The University of Texas at San Antonio, San Antonio, Texas, anticipated (month and year).

Do not list a degree from high school or any other non-higher educational institution in this category.

Work Experience. *List your work history in chronological order. Do not describe the position unless it had unique responsibilities. If you feel that it is important to describe your responsibilities add a "See Appendix A" and place "Appendix A" at the end of your resume. This is appropriate. Do not add insignificant positions such as waiter or waitressing, groundskeeper, bartender. These will not contribute to your resume.*

Work Experience

Principal, Jackson Hole High School, Jackson Hole, Wyoming. 1994–present.

Assistant principal, Lake Wilson Middle School, Lake Wilson, Wyoming, 1990–1994

Teacher, Tenth-grade U.S. history, Billings High School, Billings, Montana, 1984–1990.

Teacher, Ninth-grade world history, Billings Middle School, Billings, Montana, 1979–1984.

Related Experience. *This area demonstrates that your leadership ability and competence extend beyond the school environment. It helps to show that you are a dynamic person, one who is interested in the welfare of the community. These entries communicate that you are energetic, active, and concerned. Many people reading your resume will relate to one or more of these areas.*

Related Experience

Coordinator, Sunday School, First Baptist Church, Ames, Iowa, 1990–present.

Troop Leader, Boy Scouts of America, Palatine, Illinois, 1992–present.

Coach, Little League, Austin, Texas, 1980–1988.

Coordinator, Red Cross Blood Drive, Lafayette, Louisiana, May 1986.

Workshops: Presentations and attendance. *Educators attend workshops. It is part of the natural staff development process that exists in every school district. In this area, list all the meaningful workshops you attended as a participant or presenter. This area allows you to demonstrate that you seriously take your professional obligation to grow professionally or assist others to grow professionally. Do not include workshop attendance where there was no direct relationship to school or personal improvement. For example, you would include a workshop that taught classroom management techniques. You would not include a workshop that taught retirement planning.*

Workshops: Presentations and attendance

Presenter, "Six steps to more effective lesson plans." Region XI Educational Service Center, Alpine, Colorado, October 1993.

Participant, "Essential characteristics of good classroom management." Oakwood Independent School District, Oakwood, Minnesota, December 1996.

Committees. *Every educator understands that educational institutions do not function without committees. It is an important cultural part of your profession. Your membership on committees as a participant or as a chair is important. It shows others that you are a team player and can work effectively with other people. The committee's purpose is important. Membership on which of the following two committees is more impressive: chair of the school discipline task force committee or chair of the back-to-school night committee? Obviously, being chair of the school discipline task force committee is more important. It demonstrates leadership. Make your committee membership work for you. In each of the following entries you are either a member, chair, or cochair. Begin each entry with the correct designation of your participation.*

Committees

Member, Easton Middle School Instructional Objectives Committee, North Easton, Massachusetts, 1998–present.

Chair, Burnell Elementary School Committee on Effective Teaching Strategies, Bridgewater, Massachusetts, 1994–1995.

Innovative Programs. *This is a unique category that is virtually nonexistent on resumes. It is a category that will help to separate you from the competition for your desired position. In this category list all of the innovative programs that you have initiated. As a classroom teacher, certainly you prepared classes* *that were exceptional. These classes required intense preparation on your part. As a school administrator, you have designed and led the implementation of unique programs that made a difference for your school. Briefly describe your program in your resume and then reference it to the appendix, where you describe the innovative program in detail. Do not exceed a page when describing the program in the appendix.*

Innovative Programs

Established a community arts museum. A community arts museum was set up in Granby High School, Granby, Massachusetts, to take advantage of space from declining enrollments (see Appendix A). 1990.

Designer of the English Literary Fair, St. Joseph High School, Decatur, Missouri. All tenth-grade students were required to participate in the oral presentation of original literary works (see Appendix B). 1993.

Produced the play production of *Stone Soup*. Fourth-grade students wrote, directed, and produced a play based on the text, "Stone Soup." Wharton Elementary School, Wichita, Kansas, 1988.

Publications. *In general, educators consider this category for those in academe. It is true that those in academe are concerned with publishing. However, educators outside of academe also publish. You publish newsletters to parents, teachers, and association members. You publish curriculum guides, handbooks, and study guides. There is a wide array of potential publishing opportunities in traditional school settings. Each time you were part of a publishing team you need to record it on your resume. If you were the sole author, list only your name. If you were one of several coauthors, cite the entry as being coauthored.*

Publications

(Your name), First Grade Curriculum Guide, Mt. Pleasant School District, Mt. Pleasant, South Carolina, 1997.

(Your name), Parent Responsibility Guidelines, Las Vegas High School–East, Las Vegas Independent School District, Las Vegas, Nevada, 1996.

(Your name), coauthor, Creating smoother teacher and student relationships, *Marking Time* (School newsletter to parents), Johnson High School, Johnson City, Texas, 1995.

Honors. *Use this category to report any honors that you received in your academic or professional career. Record any honors that you may have received from civic or other social organizations within your community. This category creates an aura of prestige. Not every person has been a "teacher of the month." Not every person has received a plaque from the American Lung Association for saving the life of a choking victim. List these honors.*

Honors

President-elect, state committee for the National Association of School Principals, 1998.

Dean's list, Bellarmine College, Louisville, Kentucky, six semesters (1986–1989).

American Lung Association Award, received for saving the life of a choking victim (March 1988).

Teacher of the Month, Newton Elementary School, Newton, Oklahoma, April 1988.

Training. *Use this category to list specific training that you received related to your profession. Training is different from attending a workshop. A workshop is generally a one-day activity. Training is long term, lasting at least three days and longer. At the completion of the training period, a certificate is awarded to those who successfully complete the training.*

Training

Computer Specialist. Trained as the computer specialist to act as liaison to classroom teachers. Training took place at the IBM intensive training school, South Bend, Indiana, May 3, 1998 to May 10, 1998. Certificate received for successful completion.

Group facilitator. Trained to lead groups of young unmarried, pregnant women. Training presented by Any Woman Can, Dallas, Texas, November 4, 1997 to November 11, 1997.

Professional Memberships. *Use this category to list all of your professional memberships. These are active memberships. Do not list memberships that have lapsed. If you belong to a union or other similar organization, ask yourself if membership hinders or helps your chances of landing the position you desire. Professional memberships inform people that you are active and receive continuous updates as to what is important to your profession. Having professional memberships is an important investment in your career.*

Professional Memberships

Member, National Association of Secondary School Principals, 1990–present.

Member, American Educational Research Association, 1994–present.

Member, Phi Delta Kappa, 1993–present.

Community Activities. *This category allows you to demonstrate your active involvement in the community. It shows that you are not one-dimensional. It proves that you care about the quality of life in your community. A caution: Do not list membership in organizations that may raise political issues. You have a right to belong to these organizations. However, not everyone may share the views of these organizations. For example, if you belong to the National Association for Radical Reform, conservative members of the hiring* *committee may view you as far removed from the mainstream. Be prudent when adding organizations to your list.*

Community Activities

Member, Lincoln Interfaith Committee, Lincoln, Nebraska, 1994–present.
Member, Babe Ruth League Board of Trustees, Spring Grove, Oregon, 1995–present.
Participant, Walk for Children, Birmingham, Alabama, 1994.
Cochair, Habitat for Humanity, Key West, Florida, 1995–1998.

References. *This is an important political category. I recommend that you do not list any references, but instead place the following phrase in your resume: "References, both professional and personal, will be supplied on request." You do not want people to randomly call your references unless you are a serious candidate. You may also believe that it is prudent to maintain a low profile in your job search until you are a finalist for a position. There are times when references are required. Speak to your potential references. Ask for assurances that you will receive an excellent recommendation before listing their names. Make sure you have the correct title, address, business telephone number, and email address (if available).*

Step 3: The right package

Competent people set themselves apart from the crowd. Typically, in any review of job applications, one finds that 80 percent of the application materials are not put together in a coherent, marketable format. Instead, they are stuffed in a large envelope and sent to the prospective employer. Twenty percent of the applicants take the time to send a complete package put together with care and precision. Inevitably, interviewees are selected from this 20 percent. The difference between a competent application package and one that lacks complete competence is that the competent person understands the application process and develops an application package with the same care a major industry takes in preparing a brochure on its newest products. The application package that you develop is an opportunity to market your competence to your prospective employer.

Myth: *Allow your university placement service to handle your materials.*

Competent people understand that a student worker in a university placement office does not have an emotional investment in their success. The competent person recognizes that what is sent out to a prospective employer is a signature statement. This signature statement is the initial step in creating a competent image. Your career and reputation are on the line each time you send out an application package. What do you want people to see? The kind of package that you send is symbolic of how you view yourself and of the esteem in which you hold your professional career. A competent professional package has the following characteristics:

- **It is professional in appearance**. Present your materials professionally. Invest in a hardbound cover with a spring insert to hold your application materials. On the hardbound cover use the following format:

Credentials
Supporting the Candidacy
of
Dr. Yolanda Castro
for the
Superintendency of Longmeadow ISD

Present all materials in an organized way. There are no spelling errors, there is a consistent type font and format, and all materials are clean and clear of smudges or stains. Your materials are your mirror image!

- **The application package has the following components:**

    (a) *Letter of application.* The letter of application states your intention to apply for the position. Read the job advertisement carefully. Your letter has to speak directly to the requirements mentioned in the advertisement. Don't avoid any requirements—address them.
    (b) *Formal application if required.* Take time to be precise in completing your application. It is tedious work. If you print, print legibly. Complete all information. Your prospective employer may be required by policy to have you complete the application. Once you complete the document and return it, it has legal document status. Be accurate!
    (c) *Resume.*
    (d) *University transcripts.* Generally you are not required to send official transcripts. Student transcripts suffice. Maintain a set of student transcripts and make new copies for each application package. If you are required to send official transcripts, mention that they are forthcoming from the university.
    (e) *Letters of reference.* These letters may be specifically directed toward the prospective employer, or there may be a general reference letter addressed "To Whom It May Concern." In any event, you must be sure that any letter of reference strongly supports your candidacy. You have a right to know if you are going to receive a strong letter of support. Ask for

one. If the prospective reference is hesitant, be grateful for the hesitancy and find a new reference. One poor reference is enough to derail your chances.

(f) *Testimonials from appropriate supporters.* Include appropriate letters from parents, students, supporters, or testimonials that you have received. These provide evidence that your competence was widely recognized in your current position as well as previous positions.

(g) *Other documents that testify to your candidacy.* Maintain a scrapbook of newspaper clippings. Favorable write-ups add glamour to your candidacy. People want to hire someone who is respected by others. They want someone who has public support.

Once your package is complete, ask a trusted friend to review it. Make any final changes and mail it to the prospective employer. Normally, you will receive a form letter telling you that your materials were received. If you haven't received a form letter within ten days, contact the prospective employer and ask if the materials were received. Make no other telephone calls regarding the process. This is liminal space. You have committed action and are waiting for a response. It is a difficult time, one that tests your patience. Competent people understand the normal anxiety associated with this process. Yet, they are able to contain their anxiety—it is important to remain calm in the face of anxiety. This is a competence trait.

Step 4: The right interview
You've made the cut. You receive the telephone call. You are asked if you are still interested in the position. Your heart starts racing, and you calmly reply, YES! The interview is set. You are one of four finalists for the position you desire. Observe the following interview rules to make yourself the most attractive candidate:

Rule 1: Prepare, prepare, prepare! You cannot prepare enough for your interview. Preparation includes finding out as much as possible about the position. Visit the community; ask community members about the schools. Visit the community's library and read back issues of its newspapers to discover the issues associated with your prospective position. Remember that they want a problem solver. They want someone who understands their problems and knows how to guide them through the morass toward a viable solution.

Rule 2: Practice interview questions. You cannot anticipate all questions, but you can anticipate three questions:

Question One: Tell us about yourself. This question or a variation is generally the question that opens the interview. You need to have your response well rehearsed. Your response has to be professional and filled with energy and excitement. You want to convey your sense of excitement and energy to the interviewing parties. Speak only about your professional career; do not speak about family, hobbies, vacations, and so on. Use this opportunity to showcase your successes.

Question Two: What are your strengths and weaknesses? This typical question is asked in most interviews. Most employment specialists suggest that you offer a weakness that is a thinly veiled strength. The interviewing group is expecting this response. I recommend a different tact. Discuss your strengths at length. Then, when you address your weaknesses, admit that you have some (none specifically) but assert that your self-knowledge of your weaknesses has increased your need to involve people in a collaborative effort. This demonstrates your desire to be a team player. It demonstrates collaborative ability. The key is to be creative and move away from the traditional, expected response.

Question Three: Do you have any questions? This question signals the end of the interview. The majority of candidates will try to ask a few questions. There is a better approach. Questions at the end of the interview are an expression of anxiety. The competent person projects confidence. Questions about perquisites are not appropriate at this time—wait until you are formally offered the job. Questions about issues that were raised in your mind during the interview need to be addressed, but at a different time. Use this moment creatively. I coach my students to use the following response:

Thank you for this opportunity to be interviewed for this position. I don't have any questions at this time. However, I want to reiterate the strengths that I will bring to your organization if I am selected (here list your strengths). Again, my thanks for your attention and courtesy.

Rule 3: Appearance counts. Follow the guidelines that John Molloy suggests in *New Dress for Success*. Check your appearance in a restroom prior to the interview. Go over your appearance systematically. Your appearance doesn't help you as much as it may hurt you. Your interviewing team will make comparisons. You want to be the favorable comparison. Set the standard.

Rule 4: Be gracious. Express appreciation throughout your interview. You may feel at times that some interviewers are too "tough." Don't take it personally. They have a job to do. Thank them for their time. You may have to work with them in the future. Send personal thank-you notes to every person who interviewed you. In these handwritten notes (use professional cards) thank the person for being part of the interview and reiterate your strengths. These are the same strengths you mentioned to close the interview. Few people follow through on this advice; those that do find it highly beneficial.

Rule 5: Be helpful. Regardless of the outcome of your interview, add benefit to the organization. Approach every interview as an opportunity to give more than you receive. In this way, no interview is wasted. Every interview provides you with an opportunity to teach. Every interview provides you with the opportunity to give people the formula to solve their problems. Don't hide the formula. The outcome of the hiring process is always in doubt. You are not privy to the inner politics of the organization.

Rule 6: Use visualization. Review the rehearsal visualization in this chapter. Continued focus on visual imagery ensures peak performance.

If you followed the guidelines in this chapter, you've done an outstanding job in presenting your case that you are the best possible candidate. There is nothing more you can do. If you help them during the interview and they hire you—fantastic! If you help them and they do not offer you the position, you can take solace in the fact that you left that organization better off because they chose to interview you.

COMPETENCE CHECK

Do you understand:

- ☐ The power of optimism in your career quest?
- ☐ The formula for career success?
- ☐ The importance of applying the mental toughness strategies?
- ☐ How to use mental visualization to your personal and professional advantage?
- ☐ How to begin with the end in mind?
- ☐ How to identify your external and internal resources?
- ☐ The importance of investing in yourself?
- ☐ How to develop and implement a Plan of Action to transform weaknesses into strengths?
- ☐ The four step process in getting the right job?
- ☐ How to develop a winning resume?
- ☐ How to develop a winning application package?
- ☐ How to use the interview for mutual advantage?
- ☐ What to do after the interview?

Were you able to place a ✓ in each of the boxes in the competence check? This chapter gives you the advantage over your competent competitors. It provides the formula you can use to acquire a position in which you can use your competence to benefit the community and gain deep personal and professional satisfaction. The formula is simple, yet many people leave out critical ingredients. Imagine leaving yeast out of the dough when making a loaf of bread. The dough will not rise regardless of the quality of the other ingredients. Applying this formula for success to your professional career enables you to find the most appropriate venue for the expression of your competence. It is a mutually beneficial activity between you and your prospective employer. The final chapter, "Creating a Professional Growth Plan," provides you with the opportunity to chart out the training and strategies that will take you to the next level of competence. This will be your personal plan and it will transform your career.

NOTES

[1] Bloomfield, H., & R. Cooper. (1995). *The power of 5.* Emmaus, PA: Rodale Press (p. 449).

[2] Bloomfield, H., & R. Cooper. (1995). *The power of 5.* Emmaus, PA: Rodale Press (p. 450).

[4] Loehr, J. (1994). *Toughness training for life.* New York: Penguin Books (pp. 193–194).

[5] Mind Tools. (1997). [Online]. Available: *gasou.edu/psychweb/mtsite/imgintro. html.*

[6] Jannot, M. (1994). *Regimens: Mental training routines tailored to your . . . "Issue." Outside Magazine* (September 1996). [Online]. Available: *outside.starwave. com/magazine/0996/9609bodre.html.*

[7] Loehr, J. (1994). *Toughness training for life.* New York: Penguin Books (p. 61).

[8] Koonce, R. (1997). The 4 M's of career success. *Training and Development.* 51 (12), (p. 15).

[9] Campbell, J. (1991). *Reflections on the art of living: A Joseph Campbell companion.* Selected and edited by D. Osbon. New York: HarperCollins Publishers (p. 22).

[10] Orman, M. (1995). *18 ways to survive your company's reorganization, takeover, downsizing, or other major change.* [Online]. Available: *www.stresscure.com/jobstress/ reorg.html.*

[11] Molloy, J. (1988). *New Dress for Success.* New York: Warner.

[12] Bogdanoff, E. (1996). Dress for success, well-worn advice that's always in style. *American Agent 7 Broker.* 68 (4), (p. 15).

[13] Being values are taken directly from A. Maslow's *The Farther Reaches of Human Nature.* (1971). New York: Penguin Press (pp. 128–129).

[14] Kartje, J. (1996). O mentor! My mentor! *Peabody Journal of Education.* 71 (1), (p. 119).

[15] Calabrese, R. L. Friends along the journey. *Peabody Journal of Education.* 71 (1), (pp. 44–45).

Creating a Professional Growth Plan

In this chapter you will

- Develop a professional growth plan.
- Integrate the personal assessments taken in previous chapters.
- Create a personal ledger.
- Establish a process to systematically reduce and eliminate competence deficits.
- Create a professional abundance model.
- Eliminate any connection to a professional deficit model.

PROFESSIONAL GROWTH PLAN

A professional growth plan has two sections:

1. Analysis of personal inventory.
2. The development of a professional growth plan.

The analysis of personal inventory section describes how to integrate each of the personal assessments with your 360° Administrator Feedback assessment (see Chapter Four). The integrated use of this data is the foundation for a professional growth plan. A professional growth plan is a critical component to competence. It supports the continued evolvement of competence. Those without effective professional growth plans drift and operate with a chance-driven paradigm. Those with a flexible plan shape life's events and adapt to the changing competence demands of their environment. They recognize that there has been a significant paradigm shift in the American workforce. "The new rules . . . include the assertion that 'job homesteading' is dead because you can no longer plop on a job site and expect to stay there forever. According to the new rules, technology dominates. In addition, from now on, you should consider yourself a one-person organization and make job decisions accordingly. A number of new-rule spin-offs are dismal: income instability, long hours, a breakdown of employer–employee trust and a rise in fear and stress as you hustle from one job to another."[1] The following signify five paradigm shifts that affect all workers. Competent people are aware of these paradigm shifts. A professional growth plan enables them to use these shifts to personal advantage.

Paradigm Shifts

Job homesteading	to	**Job transitions**
Stable work environment	to	**Unstable work environment**
Job protection	to	**Job insecurity**
Organizational trust	to	**External accountability**
External placing of trust	to	**Self-reliance**

Job homesteading to job transitions. In the past, a school administrator could expect to spend her career with one organization. She changed roles from teacher to counselor to assistant principal to principal and perhaps to superintendent. Her career with the district was characterized by recognition of competence and reward by promotion to new levels of responsibility. This paradigm is no longer viable. Revolving waves of downsizing, the introduction of charter schools, and the demand for accountability has drastically altered the playing field. Lynne Waymon, career development specialist, says, "The outdated job security mind-set means being dependent on one employer and one job title. On the other hand, the quest for career security focuses all resources and energy on being ready to make a living in the marketplace no matter what organizational earthquakes erupt."[2] The competent professional realizes that personal and professional survival means having a readiness to make transitions from position to position, district to district, and from education to another field.

Stable work environment to unstable work environment. Until recently, the education profession was one of the most stable work environments. My father was pleased when I began teaching in 1966. He felt that teaching and job security went hand in hand. That may have been the case, but drastic changes have taken place in the private and public sectors. I have seen that sense of security disappear in public schools and in higher education. The loss of security exists in all professions. "A recent *Fortune* article cited layoffs of 40,000 at AT&T, 35,000 at IBM, and 12,000 at Chase as evidence of the massive changes that are occurring in the business world. This employee reduction trend has been felt in numerous service industries." The *Fortune* article advises, "Get used to it. The familiar forces driving downsizing: increased foreign competition, Wall Street's obsession with shareholder value, the changing nature of technology aren't about to go away."[3] All of us work in unstable employment environments. Global economic demands and volatile political conditions significantly influence these environments. For example, tenure in education has been questioned in public schools as well as higher education. One politician playing to constituents' emotions can create significant instability by advocating downsizing, budget reduction, or the elimination of tenure. The competent person is not fearful in this environment. The competent person accepts the unstable environment as norm rather than chaos. The competent person uses this instability as a way of creating greater personal job security.

Job protection to job insecurity. The average job-life expectancy of a school superintendent in the United States is less than five years. In some states, it is less than three years. One superintendent told me, "I expect to make five job changes before I retire. I will probably change districts every three to four years." The number of changes this superintendent anticipates is not related to his ability. It is related to the nature of the job. The American culture is an impatient culture. The culture demands solutions. Some solutions can't be achieved in a short time span. Impatience in waiting for results leads to a desire to change leaders in hopes of a quick cure. In effect, there are no longer any guarantees with a job. The only guarantee that a school administrator has is to hold the district accountable for the length of his contract. The competent person recognizes that, like a ballplayer, he is as good as his last game. This means that the one primary hedge against job insecurity is continually becoming more competent. There can be no running in place for the competent person.

Organizational trust to external accountability. The unstable political environment has lessened public trust of educational organizations to properly educate children. As a result, government agencies at the state, regional, and national levels are setting outcome performance for students. Administrator and teacher performance is being directly tied to the academic and behavioral performance of the children in their classrooms and schools. The locus of control has moved from the educators at the instructional site to people far removed from students. The competent person recognizes that the locus of control has shifted and, rather than fight the shift, anticipates future shifts and adapts her abilities to lead the shifts.

External placing of trust to self-reliance Competent people know that they can longer count on others at their work site to protect, nurture, or mentor them. These people are also concerned about survival. This is not to suggest that we have moved to a "survival-of-the-fittest" environment; yet, it does mean that self-reliance is an essential characteristic of those who survive during turbulent times. Being self-reliant means that you take personal responsibility for yourself and your career. Patricia Buhler, in her article "Managing in the 90s," says: "The new contract between employee and employer requires self-reliance on the part of employees. This means that employees must take charge of their careers. No longer will the business take the sole responsibility for managing its employees' careers. Now employees must take charge of their own careers and be prepared to manage their career progression."[4]

A school administrator becomes self-reliant by taking reasoned risks and assuming responsibility for the success of those risks. Competent people are risk-takers. They are not risk aversive. An example of risk-aversive behavior surrounded the downsizing of the U.S. military during the 1990s. Many military bases were scheduled for closing, displacing a number of workers. In some communities, the majority of workers did not look for other jobs; they placed their hopes in politicians' preventing base closings. They discovered, much to their chagrin, that their lives would have been better if they were more self-reliant and responded earlier to the career threat. Competent people are self-reliant. Competence drives self-reliance. It is the primary source of job security. As Bridges points out, "Recognizing the turbulence in the business environment, workers need to regard themselves as people whose value to the organization must be demonstrated in each successive situation they find themselves in."[5] Your commitment to competence identifies you as a survivor. Your application of the materials in this book identifies you as a proactive, competent person. Now, you have to bring the knowledge that you gained in this book into a cohesive whole to create the greatest personal benefit.

INTEGRATE PERSONAL ASSESSMENTS

The first five chapters provided a list of the assessments and their intended outcomes. Each of these assessments furnished you with critical internal or external data regarding your current state of competence. Only you can judge your current level of competence. It is safe to assume that you desire to become more competent. You recognize that increased competence means having a commitment to professional development. Conversely, no room for professional development indicates that a career has become stagnant. When we choose professional development, we assure ourselves that the learning that occurs is long term. In effect, the introduction of new paradigms of learning applies in the following sequence:

1. **Awareness of need for growth.**
2. **Acquisition of new material.**
3. **Integration of new material with already learned patterns.**
4. **Anchoring new material as a learned pattern.**

FIGURE 8.1   Adapting to a new paradigm

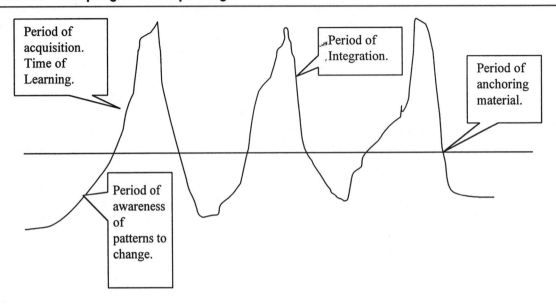

This four-step process takes time and happens sequentially. Figure 8.1 shows how we adapt to a new paradigm.

The pattern in Figure 8.1 represents the ebb and flow of competence. At some point, we become aware that our level of competence does not adequately address our current environment. We also become aware that our current level of competence does not address the foreseeable demands of a new environment (period of acquisition). We realize that our comfort with the status quo must change (time of learning). Once we are aware of the need to change and to acquire additional competence, we move into a paradigm shift and begin the process of knowledge acquisition. Knowledge acquisition is limited (period of awareness of patterns of change). We need time to assimilate and integrate what we learned (the period of integration). We make our new learning part of our experience when we anchor it to our preferred ways of seeing and responding to the world (period of anchoring material).

As you assess your strengths and areas of challenge, you will recognize that growth is essential in strengths as well as areas of challenge. You need to prioritize the targets that are the most important for your career. Only you can make a decision regarding the direction of your career.

The following table lists the assessments that are provided in this book. Each assessment provides critical data to support the goals you establish in your professional growth plan.

If you completed each assessment, you have a clear indication of your competence level. You have a clear indication of strengths and weaknesses. This knowledge is crucial in the development of your professional growth plan. Use this knowledge to create your *competence ledger*.

TABLE 8.1   Inventory of assessments

Assessment	Location	Purpose	Use in plan
Values Test	Chapter One	Awareness of values and need to move toward deeper transcending values.	Values undergird behavior. Right values lead to right action.
Journaling	Chapter One	Awareness of situations, behaviors, and consequences.	Discover basic patterns of acting. Use persistent themes to drive quest for competence.
Leadership & Competence Management	Chapter Two	Awareness of dichotomy of leadership/management focus.	Discover deficit areas in leadership and/or management and make appropriate adjustments.
Personal Competence	Chapter Two	Awareness of personal characteristics of competence.	Discover areas in which personal characteristics of competence may be missing.
Perceptual Competence	Chapter Two	Awareness of the perceptions of others regarding your competence.	Discover discrepancies between personal and perceptual views of competence.
Political Competence	Chapter Two	Awareness of state of political competence.	Discover deficits in political competence.
Baseline Competence	Chapter Two	Overview of current competence state.	Use to focus efforts on targeting increased levels of competence.
Positive Personality Traits	Chapter Three	Awareness of inherent positive personality traits.	Discover deficits in personality traits leading to career sabotage.
Derailing Personality Traits	Chapter Three	Awareness of presence of derailing personality traits.	Discover potential derailing traits to target for reduction or elimination.
Personality Style Indicator	Chapter Three	Awareness of primary personality style.	Discover how primary personality style helps and hinders professional growth.
Decision-Making Style	Chapter Three	Awareness of primary decision-making style.	Discover how the primary decision-making style helps or hinders competence.
Leadership Assessment	Chapter Three	Awareness of how well you work with others.	Discover deficits in team building and collaborative problem solving.
360° Administrator Feedback	Chapter Four	Feedback from critical sources regarding behaviors in leadership, management, decision making.	Generate accurate feedback from external sources regarding performance.
Working Relationships— Derailers	Chapter Five	Awareness of potential derailers in working with others.	Discover potential sabotaging actions in working with others.

continued

TABLE 8.1   Inventory of assessments (*continued*)

Assessment	Location	Purpose	Use in plan
Team Building—Derailers	Chapter Five	Awareness of potential derailers in building teams.	Discover potential sabotaging actions in developing and working with teams.
Transitioning—Derailers	Chapter Five	Awareness of meeting different needs in career transitions.	Discover forms of rigid behavior regarding career transitions.
Project Completion—Derailers	Chapter Five	Awareness of ability to carry projects through to completion.	Discover behavior that prevents strong follow-through on projects.
Overreliance on Authority—Derailers	Chapter Five	Awareness of dependency on protective authority.	Discover behavior that prevents assertive action.
Mediation/Negotiation—Derailers	Chapter Five	Awareness of problems associated with disagreements with others.	Discover sabotaging actions that lead to estrangement from supervisors.
Use of Time—Strengths	Chapter Five	Awareness of appropriate use of time.	Discover derailing actions in application of time management.
Relationships—Strengths	Chapter Five	Awareness of ability to forge and revitalize relationships.	Discover deficits relating to relationship building or relationship reconciliation.
Savvy—Strengths	Chapter Five	Awareness of savvy in working with and through others.	Discover limits of the innate ways in which the organization works.
Systems Thinking—Strengths	Chapter Five	Awareness of the interrelatedness of components affecting your organization.	Discover limits of systems thinking in current paradigm—understanding how to expand current level of systems thinking.
Balance—Strength	Chapter Five	Awareness of the application of balance in personal and professional life.	Discover areas in which personal and professional life is out of balance.

CREATING A COMPETENCE LEDGER

Traditionally, a ledger is a book indicating financial transactions. In this case, we want to create a ledger that lists your assets and liabilities. Assets represent the resources that you have (that's good) and liabilities represent your debts or weaknesses (that's bad). When our assets far exceed our liabilities, we have a positive cash flow balance. When our liabilities far exceed our assets, we have a negative cash flow balance. If the negative cash flow balance continues for a protracted period, then creditors take us to court and sue to collect the money that is owed to them. We can use this concept to our benefit.

Our ledger represents our competence assets and liabilities. To the degree that we have more assets in our competence ledger than liabilities, we are competent. To help you build your competence ledger review each of the assessments you have taken in this book. List current competencies as assets. Indicate the action you want to take with this competence. Do you want to strengthen it? Do you want to maintain it?

Now list your liabilities. These are areas where your competence needs to be revitalized. You may identify a derailer or a sabotaging action. Do you want to reduce your derailing behavior to a more manageable level? Do you want to eliminate it? As you move toward the generation of your development plan remember that *balance* is essential. Balance your efforts to improve assets with reducing liabilities. Total focus in either area will cause your actions to be unbalanced and reduce your competence.

The following is an example of a competence ledger. Use this competence ledger to demonstrate how to identify primary assets and primary liabilities. This ledger interacts with Table 8.1, which lists twenty-four assessments. Review each of your assessments and identify your assets and liabilities in each assessment. Follow the example of Cathy Schott, an elementary school principal.

Personal Assessment

Cathy Schott
Principal—Sensabo Elementary School

Assessment	Primary Asset (Competence)	Primary Liability (Weakness)
Values Test	Ability to say no to people. Ability to assertively lead.	Lack of sensitivity to others' needs.
Journaling	I saw a number of instances in which my leadership was invaluable to getting things done. Journaling was a confidence booster.	I discovered that under high stress times I become rigid with faculty, parents, and students. I need to handle stress better.
Leadership & Management Competence	Excellent at long-term strategic planning. Able to continuously align personal goals with organizational goals.	Too much emphasis on micromanaging. Place the completion of tasks prior to the needs of people.
Personal Competence	When I am not under stress, I am very friendly. Generally, I'm also supportive.	Need to become more truthful. Shading the truth hurts me.
Perceptual Competence	This is my weakest area. I honestly don't have good strengths.	I can jump to conclusions. Under stress, I may not listen to other people.
Political Competence	I have a strong sense of political courage. I can work well with others.	At times, I ignore the rights of others. I often fail to act with self-restraint.

continued

Personal Assessment (*continued*)

Assessment	Primary Asset (Competence)	Primary Liability (Weakness)
Baseline Competence	I had a score of 90. I do have a strong personal standard for competence.	No apparent derailer.
Positive Personality Traits	I have ten of the thirteen positive personality traits.	I am sometimes seen as not being fair-minded. I am also not seen as self-sacrificing in terms of my interests. I am not highly empathetic.
Derailing Personality Traits	Faculty realize that I keep my commitments. I am viewed as strong, one who can make decisions.	Some people see me as a loner. Some people complain about my ambition.
Personality Style Indicator	I am definitely an "A" type personality. I think this type has natural leadership qualities.	I understand now why I relish a "good fight." I understand now that I can be overly aggressive.
Decision-Making Style	I am a level 3 decision maker. I want to make the decisions. Being at level 3 means that I am an excellent planner.	I lack flexibility once I am set in my thinking. I prefer to delegate rather than to collaboratively involve others in making the decision.
Leadership Assessment	Getting along with others is crucial. I have a clear vision. I don't deviate from that vision.	I have a low tolerance of opinions that differ from mine. I am viewed as a "user" of others to get the job done.
360° Administrator Feedback	Community members gave me a high rating in the people area. Faculty scored me highest in the problem solving area. My supervisor scored me highest in the problem solving area. My colleagues scored me highest in the political area.	I was rated lowest by my supervisors, colleagues, and faculty in the people area. They made the specific recommendations: Talk to people before acting, especially when it affects them. Provide encouragement that is more personal and supportive. Be willing to negotiate differences. I can also improve in the political area according to scores of faculty and my supervisor. They recommend: Connecting with essential faculty and community leaders prior to acting. Demonstrating a greater willingness to negotiate differences that I have with people.
Working Relationships—Derailers	This is my weakest area. I need to upgrade my competence to succeed.	I often tell people "what to do." I often am accused of "intimidating" others.
Team Building—Derailers	I know how to put together strong teams. I know how to hire the right people by using objective standards.	I limit my teams. The limitations that I place on them often make people complain that I already had the outcome in mind.
Transitioning—Derailers	This is an area of strength. I recognize the macro picture. I understand my supervisor's issues.	I have a difficult time communicating my macro vision to my faculty.

Personal Assessment (*continued*)

Assessment	Primary Asset (Competence)	Primary Liability (Weakness)
Project Completion— Derailers	I am a detail person. I take a project from the idea to its successful completion. I recognize that my reputation is on the line.	I can be a severe "task master" in pushing people to make sure that projects are complete.
Overreliance on Authority— Derailers	I don't like to fail, but I try to keep a healthy distance from my supervisor. I like to think of my school as my show. I don't like outside interference.	I may go a little too far in not involving my supervisor. Sometimes he is blind-sided by my actions. I have to watch this.
Mediation/ Negotiation— Derailers	I work well with my supervisor. I am able to disagree and challenge my supervisor and negotiate in the best interests of my school.	I am fortunate to have a fantastic super-visor. I don't know the level of my nego-tiating skill with a supervisor who may not be supportive. I need to improve this area—just in case.
Use of Time— Strengths	Time management is a high strength area. I feel like I am the master of my time. I make it work for me.	I really don't have weaknesses in this area. I teach workshops on time management.
Relationships— Strengths	This is my weakest area.	I don't try to understand others. I don't spend time with faculty to enter a rela-tionship. I have a difficult time laughing at myself.
Savvy— Strengths	I have excellent savvy in intuiting where my school should position itself for the future. We are always out in front of other schools in the district.	I need to use my strength in terms of savvy to understand the needs of the members of my organization.
Systems Thinking— Strengths	I can see my school as an inter-dependent system.	I can't get other people to understand the needs for systems thinking. I find this terribly frustrating.
Balance— Strength	This is a major weakness area. I don't have a fully balanced life. To date my personal relationships or health have not suffered. I feel strong. I don't know how long I can last.	I only work. Work is my primary focus. I seldom relax. Even when I am not working, I am reading something that will help me at work. I drive others as I drive myself—without mercy.

Cathy Schott has completed her summary of the twenty-four assessments. She is aware of her primary competencies (assets) as well as her primary challenges (liabilities). Armed with this information, Cathy can build her competence ledger. Once completed, the competence ledger is the trigger for Cathy's professional growth plan. Using the competence ledger eliminates the guesswork and reliance on intuitive hunches as to the direction of her professional growth. A competence ledger is available at the end of this chapter for you to copy.

Competence Ledger

Strengths (Assets)	Strengthen	Maintain	Challenges (Liabilities)	Reduce	Ignore	Eliminate
Assertiveness		Yes	Increase of insensitivity.	Yes		
Journaling (This has been a big help).		Yes	Aggressiveness under stress.			Yes
Alignment of personal goals with organizational demands.	Yes		Too narrow locus of control.	Yes		
Political courage.		Yes	Perception as a loner.	Yes		
Commitment keeper.	Yes		Too work focused.	Yes		
Level 3 decision maker.	Yes		Nonformal involvement of others in decision making.			Yes
Sense of vision and mission.		Yes	Low tolerance of different opinions.	Yes		
Organizing strong teams.	Yes		Interpersonal relationships.	Yes		
Having a macro picture of the organization.		Yes	Low communication skills.			
Organizational capacity. I understand the intricacies of a project.	Yes					
Self-reliance.		Yes				
Working relationship with supervisor.	Yes					

Cathy's asset (strengths) sheet is larger than her liability (challenge) sheet. When Cathy reviewed the summary of her assessment, she realized that her major challenges were in three areas: communications, interpersonal relationships, and personal ambitious drive. Cathy's mentor suggested that her high personal ambition drive was the source of her challenges in other areas. At first, Cathy became defensive. After all, she believed her drive had gotten her to this point in her career. She was clearly on the move. Cathy's mentor suggested that all Cathy said was true. The mentor told Cathy that she was on the verge of sabotaging her career by adopting derailing strategies. Cathy's mentor assured her that there was nothing wrong with her ambitious drive. He suggested that Cathy's personal career goals would be achieved more easily by focusing on relationships and communication. Cathy trusted her mentor. She knew her mentor always provided excellent advice. She chose to take a trust walk and follow her mentor's advice. Together they sat down and developed a professional growth plan.

This professional growth plan will lead you through a process to enable you to identify your personal and professional goals. Each component is essential. The effort you put into identifying your personal and professional goals will enable you to gain maximum personal and professional benefit. Follow Cathy Schott through the development of her professional growth plan. A professional growth plan for you to complete can be found at the end of this chapter.

PROFESSIONAL GROWTH PLAN

Cathy Schott
(List School Year)
School Administrator—Sensabo Elementary School

Description: A professional growth plan is a personal statement that describes the direction in which you intend to grow over a period of time. Although the time is arbitrary, it is best to focus professional growth over one year. This professional growth plan will lead you through a process to enable you to identify your personal and professional goals. Each component is essential. The effort you put into identifying your personal and professional goals will enable you to gain maximum personal and professional benefit.

All professional growth plans are grounded in a personal mission. This mission is driven by *clear goals* linked to well-defined *objectives* that are delineated with specific *indicators*. In a professional growth plan you:

1. Choose the areas for your professional development.
2. Choose development activities.
3. Choose the outcomes associated with each activity.

Mission

Professional growth plans are centered in a personal mission. A personal mission is filled with passion. It has a sense of destiny. One's experience, knowledge base, and competence drive a mission. It acts as a motivating force. Stephen Covey says that the creation of a meaningful mission statement is "without question, one of the most powerful and significant things you will ever do to take leadership of your life. In it you will identify the first, most important roles, relationships, and things in your life—who you want to be, what you want to do, to whom and what you want to give your life, the principles you want to anchor your life to, the legacy you want to leave. All the goals and decisions you will make in the future will be based upon it. It's like deciding first which wall you want to lean your ladder of life against, and then beginning to climb. It will be a compass—a strong source of guidance amid the stormy seas and pressing, pulling currents of your life."[6]

Cathy Schott's Mission: My ultimate goal is to significantly contribute to the lives of minority students in an urban environment by improving the quality of education they receive.

Determine the "Why"

Why is this mission important to accomplish? What are the consequences for you, others, and society if you don't accomplish your mission? What are the consequences for you and society if you do accomplish your mission? How will you feel if you don't accomplish your mission? How will you feel if you do accomplish your mission? How will those who are important in your life feel about you? When we discover the why behind our mission, we provide our mission with power and energy. When we have a why, we can always find a way to achieve our mission.

Cathy Schott's "Why": A single mother raised me in a ghetto. My mother made sure I studied. She monitored the friends I associated with, and made sure I focused on going to college. My grandmother and grandfather sent me money each month to help take care of my expenses while I was away at college. It is payback time. I no longer live in a ghetto, but my commitment is strong. I will do for others what my mother and grandparents did for me.

Identify your professional goal

Our professional goal is tied directly to our mission. Applying professional goals to our mission is one way we work toward completing our mission. Identify your professional goal. Think beyond your current position. If your current position is your ultimate professional goal, then reflect on your ultimate goal within that role. Make sure the goal you choose is appropriate to your current context. That is, given your experience, socialization, and knowledge base, are you choosing a goal that fits who you are and where you want to direct your life? Viktor Frankl states: "For the meaning of life differs from man to man, from day to day and from hour to hour. . . . To put the question in general terms would be comparable to the question posed to a chess champion: 'Tell me, Master, what is the best move in the world?' There simply is no such thing as the best or even a good move apart from a particular situation in a game and the particular personality of one's opponent. The same holds for human existence."[7] When you commit your professional goal to writing, be sure to state it as a performance goal and not as an outcome goal.

Cathy Schott's professional goal: My professional goal is to be fully prepared to be a superintendent of schools of a large urban school district in Texas. I will begin applying for superintendent positions no later than four years from today.

- Be *precise* in *writing* your goal.
- Make sure your goal is *measurable.*
- Make sure your goal is *attainable.*

Identify the steps to your professional goal

(Note: These are Cathy Schott's responses.)

Goal Step One: I will apply for admission to major university doctoral programs that specialize in preparing superintendents for urban environments. I will complete the application process by the end of this fall semester. **Why**: This is the first step I need to take to realize my ultimate goal of shaping the education of a large urban environment.

Goal Step Two: I will organize and work with my faculty to review the impact that my current school has on minority students. I will complete this review by the end of the fall semester. **Why**: Each step of my journey toward my ultimate goal must provide benefit to minority students. At each successive level of responsibility, I will increase my focus on bringing benefit to minority students.

Goal Step Three: I will make myself aware of the challenges I discovered in the twenty-four assessment areas. I will focus on gaining competence in my top five priorities. I will complete this by the end of this academic year. **Why**: I am a competent person. I intend to become more competent. How can I help my people if I am not as competent as possible?

Goal Step Four: I will apply for secondary school principal positions. I will complete the application process by the end of April of this coming school year. **Why**: If I am going to have an impact on minority education in an urban environment, I need to have leadership experience at multiple levels. I have successful elementary experience. Now is the time to move forward.

Determine your level of commitment

Identify your level of commitment to achieving these goals on a scale of one to ten: one being a very low commitment and ten being a rock-solid, nothing-can-shake-me commitment.

Cathy Schott's level of commitment: My level of commitment toward reaching these goals is a seven on a scale of ten. I want to say ten, but to be honest, there are times when I am filled with doubt.

Identify barriers to commitment

Cathy Schott's response: My family is supportive of my career. My husband has chosen a career that allows him to be mobile and move to where my career will take me. However, I have lingering doubts about whether I can make it in the "big leagues." After all, I'm the only one I know who made it out of the projects. Do I really have what it takes?

Identify strategies to attain commitment

Cathy Schott's response: I have a clear vision in my mind of urban education. I can see, in my mind's eye, black students accepting academic scholarships to major four-year universities because they are academically talented. This picture is so clear, so real, that whenever I get down on myself I bring this picture into focus.

Identify strategies to eliminate barriers to commitment

Cathy Schott's response: The biggest consideration is my self-doubt. Ironically, others don't have doubt in my abilities or in me achieving my dreams. I am going to review and write my history of achievement from my earliest memories to the present. My history will confirm a lifetime of successes. I can use this history to erase any self-doubts that remain in me.

Identify five ways to bring about healthy pressure on yourself to increase your commitment

Cathy Schott's response:

1. I am going to revisit the projects where I grew up. I want to remember the sights, sounds, smells, and tastes of the projects.
2. I am going to share my story and goals with a wider group. This means I will share my story and goals with my faculty at our first faculty meeting of the school year. This is a leap of faith, to make my life so public.
3. I am going to join minority advocate groups. I have refrained from this in the past. It is now time to bring my experience and competence to other organizations that are trying to make a difference.
4. I am going to take the goals in my professional growth plan and translate them into yearly, monthly, weekly, and daily goals. I will review these daily and post them in prominent places.
5. I am going to ask the leaders in the projects where I grew up if I can be of assistance in any way. This public commitment to move out of my career and to serve in a lesser capacity in the projects will be invaluable to me.

Alignment of Goals

Align your professional goals with those of your school, district, and state. Creating a consistency within this alignment will facilitate your success. (Note: These are Cathy Schott's responses.)

Identify your school's primary goals

Instruction related primary goal(s): I will take the leadership responsibility for raising faculty awareness toward increasing minority achievement in Sensabo Elementary School. My primary instruction related goal is to work with faculty to provide a series of workshops to increase faculty awareness of minority learning styles and of African American culture.

Parent related primary goal(s): I will take leadership responsibility in encouraging minority parents to supervise their children's homework. My primary parent related goal is to establish a set of meetings in the projects surrounding my school to enlist parent support in improving their child's academic performance.

Student related primary goal(s): I will take leadership responsibility in changing student visions of success. My primary goal is to work with the community and faculty and organize ongoing small group meetings with students to create a sense of academic toughness and personal determination to succeed.

Teacher related primary goal(s): I will take leadership responsibility for increasing faculty awareness of the culture of the students in my school and how that culture impacts learning strategies. My primary goal is to create an agenda among faculty that dramatically increases minority student achievement. This is a critical part of our mission. I will constantly speak of this at all faculty meetings, team meetings, and in observation conferences.

Resource related primary goal(s): I will take a leadership responsibility for increasing the needed resources to improve the instructional outcomes for minority students in my school. I will create an achievement team comprising community and school leaders to advocate for resources. My primary goal is to generate resources for staff development and to change student perceptions of success.

Identify your district's goals

Instruction related primary goal(s): The district's primary instructional goal is to increase student achievement scores on the state-mandated achievement tests. Raising minority scores is a primary component of this instructional goal.

Parent related primary goal(s): The district's primary parent related goal is to increase the participation of parents as partners with teachers to improve instructional performance. Training parents to provide appropriate instructional intervention is an important component of this goal.

Student related primary goal(s): The district's primary student related goals are related to achievement and attitude. The district has set a five-year goal to have 95 percent of high school graduates attending postsecondary education. It also has a goal of making academic achievement awards the most prestigious and sought-after by students.

Teacher related primary goal(s): The district's primary goal is to upgrade teacher competencies to meet new state standards within three years. A primary ingredient of this component is that urban teachers will have to have a clear understanding of successful instructional strategies targeted toward minority students.

Resource related primary goal(s): The district's primary resource related goal is to have a bond issue passed by voters this year. Continuous student improvement in measurable academic areas is crucial to the public's support of the bond issue. The district is linking the bond to continued instructional growth.

Identify the knowledge base and performance skills you need

Knowledge Base

A knowledge base is the core of technical knowledge that is gained through study or experience. This knowledge base becomes a resource for reference when confronting new situations. To achieve the professional goals you have identified, you have to increase your knowledge base. The most effective way to increase your knowledge base is to target your efforts to the essential technical knowledge and experience that you need to acquire to become more competent. This book gives you targeting tools. Refer to your Personal Assessment to accurately target your efforts.

Cathy Schott's response:

1. Increase team-building skills.
2. Increase relationship-building skills.
3. Increase communication skills.
4. Increase flexibility.
5. Improve reactions when under stress.
6. Increase ability to work and relate effectively in chaotic situations.
7. Increase ability to move my locus of control from rigid personal control to a loose–tight coupling with faculty.

Performance Skills

Performance skills are specific skills you want and need to acquire or sharpen. It is important that you are coached in the acquisition of these skills. You may acquire a skill and practice it the wrong way. If you practice the skill in the wrong way, you end up having the right tool but using it inappropriately. It is much like hitting golf balls on a driving range. If you do not have a golf pro to correct your swing, you may hit two hundred golf balls with the incorrect swing, reinforcing bad habits. (Note: These are Cathy Schott's responses.)

Performance Skill 1: I will talk to people before I act, especially when my prospective action impacts their working conditions. I will practice dialoguing with faculty and asking for opinions rather than just telling people what to do. I will need constant feedback to monitor my actions. I will ask the faculty for help.

Performance Skill 2: I will delegate important issues to qualified faculty members. I will learn how to delegate effectively.

Performance Skill 3: I will become more aware of the consequences of my actions, especially how those actions impact the lives of my faculty. I am so focused that I am often unaware of the ripple effects of my actions. I need to slow down and consider the positive and negative consequences of my actions before acting.

Performance Skill 4: I will connect with key community and faculty leaders. I have made it a point in my life to push ahead without consulting or involving others. If I want to achieve my ultimate goal, I have to change. Acquiring this performance skill is essential to my growth.

Performance Skill 5: I will handle stress more effectively. School leadership has a large amount of inherent stress. I need to be in control of my emotions, not allowing my emotions to be in control.

Strengths and Challenges

The 360° Administrator Feedback, along with the other twenty-three assessment areas, targets specific areas to address in terms of your knowledge base or performance skills. Refer to your summary of assessments and your competence ledger to determine strengths that need to be maintained or improved and challenges that need to be reduced or eliminated.

The following chart shows how Cathy Schott prioritized her strengths and challenges.

Prioritized Strengths and Challenge Areas

Strengths and Challenge Areas	Strength	Challenge	Priority
Lack of sensitivity to others.		Yes	1
Rigidity under stress.		Yes	6
Strategic planning.	Yes		11
Ignore the complaints and rights of faculty.		Yes	4
Political courage.	Yes		10
Lack of empathy toward faculty.		Yes	5
Keeper of commitments.	Yes		9
Overly aggressive toward others.		Yes	7
Clear sense of vision and mission.	Yes		8
Lack of people skills.		Yes	2
Having a macro picture of the organization.	Yes		12
Maintain healthy distance from superordinates.	Yes		13
Lack of appropriate professional relationships.		Yes	3

Note: Cathy has identified her strength and challenge areas. Rather than scatter her energy, Cathy assigns a priority to each item on her list. Cathy intends to begin working on her first three priorities.

Identify specific categories of potential growth

Base these on the 360° Administrator Feedback. Always state responses in a positive voice.

Cathy Schott's response: I will be more decisive. I will to focus on the source as well as the symptoms of problems. I will seek all pertinent data before choosing to offer my support to a person or group.

Areas of strength that will be maintained

Cathy Schott's response:

1. Increase knowledge of strategic planning especially as it ties to district plans.
2. Increase knowledge of the circumstances of disenfranchised students.
3. Increase my understanding of vision and mission. I want to make sure that my sense of vision and mission are closely aligned to well-grounded values.
4. Increase my awareness of the macro picture of the organization. This will expand my systems thinking perspective and allow me to understand the various forces that influence district policy.
5. Increase my ability to maintain a loose–tight fit with my supervisors. I want to be independent, yet I need their support. This is important to me.

Areas in which professional growth will be sought

Cathy Schott's response:

1. Effective interpersonal communications.
2. Stress management.
3. Effective interpersonal relationship strategies.
4. Effective strategies in working with teams.

Performance skills that will be maintained

Cathy Schott's response:

1. Maintain my journaling. This is a big help as I reflect on the day's activities.
2. Maintain my leadership focus. I have a true sense of what needs to happen. My leadership provides the catalyst that is necessary for constructive action.

3. Maintain my assertive behavior. I am able to set constructive limits. I do not have a difficult time saying no to ideas, proposals, or requests that fall outside of our mission.
4. Maintain my relationship with parents in the community. They gave me a high score in my 360° Administrator Feedback.

IMPLEMENTATION OF THE PROFESSIONAL GROWTH PLAN

The following chart enables you to list your four primary goals, identify the objectives (reasons) for each goal, and to identify specific indicators to mark goal attainment. The following examples will help you word your goals, objectives, and indicators. Your indicators are specific strategies and tactics to accomplish your goals and objectives. Employ the SMART system (Specific, Measurable, Attainable, Relevant, Time dimension) when writing your goals.

Goal Planner

Goal	Objectives	Indicators
To get a doctorate degree with a specialization in urban superintendency.	Become accepted into one of these programs. Receive a fellowship or grant to attend.	Complete four applications by December. Complete financial aid forms by January. Visit each campus and talk with appropriate professors.
Organize faculty to understand impact on minority students.	Increase faculty awareness of school's effect on minority students. Increase student achievement among minority students.	Schedule full day planning session for faculty on minority issues. Faculty will draw up a specific plan to increase minority achievement scores. Schedule staff development for faculty on specific instructional strategies for minority students.
Target top five priorities on Personal Assessment for immediate action.	Increase competence in areas of significant challenge. Increase competitiveness through increased competence.	Attend specific workshops for interpersonal communications. Read two books on improving interpersonal relationships. Begin taking yoga classes to manage stress. Seek a mentor to help with delegation strategies.
Become a secondary school administrator.	To become more competitive for an urban superintendency. To gain a greater breadth and depth of experience in a school district.	Identify all secondary school administrator openings in immediate area. Make applications for all openings. Make contact with successful secondary school administrators to learn more about issues.

Reminders
- Does your plan focus on professional growth?
- Do your goals, objectives, and indicators relate to school leadership?
- Do you feel as if you have ownership in this plan?

SUMMARY

Congratulations! You have completed your professional development growth plan. You are now ready to take your professional career to higher levels of competence. There is one more step. Do you have the will to move from potential to action? If you've read this book, I believe you do. Once you put your plan into action, nothing will stop you from adding benefit to your community through increased competence. You will be a model for others and a highly sought-after mentor. As your competence increases, your responsibility to contribute to society also increases. This will be another challenge. It will be a challenge that you can easily meet by following your professional growth plan. Work this plan. Review your plan regularly. It will be your history as you chart your destiny.

SAMPLE FORMS

Competence Ledger - Personal Assessment

Assessment	Primary Asset (Competence)	Primary Liability (Weakness)
Values Test		
Journaling		
Leadership & Management Competence		
Personal Competence		
Perceptual Competence		
Political Competence		
Baseline Competence		
Positive Personality Traits		
Derailing Personality Traits		
Personality Style Indicator		
Decision-Making Style		
Leadership Assessment		
360° Administrator Feedback		
Working Relationships—Derailers		
Team Building—Derailers		
Transitioning—Derailers		
Project Completion—Derailers		
Overreliance on Authority—Derailers		
Mediation/Negotiation—Derailers		
Use of Time—Strengths		
Relationships—Strengths		
Savvy—Strengths		
Systems Thinking—Strengths		
Balance—Strength		

Competence Ledger

Asset	Strengthen	Maintain	Liability	Reduce	Ignore	Eliminate

PROFESSIONAL GROWTH PLAN[8]

Name:
(List School Year)
Title/Position

Description: A professional growth plan is a personal statement that describes the direction in which you intend to grow over a period of time. Although the time is arbitrary, it is best to focus professional growth over one year. This professional growth plan will lead you through a process to enable you to identify your personal and professional goals. Each component is essential. The effort you put into identifying your personal and professional goals will enable you to gain maximum personal and professional benefit.

All professional growth plans are grounded in a personal mission. This mission is driven by *clear goals* linked to well-defined *objectives* that are delineated with specific *indicators*. In a professional growth plan you:

1. Choose the areas for your professional development.
2. Choose development activities.
3. Chose the outcomes associated with each activity.

Personal Mission:

Professional growth plans must be centered in a personal mission. A mission is filled with passion. It has within it a sense of destiny. Experience, knowledge, and competence drive one's mission. It acts as a motivating force.

Personal Mission: _____

_____

_____

Determine the "Why"

Why is this mission important to accomplish? What are the consequences for you, others, and society if you don't accomplish this goal? What are the consequences for you, others, and society if you do accomplish this goal? How will you feel if you don't accomplish this goal? How will you feel if you do accomplish this goal? How will those who are important in your life feel about you? When we discover the why behind our goals, we provide them with power. When we have a why, we can always find a way to achieve the goal.

Why: _____

_____

_____

Identify your professional goal

Our professional goal is tied directly to our mission. It is one way that we work toward completing that mission. Identify your professional goal. Think beyond your current position. If your current position is your ultimate professional goal, then reflect on your ultimate goal within that role. The goal you choose is appropriate to your current context. That is, given your experience, socialization, and knowledge base, you are choosing a goal that fits who you are and where you want to direct your life. Viktor Frankl states: "For the meaning of life differs from man to man, from day to day and from hour to hour. . . . To put the question in general terms would be comparable to the question posed to a chess champion: 'Tell me, Master, what is the best move in the world?' There simply is no such thing as the best or even a good move apart from a particular situation in a game and the particular personality of one's opponent. The same holds for human existence."[9] When you commit this goal to writing, state it as a performance goal and not an outcome goal.

Professional Goal: _____

_____

_____

- Be *precise* in *writing* your goal.
- Make sure your goal is *measurable.*
- Make sure your goal is *attainable.*

Determine the "Why"

Why is this goal important for you to accomplish? What are the consequences for you, others, and society if you don't accomplish this goal? What are the consequences for you, others, and society if you do accomplish this goal? How will you feel if you don't accomplish this goal? How will you feel if you do accomplish this goal? How will those who are important in your life feel about you? When we discover the why behind our goals, we provide them with power. When we have a why, we can always find a way to achieve the goal.

Your why: _____

_____

_____

Identify the steps to your professional goal

Goal Step One:

_____

_____

_____

Goal Step Two:

_____

_____

_____

Goal Step Three:

_____

_____

_____

Goal Step Four:

_____

_____

_____

Determine your level of commitment

Identify your level of commitment to achieving this goal on a scale of one to ten: one being a very low commitment and ten being a rock-solid, nothing-can-shake-me commitment.

Level of Commitment:

Identify barriers to commitment

_____

_____

_____

_____

Identify strategies to attain commitment

_____

_____

_____

_____

Identify strategies to eliminate barriers to commitment

_____

_____

_____

_____

Identify five ways to bring about a healthy pressure on yourself to increase your commitment

1.

2.

3.

4.

5.

Alignment of Goals

Align your professional goals with those of your school, district, and state. Creating a consistency within this alignment will facilitate your success.

Identify your school's primary goals:

Instruction related primary goal(s)

_____

_____

_____

Parent related primary goal(s)

_____

_____

_____

Student related primary goal(s)

_____

_____

_____

Teacher related primary goal(s)

_____

_____

_____

Resource related primary goal(s)

_____

_____

_____

Identify your district's goals:

Instruction related primary goal(s)

_____

_____

_____

Parent related primary goal(s)

_____

_____

_____

Student related primary goal(s)

_____

_____

_____

Teacher related primary goal(s)

_____

_____

_____

Resource related primary goal(s)

_____

_____

_____

Identify the knowledge base and performance skills you need

Knowledge Base

A knowledge base is the core of technical knowledge that is gained through study or experience. This knowledge base becomes a resource for reference when confronting new situations. To achieve the professional goals you have identified, you have to increase your knowledge base. The most effective way to increase your knowledge base is to target your efforts to the essential technical knowledge and experience that you need to acquire to become more competent. This book gives you targeting tools. Refer to your Personal Assessment to accurately target your efforts.

1.

2.

3.

4.

5.

6.

Performance Skills

Performance skills are specific skills that you want and need to acquire or sharpen. It is important that you are coached in the acquisition of these skills. You may acquire a skill and practice it the wrong way. You end up being skilled with the right tool but in its wrong application. It is much like hitting golf balls on a driving range. If you do not have a golf pro to correct your swing, you may hit two hundred golf balls with the incorrect swing, reinforcing bad habits.

Performance Skill 1

_____

_____

_____

Performance Skill 2

_____

_____

_____

Performance Skill 3

_____

_____

_____

Performance Skill 4

_____

_____

_____

Performance Skill 5

_____

_____

_____

Strengths and Challenges

The 360° Administrator Feedback, along with the other twenty-three assessments, will target specific areas to address in terms of your knowledge base or performance skills. Refer to your summary of assessments and your competence ledger to determine strengths that need to be maintained or improved and challenges that need to be reduced or eliminated. Prioritize your strengths and challenges on the table below.

Prioritized Strengths and Challenge Areas

Strengths and Challenge Areas	Strength	Challenge	Priority

Identify specific categories of potential growth

Base these on the 360° Administrator Feedback. Always state in positive voice. For example, I will be more decisive. I will focus on the source as well as the symptoms of problems. I will seek all pertinent data before choosing to offer my support to a person or group.

Areas of strength that will be maintained

1.

2.

3.

4.

5.

Areas in which Professional Growth will be sought

1.

2.

3.

4.

5.

Performance skills that will be maintained

1.

2.

3.

4.

5.

Implementation of the Professional Growth Plan

The following chart enables you to list your four primary goals, identify the objectives for each goal, and specific indicators that you can use to mark goal attainment. The following examples will help you word your goals, objectives, and indicators. Your indicators are specific strategies and tactics to accomplish your goals and objectives. Employ the SMART system (**S**pecific, **M**easurable, **A**ttainable, **R**elevant, **T**ime dimension) when writing your goals.

Examples

Goal 1:	I will communicate more effectively with parents.
Objective One:	I will attend a workshop to improve parent/administrator communications.
Indicator:	I will submit an executive summary on what I've learned at this workshop to my supervisor.
Objective Two:	I will seek parent input on how to improve my communication methods.
Indicator:	I will send out a needs assessment to all parents seeking their input on school/parent communications.
Goal 2:	I will gain greater mastery of curriculum issues.
Objective One:	I will take a curriculum course at The University of Texas.
Indicator:	I will complete this course and show my transcript to my supervisor.
Objective Two:	I will attend a workshop related to curriculum and student achievement.
Indicator:	I will provide my supervisor with an executive summary of what I learned at this workshop.

Goal 3:	I will increase my problem solving capacity.	
Objective One:	I will attend a problem solving workshop for school administrators.	
Indicator:	I will provide an executive summary on what I've learned at this workshop.	
Objective Two:	I will read a book on administrative problem solving.	
Indicator:	I will discuss this book with my administrative team.	

Goal Planner

Goal	*Objectives*	*Indicators*
Goal 1:	Objectives:	Indicators of goal achievement:
Goal 2:	Objectives:	Indicators of goal achievement:
Goal 3:	Objectives:	Indicators of goal achievement:
Goal 4:	Objectives:	Indicators of goal achievement:

Reminders:

- **Does your plan focus on professional growth?**
- **Do your goals, objectives, and indicators relate to school leadership?**
- **Do you feel as if you have ownership in this plan?**

NOTES

[1] Kennedy, J. L. (June 28, 1998). To stay ahead in the future job market, get "upskilled" now. *The Dallas Morning News.* Sunday (Page 1, Section D).

[2] Lynne Waymon quoted in M. Fuertes. Moving up, moving on. *Government Executive. 30* (9), (p. 30).

[3] Pannesi, R. (1997). Personal strategies for maximizing your value in an uncertain future. *Hospital Management Quarterly. 19* (2), (p. 46).

[4] Buhler, P. (1995). Managing in the 90s. *Supervision. 56* (7), (p. 25).

[5] Bridges, W. (1995). A nation of owners. *Inc. 17* (7[Special Issue]), (p. 90).

[6] Covey, S. *Mission statement builder.* [Online]. Available: *www.covey.com/customer/missionform.html.* Accessed: February 11, 1999.

[7] Frankl, V. (1984). *Man's search for meaning.* New York: Touchstone Books (p. 113).

[8] Copyright © 1999 by Dr. Raymond L. Calabrese. Permission is given to make copies for personal use only and/or for submission of contents as part of a Professional Growth Plan. No other copies are permitted without the express written permission of Dr. Calabrese.

[9] Frankl, V. (1984). *Man's search for meaning.* New York: Touchstone Books (p. 113).

Index